DIASPORA AND TRUST

DIASPORA
AND TRUST

CUBA, MEXICO,
AND THE RISE OF CHINA

ADRIAN H. HEARN

Duke University Press   Durham and London   2016

© 2016 Duke University Press
All rights reserved
Typeset in Warnock Pro and Trade Gothic by Graphic
Composition, Inc., Bogart, GA

Library of Congress Cataloging-in-Publication Data Hearn,
Adrian H., [date] author.
Diaspora and trust : Cuba, Mexico, and the rise of China /
Adrian H. Hearn.
pages cm
Includes bibliographical references and index.
ISBN 978-0-8223-6057-5 (hardcover)
ISBN 978-0-8223-6073-5 (pbk.)
ISBN 978-0-8223-7458-9 (e-book)
1. China—Foreign relations—21st century. 2. Chinese
diaspora. 3. China—Relations—Cuba. 4. Cuba—Relations—
China. 5. China—Relations—Mexico. 6. Mexico—
Relations—China. 7. Chinese—Cuba—Ethnic relations.
8. Chinese—Mexico—Ethnic relations. I. Title.
DS779.47.H44 2016
303.48'251072—dc23 2015031596

Cover art: Chinatown in Havana, Cuba, 2015. The building is
the historical headquarters of the Wong Family Association.
© Elisabeth Blanchet / Alamy Stock Photo.

CONTENTS

ILLUSTRATIONS

ACKNOWLEDGMENTS

The time and insight of many people guided this work. I especially thank my Chinese-Cuban and Chinese-Mexican colleagues for encouraging me to see current affairs in the light of historical tradition; María Teresa Montes de Oca Choy, Enrique Dussel Peters, and Catalina Velázquez Morales for connecting me with their friends and colleagues; Gisela Fosado, Valerie Millholland, Danielle Houtz, Jeanne Ferris, and the Duke University Press team for steering the project to publication; the manuscript reviewers for foregrounding the interplay of local and global influences; the Australian Research Council, the Worldwide Universities Network, the German Institute for Global and Area Studies, and the University of Melbourne for funding the research and writing; my family for tolerating my long periods away collecting information and writing it up; and Echú Alaguana for keeping me on track.

Three booking agents and two assistants were on duty at 4:30 PM when a brick shattered the window of the China Viaje travel agency in Tijuana's business district. At 6:00 PM all five were sitting in a row before their manager and two representatives of the Chinese Association of Tijuana. Pedro, the owner of the business, spoke to me in a surprisingly calm voice: "Now do you see? This is what I was telling you about: it's been happening more and more to Chinese businesses. This has been a bad year. Is it because our employees are Chinese? When these things happen we try to hold our heads high and carry on without retaliating, and without drawing attention to ourselves. You're the anthropologist, so you tell me, what's going on? Have we done something wrong?" (interview, October 16, 2008).

The incident at China Viaje was not isolated. In November, a month earlier, a Chinese supermarket three blocks away had been vandalized and robbed, and the owners of a local department store specializing in imported Chinese home appliances discovered the words "*pinche Chinos*" (damn Chinese) spray painted on its front window. When the mayor announced his support for the establishment of a Chinatown in downtown Tijuana, the opinion pages of local newspapers showed strong opposition: "How ridiculous, the damn Chinese have already inundated us with commercial piracy, and now they want to put a Chinatown in

Tijuana" (Salinas 2008). A similar comment appeared in relation to the newly established Chamber of Chinese Enterprises in the nearby city of Mexicali: "First they invade us [and] now they are getting organized to demand guarantees?? I hope the people of Sinaloa don't plan to do the same" (Minor 2010). Comments like these, and the hostile actions that accompany them, reveal profound insecurity about China's cultural and economic impact in Mexico.

Eighteen hundred miles away a distressed group of Chinese descendants convened at a popular restaurant in Havana's Cuchillo Lane, the heart of Latin America's oldest Chinatown. Public hostility, inadequate legal protection, and official neglect were not among their concerns. On the contrary, they were worried about the growing attention and incessant commercial regulations they had attracted from the Cuban state. The goal of their meeting was to appraise, five years on, the 2006 dissolution of the district's coordinating body, the Grupo Promotor de Barrio Chino (Promotion group of Chinatown) and the assumption of its administrative responsibilities by a government institution called the Office of the Historian of the City. Everything from foreign donations to proposals for cultural festivals and tourism development had since been assessed and regulated by the Office, signifying a total reorganization in the conduct of local business and politics.

Attending the meeting were Yrmina Eng Menéndez, Julio Hun Calzadilla, and Carlos Alay Jó, three founding members of the Grupo Promotor. Each had been instrumental in the revival of Havana's Chinatown (hereafter Barrio Chino) in the 1990s and early 2000s, and each believed that the Office's centrally devised plan for growth and development had weakened the district's cultural and economic potentials. The irony of their predicament, they said, was plain to see: "The tourists come here to see the new gift shops, the restored restaurants, and streets with fashionable cafés. What they don't see is the human cost below the surface. Our social activities are not supported, our elderly residents are neglected, and our restaurants are paying higher taxes than ever. . . . The bureaucrats behind all this become suspicious whenever we try to do something really useful for our community" (interview, February 22, 2011).

In both Cuba and Mexico, Chinese immigrants and their descendants are confronted by a common problem: their commercial activities are believed to be strongly bound up in ethnic favoritism and therefore adverse to national interests. It is a recurring narrative that has resurfaced in both countries during times of economic hardship, most powerfully in the 1930s when the Great Depression provoked the forced closure of Chinese businesses in Cuba and the expulsion of some ten thousand Chinese people from Mexico. Today the narrative is fueled by China's growing global influence and the role that overseas Chinese communities are thought to play in it.

It is striking that similar preoccupations should emerge in Cuba and Mexico, countries at opposite ends of the spectrum in terms of economic openness and political ideology. A combination of downward coercion and upward nationalism continues to maintain the Cuban state's firm grip on civic and economic administration. In contrast, three decades of privatization in Mexico have eliminated nearly all forms of state intervention. China's growing impact has exposed problems with both approaches. In Cuba, nascent bilateral trade and investment agreements have provoked a grudging awareness that uncompromising state control is ill suited to post–Cold War economic rationalism. In Mexico, unrelenting Chinese commercial competition has fueled new accusations of inadequate industrial policies and insufficient state support for manufacturers.

China's rise and the so-called Asian Century it heralds are forcing politicians, businesspeople, and researchers to debate and formulate fresh solutions to an old problem: what balance of state, market, and civic inputs can best harness the world's shifting economic currents? While Cuban and Mexican policy makers approach this question from contrasting ideological systems, all of them recognize a need for forms of public-private cooperation that diverge from conventional development models. As both countries attempt to respond to the challenges and opportunities brought by China, there is a growing awareness that more mixed approaches are needed to diversify productivity and to leverage the capacities of resident Chinese communities.

Integration with China is prompting the governments of Cuba, Mexico, and most other countries to rethink the structure of their economies. The Cuban government's 2011 *Lineamientos de la política económica y social del partido y la revolución* (Economic and social policy guidelines of the party and revolution) articulates the need to connect large state-owned enterprises with emerging private businesses, just as China began to do in the 1980s. Chinese advisors have long recommended this course to their Cuban counterparts, who are in no position to disagree as their nation becomes increasingly reliant on Chinese trade, investment, and loans. In Mexico, the administration of President Enrique Peña Nieto has acknowledged that long-established tax concessions and financial incentives for the most powerful and successful sectors must be balanced with greater access to loans, information, and logistical support for small and medium-size enterprises (SMEs). China has taught Mexico this lesson not by example but by force: as Mexican textiles, electronics, and even automobiles face growing Chinese competition in the U.S. market, empowering the nation's acutely underresourced SMEs is not only desirable but critical.

In social engagement, too, China's rise is pushing the Cuban and Mexican governments to explore less top-down approaches. Cuban politicians and administrators have largely overlooked their nation's Chinese community for decades—some would say since the mid-nineteenth century. As Chinese diplomats and businesspeople forge new ties with Havana's Chinese diaspora, particularly its enthusiastic descendant population, the Cuban government has had to accommodate local demands for resources or risk being bypassed. Mexico's government has been slower to act, but it too is beginning to engage with its Chinese residents. It is doing so more out of necessity than by choice: engagement offers the best hope for containing unregulated trade in goods, services, and people.

How are we to make sense of this forced disposition of governments to engage more assertively with their economies and societies? This book attempts to do so through concepts like public-private cooperation, synergy, linkage, and social capital. The first two invoke vertical notions of state-society engagement, and the last two horizontal conceptions of community solidarity. The book argues that a convergence of these vertical and horizontal forces is necessary to unlock the opportunities for development and prosperity brought by China's rise. The catalyst for this convergence, I argue, is trust.

Chapters 1 and 2 examine how pressure is growing on the Cuban and Mexican governments to reach out beyond national champions to SMEs, and in the process reap the political and economic dividends generated by independent cooperation at the grass roots. Chapters 3 and 4 show that government engagement with Chinese communities in Cuba and

Mexico is beginning to simultaneously leverage and engender purposeful solidarity within Chinese neighborhood associations. In all cases, vertical state-society synergies and horizontal community linkages are interacting in new ways to condition economic and social life, a process of convergence stimulated—and compelled—by China's rise.

As China reaches out to international markets and diasporas, governments cannot hope to contain the resulting exchanges in official programs. Instead they must design more flexible development agendas that simultaneously accommodate global change, attract local participation, and build trust. The book explores how two nations with deeply contrasting economic and political orientations are responding to this challenge. It shows that their responses reflect different histories, cultures, and political structures but also a common convergence toward a more centrist balance of state, private, and civic power. This is not simply because the Chinese government is encouraging them along this path or because of their independent political evolution, but also because rebalancing these structural forces is a necessary response to China's global expansion.

ECONOMIC RELATIONS WITH CHINA: LIKE A BICYCLE

After Venezuela, China is Cuba's second largest trading partner: their bilateral trade reached $1.39 billion in 2014, one-third of which consisted of Cuban exports. China is also Mexico's second largest trading partner (after the United States): trade reached $72.24 billion in 2014, but only $5.98 billion of this flowed in Mexico's favor (United Nations Commodity Trade Statistics Database 2015). Neither Cuba nor Mexico exports large quantities of natural resources to China, making them exceptions in Latin America—a region whose rich endowment of commodities has seen trade with China grow from $10 billion in 2000 to over $250 billion in 2014. The flow of mineral, energy, and agricultural products westward across the Pacific is reciprocated by an eastward flood of toys, clothes, home appliances, and industrial equipment from the factories of southern China. Cuba and Mexico do not share their neighbors' concerns about resource dependency on China, but both are witnessing an unprecedented influx of Chinese consumer goods, with the full range of reactions this brings.

Cuba's relationship with China is now more harmonious than Mexico's, but it has not always been. In 1960 Cuba's new revolutionary government became the first in the Americas to officially recognize the People's Republic of China. However, against Mao Zedong's wishes, Fidel Castro soon drew closer to the Soviet Union, whose leadership of international communism was disputed by China. Despite their contrasting relationships with the Soviet Union, Cuba and China never broke diplomatic ties with each other. When the Soviet Union collapsed in 1989–90, China replaced it as Cuba's main foreign ally, enabling the Castro government to keep its struggling economy afloat. Asking its citizens for renewed austerity and self-sacrifice to overcome the warlike conditions of the so-called Special Period in Time of Peace, Cuba might well have imploded without Chinese support. Sustained by Chinese President Jiang Zemin's determination to "save Cuba's revolutionary project," the two countries commenced what a Chinese government newspaper called a "period of completely new and steady development" (*People's Daily* 1996).

The Chinese government has taken interest in the discovery of oil off Cuba's north coast. As well as securing exploration rights, the Huanqiu Contracting and Engineering Corporation (owned by the Chinese state and a subsidiary of the oil giant China National Petroleum Corporation) is the lead financier of a $5.5 billion refinery in Cienfuegos. Furthermore, Chinese trade credits and unsecured loans have helped Cuban gross domestic product to rebound, according to the World Bank (2015b), from $32 billion in 2004 to $234 billion in 2014 (measured as purchasing power). This financial support has enabled Cuba to buy Chinese buses and trains to help alleviate the island's transportation crisis, as well as consumer goods ranging from clothing to home appliances and computers.

As is the case in other Latin American nations, China's impact is pervasive in the daily lives of ordinary Cubans. However, unlike in Mexico, Brazil, Argentina, and many other countries, in Cuba China's growing influence has not given rise to public hostility toward Chinese products and people. China poses no threat to Cuba's domestic industries, and furthermore, the Cuban government goes to great lengths to emphasize China's standing as a historical friend and ally. Televised documentaries and mainstream literature often invoke Beijing's loyalty in the wake of the Soviet meltdown.

Despite the apparent resonance of their political philosophies, China and Cuba no longer look to socialist solidarity as the prime mover of their relationship. Pragmatism is replacing ideology, in the process redefining the basis for trust between the two nations and reconfiguring the structure of the Cuban economy. China's prior experience with reform and opening—professed by a constant stream of advisors from Beijing—provides Cuban leaders with insights into the making of a market economy. As chapter 1 shows, the countries' newfound common interest in market socialism is producing impressive results, but as yet neither China nor Cuba trusts nonstate actors to exchange goods, services, and ideas.

Unlike Cuba's relationship with China, Mexico's has suffered from a lack of political engagement and economic complementarity. The impact of Chinese exports on Mexico has been severe, displacing Mexican producers of clothing, toys, shoes, and other manufactured products at home and in the U.S. market. Mexican manufacturers argue that for every two products they export, ten enter the country from China, and that consequently, between 900,000 and one million workers have lost their jobs (*El Mural* 2011).

Chinese officials insist that to remedy the chronic bilateral imbalance, Mexico should permit Chinese investment in the oil sector. Peña Nieto's energy sector reforms may advance this prospect, but Chevron, Exxon, and other established multinationals have been waiting at the front of the line for contracts ever since President Lázaro Cárdenas expelled them during his 1938 oil nationalization program. With oil unlikely to bring balance to Sino-Mexican trade relations, Presidents Peña Nieto and Xi Jinping have turned instead to tequila, pork, and tourism. Here too, though, the search for complementarity will be an uphill journey. Even if the Chinese government reduces agricultural tariffs, encourages its citizens to visit the Mayan pyramids, and awards safety approval to Mexican foods and drinks, Mexican firms are in a poor position to grasp resulting opportunities.

With little access to loans, tax breaks, overseas promotion, and government start-up grants, most Mexican companies are struggling to compete in their own market, let alone in China. Their predicament reflects the legacy of an outdated industrial policy, introduced by President Miguel de la Madrid in response to Mexico's 1981 oil crisis and the (consequently) unsustainable spending of his predecessor. Joining the international wave of state retrenchments and privatizations of the 1980s, Mexico internalized the economic ideology championed by U.S. president Ronald Reagan and UK prime minister Margaret Thatcher. Ever since then, government assistance in Mexico has focused on a narrow set of leading private firms in sectors such as automobiles, banking, and media. Represented by powerful industry associations, these enterprises secure tax concessions and the lion's share of government funding for research and expansion (Schneider 2002).

Chinese competition has hit Mexico hardest in the manufacturing sector, which has lobbied against the relaxation of tariffs on Chinese imports and for greater government protection from the so-called China threat. Conscious that the sector accounts for 20 percent of Mexico's $1.1 trillion gross domestic product, politicians eager for votes have heard the manufacturers' call and have kept tariffs on most Chinese items at 35 percent. But in a nation beset by inadequate law enforcement and organized crime, high import duties have bred illegal countermeasures. Falsification of documents, collusion between Chinese exporters and the informal sector of the Mexican economy, and bribery of customs officials are commonplace, undermining public trust in the state's ability to govern. A more effective industrial policy would rely less on import tariffs, broaden the tax base, and extend the funding and concessions enjoyed by big business to smaller, more dynamic enterprises. Chapter 2 shows that such an adjustment is tentatively beginning, and that its full implementation over time would build trust and cooperation where they are needed most: horizontally between Mexican businesses and citizens, vertically between state and society, and broadly between Mexico and China.

For Cuba and Mexico, China's economic impact reaches beyond trade and investment to the heart of industrial relations. Large enterprises— whether state owned or private—cannot by themselves effectively design and implement national responses to twenty-first-century globalization. The monolithic state-owned enterprises behind Cuba's agriculture and energy sectors, for instance, are not efficient and competitive enough to meet domestic demand, let alone profit from China's hunger for food and oil. Similarly, the small group of elite private firms at the helm of Mexico's automobile sector faces unprecedented challenges as Chinese car makers establish factories in Latin America and set their sights on the U.S. market.

Small businesses have an increasingly important role to play in Cuba and Mexico, but they will require support if they are to generate jobs, confidence, and stability. Both governments recognize this dynamic and are experimenting with policies to widen access to permits, finance, and markets. The reforms outlined in the Cuban government's *Lineamientos* encourage self-employment in sectors ranging from tourism to education, particularly if independent providers can efficiently supply larger state-owned enterprises (República de Cuba 2011). Meanwhile, Mexico's reforms seek, among other things, to lower the cost of electricity, telecommunications, and finance for small businesses. These initiatives respond as much to domestic pressures as they do to global circumstances, including the erosion of citizens' trust in the capacity of their nations' public and private sectors to create economic opportunities.

In both countries the need for economic diversification, and proposals for achieving it, are documented in government statements, independent position papers, and academic literature. However, the pathway from publication to policy is less certain. Chapter 1 shows that the pace of Cuba's economic liberalization has been slowed by its expansive informal sector, which will continue to grow in the absence of functional wholesale supply chains. Chapter 2 points out that Mexican reforms that would augment opportunities for small businesses face competition from powerful lobby groups such as the Consejo Coordinador Empresarial (Council for Business Coordination) and the Consejo Mexicano de Hombres de Negocios (Mexican Council of Businessmen). These domestic dynamics highlight a broad challenge facing both countries: to see through policies that stimulate local initiatives in ways that build trust rather than erode it.

The chapters that follow show that government support should not be overbearing, even when it is needed to pull through the bad times, but neither should it fade away into complacency in the good times. As the economist Robert Reich once wrote, "economies are like bicycles. The faster they move, the better they maintain their balance unaided" (1982, 852). Cuba has found that economic bicycles do not accelerate under a domineering rider, while Mexico has found that when the road goes uphill bicycles cannot ride themselves.

HARNESSING OVERSEAS CHINESE NETWORKS

As global economic dynamism shifts to Asia, comprehensive responses require government engagement not only with businesses but also with people, especially those with professional and personal knowledge of China. To this end, the worldwide Chinese diaspora is a powerful but often overlooked human asset. Its associations, small enterprises, and cultural activities are the human face of China, and when appropriately supported, they have begun to play a critical role in the formation of bilateral trust.

For overseas Chinese actors, brokering trust across borders means balancing allegiances among their homelands, host countries, and local communities. David Palumbo-Liu writes that this "political strategizing" animates diasporic identities at least as much as nostalgia for home does (2007, 283). As the book's case studies demonstrate, widespread perceptions that Chinese expatriates and descendants are eternally loyal to the Chinese motherland fail to appreciate their disposition to pursue the new opportunities for internal and external collaboration generated by China's rise. Chinese authorities are partly responsible for perpetuating exaggerated notions of nationalist loyalty among overseas Chinese communities, describing them since imperial times as *huaqiao* (华侨). This term, writes Wang Gungwu, "was never used to depict the usual reasons for leaving home, such as to make a living, to trade, to seek one's fortune, or to migrate in search for a better place to settle. Instead, it captured a sense of doing what had to be done, fulfilling duty. . . . But one thing is clear. Assimilated or not, the Chinese overseas did change. They have been variously adaptable, and they have demonstrated that the idea that 'once a Chinese, always a Chinese' is simply not true" (2000, 39 and 47).

Chinese migrant workers have been building bridges to Latin America since the sixteenth-century voyages of the Manila Galleons, which for over two centuries brokered trade between the Chinese and Spanish empires (see chapter 4). By the mid-nineteenth century Chinese migration to Latin America had begun in earnest, underpinning Philip Kuhn's observation that "emigration has been inseparable from China's modern history . . . neither Chinese history lacking emigration nor emigration lacking the history of China is a self-sufficient field of study" (2008, 5).

To establish a foothold in Latin American economies, Chinese immigrants endured and sometimes overcame repressive work regimes and discriminatory commercial regulations. But their hard-won progress, writes Evelyn Hu-Dehart, provoked harsh responses: "The eventual success of Chinese in converting themselves into small urban business proprietors and the influx of free Asian immigrants to Latin America in ensuing decades were accompanied everywhere by anti-Asian agitation and mob action, as well as more organized state campaigns and persecution. In emulation of the U.S. Exclusion Act, Latin American governments in the early twentieth century enacted laws to severely limit further Asian, especially Chinese, immigration" (2007, 51). Discriminatory laws influenced Chinese patterns of trans-Pacific immigration, settlement, and commerce, but as Adam McKeown has argued, the impact of such laws was conditioned by specific contexts of place, time, and hierarchy (2001, 26–27). Social forces were as important as legal codes, evident in the formation of solidarity networks to navigate and circumscribe official rules. Membership in mutual aid associations provided protection from discrimination, pathways to employment, and finance for small business development. But the same associations also deepened the segregation of their members from broader civic and social landscapes, perpetuating a vicious circle of external hostility and internal protection. Every rotation of this circle broadened the perception that resident Chinese groups were closed and self-serving (Chang 1973; Hira 2007, 64–66; Oxfeld 1993).

Twenty-first-century anxieties about China's growing global influence, intensified by the competitive apprehension of domestic manufacturers, have brought new pressures to bear on overseas Chinese communities. Ethnic associations continue to fill protective functions for their members, including providing alternative pathways for economic advancement, defense against discrimination, and mechanisms for bypassing regulations that are perceived to be inappropriate or unfair. Where external pressure has fomented in-group solidarity and loyalty over time, fairness is conceived not only in terms of individual advancement but also as the promotion of collective cultural and economic security (Hu-DeHart 2010; Velázquez Morales 2001). Family ties and ethnic allegiances have furnished network members with benefits such as start-up capital, market access, a flexible labor force, a loyal customer base, and informal advice about opportunities (A. Smart 1993; A. Smart and Hsu 2004; Y. Yan 2009).

While Chinese networks have sustained collective notions of exchange, loyalty, identity, and fairness, their informality and ethnic partiality have led them into conflict with host country laws and public values. Internal affinities among Chinese people and their descendants in Indonesia and Malaysia, for instance, provoked riots against them in the late 1960s and continue to complicate the multicultural agenda in both countries (Yahuda 1985, 222–23). Recent studies show that perceptions of ethnic favoritism have also generated hostility toward Chinese immigrants across Africa and parts of Latin America. Governments, businesses, and societies in both regions have struggled to incorporate Chinese immigrant groups into domestic structures of governance and commercial compliance.

The following chapters show that entrenched ideologies, in support of state socialism or market liberalism, have impeded government engagement with Chinese communities. Centralized regulations in Cuba are unable to accommodate the grassroots priorities and productive capacities of Chinese ethnic associations and neighborhood leaders. Meanwhile, the hypersensitivity of Mexican politicians and businesspeople to the opinions of voters and customers has prevented them from openly collaborating with resident Chinese entrepreneurs to leverage their unique potentials. Both states' vertical linkages are too narrow to harness the capacities of the Chinese diaspora.

In Cuba, the revolution of 1959 led to the nationalization of Chinese businesses, the emigration of Chinese entrepreneurs to the United States, and mandatory recognition of the People's Republic of China by Chinese ethnic associations. Twelve associations and their coordinating body, the Casino Chung Wah, survived these pressures and in the early 2000s were reinvigorated by the induction of over 2,500 enthusiastic second-, third-, and fourth-generation descendants. Biologically and socially integrated with Cubans of European and African origin, the island's Chinese descendants have gradually climbed through the ranks of the associations and initiated a range of dynamic initiatives. These include hosting international conferences on Chinese cultural influences in Cuba, converting the associations' canteens into thriving restaurants with investments from the state and foreign sources, and increasingly conducting commercial exchange with partners in mainland China. As the number of visiting Chinese diplomats and businesspeople grows, the Cuban state's traditional strategies for inserting itself as an intermediary between local actors, foreign nongovernmental organizations, and visiting delegations cannot keep pace. Instead, as chapter 3 demonstrates, government officials are increasingly forced to deal with Chinese associations on their own terms, which include demands for recognition and resources.

In Mexico, macroeconomic tensions with China have not stopped enterprising Chinese community leaders from reaching out both to their motherland and to the Mexican state. In the northern state of Baja California, they have worked with the city governments of Tijuana and Mexicali to create trade networks that are beginning to produce concrete benefits. In contrast to the situation in Cuba, the number of first-generation Chinese immigrants in Mexico has grown rapidly since the mid-twentieth century, but owing to the undocumented status of many of them, Mexican scholars have little faith in official statistics. While the census of 2010 reports 6,655 Chinese-born people residing in Mexico, the Chinese embassy in Mexico counts three thousand as well as twenty thousand Mexicans of Chinese origin—with the majority of both groups employed in the food industry, trade, and to a lesser extent, bureaucratic professional services. The Overseas Chinese Affairs Office in Beijing calculates only half the number of naturalized Chinese people in Mexico, living primarily in the northern border cities of Tijuana and Mexicali, the urban metropolis of Mexico City, and the southern state of Chiapas. Unofficial counts from Tijuana and Mexicali indicate that these two cities alone are respectively home to 25,000 and 35,000 Chinese immigrants and their descendants, many of whom arrived since 2000 and are not legally registered. Whether in Mexico City or on the northern border, Chinese people speak of a division between old and new arrivals, the former descending from the Cantonese-speaking immigrants of the nineteenth and twentieth centuries, with corresponding ties to the Chinese National People's Party (the Kuomintang, or KMT), and the latter hailing from the Mandarin-speaking urban centers of eastern China.

China's growing influence in Mexico has subdued some of the differences between old and new arrivals and aggravated others. Since 2000 the Chinese government has offered commercial partnerships and orchestrated prestigious visits from senior officials to persuade Mexico's Chinese associations to renounce recognition of the KMT and adopt Mandarin as their official operating language. However, the recent wave of Chinese immigrants, most of whom are Mandarin-speaking young people with little interest in traditional ethnic associations, remains disengaged from the older Cantonese-speaking communities and from Mexican society in general. These recent immigrants have generally focused on commercial activities, such as importing and retailing low-cost Chinese consumer goods, and have consequently drawn their predecessors' scorn.

A string of conservative Mexican governments has been reluctant to engage with the nation's Chinese diaspora. Chapter 4 shows that the need to integrate Chinese commercial activities into an enabling and clearly governed environment is becoming more urgent. The bilateral trade deficit, the expansion of the black market, and the growing tide of negative attitudes toward China are all good reasons for more assertive leadership from above. An even more poignant call to action is the illegal exploitation of Chinese workers in Mexican factories, a practice that Chinese associations have done little to stop and have sometimes supported.

The poor track record of Cuban and Mexican officials in working with Chinese communities is conditioned by contrasting ideological orientations, the Cubans favoring top-down control and the Mexicans almost complete neglect. As Chinese communities deepen their ties to the mainland, however, both governments are assessing the merits of closer engagement with the Chinese diaspora. This growing disposition to engage is motivated in part by fears that unregulated commercial exchanges could increase in step with deepening interpersonal ties, but it is also driven by hopes of leveraging local capacities to strengthen relations with China. Fueling these fears and hopes is a growing appreciation of the threats and opportunities posed by *guanxi*, social capital, and trust.

GUANXI, SOCIAL CAPITAL, AND TRUST: PERSONAL FAVORS OR PUBLIC GOODS?

The term "guanxi" (关系, meaning relationship or connection) encompasses a wide range of formal and informal exchange practices that are pursued for both affective and instrumental reasons. Traditions of reciprocity vary widely in meaning and purpose, but in most cases the "relationship must be presented as primary and the exchange, useful as it may be, treated as only secondary" (A. Smart 1993, 399). In the gradual construction of guanxi, each transaction should be treated as a step in a series of interactions designed to deepen the relationship and foment certainty, especially when formal legal and financial institutions are weak

(M. Yang 1994). In such contexts, guanxi has fostered the confidence necessary for foreign investment, informal loans, community mutual aid, and business partnerships (Hsu 2005; Keister 2002; J. Smart and A. Smart 2009; Velázquez Morales 2001). Unlike many Western conceptions of gifting, in which instrumental considerations taint supposedly pure emotional ties, Chinese Confucianism envisions the formation of affective relationships through the exchange of useful goods and helpful actions (Carrier 1999; Lo and Otis 2003).

Chinese business practices developed in domestic and foreign contexts where legal and financial institutions were deficient and antagonistic. Contracts were difficult, if not impossible, to enforce through legal means (A. Chen 1999). Small business owners had little recourse against harassment from police and more influential competitors, and banks generally refused to loan them capital (Tsai 2002). Guanxi compensated for insecure contracts, weak institutional guarantees, and closed doors. Through ever-expanding networks of friends, aspiring business owners could raise capital, form partnerships, seek suppliers, gather information, and conduct relatively secure transactions.

Drawing on guanxi relationships, investors from prospering communities in the Chinese diaspora (particularly in Hong Kong, Taiwan, and Southeast Asia) were able to make connections and build cooperative relationships with actors in China. These investors were willing to send their capital "home" despite the lack of legal protections because guanxi provided grounds for security (Hsing 1998). Guanxi networks allowed them to penetrate the Chinese market more quickly and successfully than other investors, and as China began to integrate itself into the capitalist world economy, these overseas compatriots became key sources of finance, connections, and information. Ironically, insecure property rights and ambiguous or lax legal regulations for investors, along with widespread distrust of the system, encouraged reliance on personal relationships, which helped produce one of the fastest growing economies in history (Hearn, Smart, and Hernández Hernández 2011).

The unwritten rules of guanxi constitute mechanisms of coordination, enforcement, and dispute settlement that are commonly known and relatively openly practiced in China (Bell 2000; X. Chen and C. Chen 2004; Hurst 2002, Wang H. 2000). Guanxi therefore differs from Western forms of reciprocity not only because it more seamlessly blends instrumental goals with affective bonds, but also because liberal democracies publicly regard nepotism as antithetical to the principle of equal opportunity. In practice, meritocracy rarely exists free from bias anywhere in the world, but it is formally enshrined in Western codes of conduct from the law court to the company boardroom. Hence, as globalization exposes Chinese enterprises to Western norms, Douglas Guthrie posits "the declining significance of guanxi" (1998).

Despite its more open public expression, guanxi has much in common with Western formulations of social capital. Wherever we live, we can all agree that well-connected friends are a valuable resource—if we have them. However, if we do not, we may conclude that social capital, like guanxi, impedes upward mobility and maintains the status quo. Nan Lin (2001, 24) sees a theoretical reflection of this rift in the contrast between Émile Durkheim's cross-societal "organic solidarity" and Karl Marx's class antagonism. While the former concept evokes the biological metaphor of individual organs functioning cooperatively for the benefit of the larger organism, the latter focuses on the economic inequalities that result from the domination of some sectors by others and the construction of exclusionary social boundaries between them. This core tension finds contemporary expression in analytic distinctions between social capital's exclusive and inclusive dimensions.

Robert Putnam describes the exclusive, inward-oriented loyalties of a given network's members as "bonding social capital," in contrast to a more outward-oriented (and uncommon) form of solidarity that may extend to nonmembers, which he calls "bridging social capital" (2000, 22–23). Case studies from around the world generally substantiate this distinction, demonstrating the tendency of strong internal bonds to discourage the formation of external relationships. Alejandro Portes and Julia Sensenbrenner (1993) for instance, find across a range of immigrant communities that exclusion of outsiders is related to the pressures of group membership. Among these pressures are demands for subjects' time and resources, restrictions on individual freedoms, and "downward leveling norms" that gradually drain members' confidence and capacity to find common cause with those beyond their reference group (Portes 1998, 15). Putnam acknowledges these constraints, but more recently he has argued that bonding and bridging social capital are not mutually exclusive: "Without really thinking about it, we assume that bridging social capital and bonding social capital are inversely correlated in a kind of zero-sum relationship: if I have lots of bonding ties, I must have few bridging ties, and vice versa. As an empirical matter, I believe that assumption is often false. In other words, high bonding might well be compatible with high bridging, and low bonding with low bridging. . . . Bonding social capital can thus be a prelude to bridging social capital, rather than precluding it" (2007, 143–44 and 165).

The prospect of mutually supportive bonding and bridging social capital raises a pressing policy question for community development institutions, articulated by Michael Woolcock: "Do the high levels of integration characterizing indigenous social relations in many poor communities actually constitute a resource that can be used as a basis for constructing substantive development programs? If so, how?" (1998, 181). Scholars who study diasporas do not deal with "indigenous social relations" in a conventional sense, but they are well placed to explore this question, and the growth of Chinese communities around the world provides a valuable source of insight. As Rhacel Parreñas and Lok Siu observe, the inward pull of ethnic affinity among overseas Chinese communities does not necessarily impede their outward cooperation with external actors: "there is nothing inherent in diasporic identifications that prevents the formation of broader political alliances. It does not have to be one or the other, but both forms of collective identification can coexist" (2007, 10).

In the Cuban and Mexican Chinese diaspora, people who simultaneously forge horizontal linkages within their community and vertical synergies with the public and private sectors are rare. As Mark Granovetter observed forty years ago, this is because such people possess an unusual ability to work at arm's length from the communities they bridge, enabling them to leverage the "strength of weak ties" (1973). Anthropologists are trained to seek out such liminal people precisely for their ability to explain and broker local relationships (Rabinow 1977). Chapter 3 shows that the difficulties of balancing allegiances to community and state in Havana's Barrio Chino have spelled the undoing of several would-be intermediaries. Similarly, chapter 4 shows how Chinese community leaders in Mexico who have developed strong ties with the export-processing maquiladora sector have seen their interests come into conflict with those of the immigrant Chinese workers they ostensibly protect.

Intermediaries demonstrate the embodied nature of social capital, for however widely and densely connected they may be, their personal identities underpin its efficacy. Like guanxi, social capital requires direct interactions between individuals who know each other or wish to, and it is therefore limited by the scope of the networks in which it operates. Social capital may generate "positive externalities" (Fukuyama 2000, 15), and societies with greater stocks of social capital are said to function more effectively and inclusively (Coleman 1988; Fedderke, de Kadt, and Luiz 1999; Woolcock 1998). However, these stocks consist not of a collective public good, but of a cumulative reserve of personal favors to be reciprocated and of rewards and sanctions to be expected. Reserves of social capital are accessible only to group members and consequently are not fungible across distinct communities. Unlike financial capital, writes Ariel Armony, "social capital does not have the same portability; therefore, it cannot be easily transferred from one setting to another" (2011, 49).

Trust relates better to collective scenarios than guanxi or social capital do, providing a more encompassing and inclusive organizing principle for responding to China's rise. Long associated with efficiency, productivity, and prosperity, trust can take a "particularized" form between individuals who know each other but also a "generalized" form between "those whom we don't know and who are different from us" (Armony 2004, 21; also see Arrow 1974, 26; Uslaner 1999, 124–25; Yamagishi and Yamagishi 1994). Lin describes trust as a public resource necessary for civic order: "Societies must have consensual rules and collective trust for them to function" (N. Lin 2001, 148). Similarly, Francis Fukuyama argues that "one of the most important lessons we can learn from an examination of economic life is that a nation's well-being, as well as its ability to compete, is conditioned by a single, pervasive cultural characteristic: the level of trust inherent in the society" (1995, 7).

It is widely agreed that generalized trust, untethered to specific exchanges between associated individuals, is an asset to any society, but pathways from personal favors to public goods are harder to define. Johannes Fedderke, Raphael de Kadt, and John Luiz argue that governments should encourage the assimilation of community-level allegiances and loyalties into a wider national system of regulated exchange. This "rationalization of social capital" involves the "the gradual replacement of informal associations and networks by formal administrative structures, and the impersonal market mechanism no longer tied to individual identities of trading agents" (1999, 719). Particularized trust based on informal reciprocity (for example, the exchange of gifts and favors) thus evolves into generalized trust based on formal transactions and codified civic norms (such as contracted exchanges of goods and services). Governments can encourage and benefit from this evolution by investing in family, community, and education programs that build understanding, skills, and human capital appropriate to national development priorities (ibid., 736–38). As Theda Skocpol has argued, associational activity, entrepreneurial initiative, and the welfare state can thus reinforce each other in "close symbiosis" (1996, 20).

Others are skeptical that governments can inspire citizens to trust in each other and in shared civic norms. Fukuyama warns that state intervention is futile because excessive "legal apparatus" is a "substitute for trust" (1995, 27). In a working paper for the International Monetary Fund, he supports this argument with historical examples:

> If the state gets into the business of organizing everything, people will become dependent on it and lose their spontaneous ability to work with one another. France had a rich civil society at the end of the Middle Ages, but horizontal trust between individuals weakened as a result of a centralizing state that set Frenchmen at each other through a system of petty privileges and status distinctions. The same thing occurred in the former Soviet Union after the Bolshevik Revolution, where the Communist Party consciously sought to undermine all forms of horizontal association in favor of vertical ties between party-state and individual. This has left post-Soviet society bereft of both trust and a durable civil society. (2000, 15–16)

The conservative commentator George Will offers a similar zero-sum assessment of state intervention and trust: "as the state waxes, other institutions wane" (quoted in Skocpol 1996, 20; also see Schambra 1994). From this perspective, the state's monitoring and compliance regulations impose cumbersome expenses and transaction costs while undermining the natural inclination of private actors to trust and cooperate with each other.

China's impact in Cuba and Mexico opens a window into the politics of trust. The need for fresh development models in both countries is forcing governments, businesses, and citizens to interact in new ways. To leverage benefits from these interactions requires smart policy making that is sensitive to social dynamics. Concepts like synergy, linkage, and public-private cooperation can help formulate government policies, but they are ultimately social propositions that envision distinct communities working together for a greater good. If they are to gain any traction on the ground, these concepts and the policies they inform must be used to build trust between strangers.

Whether the resources and responsibilities for participatory development should come from the top down, the bottom up, or both has long been a matter of intense disagreement. Conflicting political philosophies have prevented academic theorists from finding common ground on this point, but entrenched ideologies have too often inhibited politicians from even debating it. The pressures and opportunities generated by China's rise are stimulating more open public discussions about the optimal balance of state, market, and civic power. Setting out from contrasting political and economic systems, Cuba and Mexico show that forming more inclusive industrial policies (see chapters 1 and 2) and achieving civic engagement with resident Chinese communities (see chapters 3 and 4) are challenges that governments of all ideological stripes must address.

BLACK MARKETS: THE DARK SIDE OF TRUST

There is no single formula for optimizing the balance of public, private, and civic inputs, but there are more and less effective blends for addressing specific challenges. The informal sector is a case in point. In Cuba, the gradual opening of consumer retail to small private entrepreneurs reflects a slow top-down process of decentralization, creation of regulated supply chains, and assessment of results. Increasingly reliant on Chinese manufactured products and finance, this state-guided process aims to contain the expansion of the black market—a prerequisite for further liberalization (see chapter 1). In Mexico, high import tariffs on Chinese textiles, handicrafts, and other products have encouraged smuggling and fraud. Evidence is mounting that more sophisticated forms of state support, such as easier access to loans for small businesses and official sponsorship of trade fairs, would better assist affected sectors of the economy (see chapter 2). While deepening commercial connections with

China are affecting the Cuban and Mexican informal sectors in different ways, they are exposing a common need for more innovative government policies.

A careful balance of state regulation and private initiative will also be necessary if the activities of Chinese diasporic communities are to be leveraged in support of national development. For a century and a half, Chinese associations in Cuba and Mexico have drawn on informal networks, personal determination, and trust to sustain connections with their motherland. Premised on shared ethnicity, these relationships have deepened in the twenty-first century, joining together people on opposite sides of the Pacific who often have little or no personal knowledge of each other. It is not unusual for mainland Chinese exporters and investors to take risks, brokered by intermediaries, with diasporic business partners they have never met. In these circumstances, writes Steffen Mau, trust is at once inclusive and exclusive: "Transnational trust is a form of generalized trust in the sense that it is extended to individuals whom we do not know and who are unlike us. And yet, it does not extend to an abstract other, but to a specific nationally defined group" (2010, 110). With consensual policy making the state may harness the elusive social connections of Chinese and other diasporic communities for use in official development projects, but as the Cuban and Mexican governments have found, administrators are hard pressed to regulate—let alone control—the deployment of trust.

Less reliant on preexisting exchanges between specific people, trust within the transnational Chinese diaspora is more mobile and fungible than guanxi and social capital. Shared ethnic roots, real or imagined, constitute an affinity among some fifty million overseas Chinese people spread around the globe. But even globalized ethnicity does not define the outer limits of collective trust. Broadly shared experiences—for instance, of life and livelihood in the developing world—can also provide a platform for common cause. The convergence of distinct yet overlapping practices, such as the Chinese tradition of conducting business through the "back door" (*hou men* 后 门), the Cuban custom of resolving problems "below the cover" (*bajo el tapete*), and the Mexican convention of "leveraging" favors (*palanca*), provides a basis for informal cooperation between people who may otherwise have little in common. Such a convergence could pose new challenges to the rule of law in Latin America as Chinese diasporic communities relink themselves with the mainland (Armony 2011, 40–41; Tokatlian 2008, 77).

Enabling foreigners to find their social bearings, generalized trust built on similar precursor experiences—what Armony calls "GPS capital" (2011, 27)—provides common ground between strangers. As this ground is traversed, though, strangers become friends and their trust evolves. Whether or not their relationship draws strength from ethnic solidarity, they likely belong to independent social capital networks whose goals and priorities may or may not overlap. Should the priorities of their broader networks intersect, the strangers-*cum*-friends may become channels of intergroup contact and mediation. For example, some Chinese community leaders in northern Mexico have become well connected with the region's political and economic elites and now broker partnerships for them with mainland Chinese wholesale suppliers and labor contractors. These exchanges may have originated in generalized trust built on ethnic affinity, shared experiences of development, familiarity with informality, and even appreciation of Chinese art (as in one case discussed below), but over time they have become more instrumental and focused. The material benefits they generate are unevenly distributed among managers, intermediaries, and factory workers, and the trust underpinning them has become exclusive and particularized.

The transformation of generalized trust into more particularized forms casts new light on Guthrie's argument for the "declining significance of guanxi" brought on by China's integration into the global economy. Instead, as Mayfair Yang has argued, "*guanxi* practices may decline in some social domains, but find new areas to flourish" (2002, 459). Drawing both on ethnic solidarity and "GPS capital," trust is fomenting new links between China and the Chinese diaspora in Cuba, Mexico, and elsewhere. As these linkages deepen, guanxi may find new grounds for consolidation.

From a policy perspective, the business generated by resident Chinese communities can augment tax revenue and widen trade networks, but only when it operates within the law. When it does not, ethnic entrepreneurship can evolve into organized crime, and broad-based benefits into private profiteering. As Alejandro Portes puts it, "the capacity of authorities to enforce rules (social control) can [be] jeopardized by the existence of tight networks whose function is precisely to facilitate violation of those rules for private benefit" (1998, 15). Inward-looking informal networks impede the efforts of governments and markets to harness domestic talent and scale up local capacities for an ostensibly greater national good. The policy challenge, once again, is to intervene in ways that leverage trust rather than destroy it.

Government programs the world over attract public trust when they affirm community values. As a series of papers from the John F. Kennedy School of Government argues, regulatory frameworks are most effective when they are socially "embedded" and "tailored to take account of the culture, education, and priorities of intended audiences" (Fung et al. 2004, 4 and 5; also see M. Graham 2001; Weil 2002). This book finds that responsiveness to bottom-up demands is becoming more central to the capacity of the Cuban and Mexican governments to establish and sustain the rule of law. Unofficial connections to China, whether through illicit trade networks or diasporic communities, require more refined policies of social engagement.

THE POLITICS OF WRITING TRUST

China's profound impact on Latin America has generated a rich literary response. Trade is the most quantifiable dimension of this impact, as is evident in the early appearance of reports from the Inter-American Development Bank (Agosin, Rodas Martini, and Saavedra-Rivano 2004), the Organisation for Economic Co-operation and Development (Blázquez-Lidoy, Rodríguez, and Santiso 2006), and the World Bank (Lederman, Olarreaga, and Perry 2008). Kevin Gallagher and Roberto Porzecanski's *The Dragon in the Room* draws on these efforts to spell out the economic pressures that China has brought to bear on the region. China's unprecedented demand for its natural resources, the authors argue, has kicked away the ladder that might otherwise lead to upgraded industries and value-added exports (2010).

The political implications of Sino–Latin American engagement have also attracted attention. Joshua Kurlantzick's *Charm Offensive* (2007) presents interviews, media excerpts, and survey data that reveal the Chinese government's soft power initiatives in Latin America and elsewhere, from Confucius institutes to sports infrastructure. *China in Latin America* (2009) by R. Evan Ellis zeroes in on the strategic positioning of

Chinese state-owned enterprises in the region and the security dilemmas they may arouse. The seven case studies that constitute *Latin America Facing China* (2010a), edited by Alex Fernández Jilberto and Barbara Hogenboom, illustrate the risks of unbalanced Sino–Latin American trade, which emerged in sobering clarity when commodity prices collapsed in 2008. The need for longer-term planning and coordination, the editors conclude, has fomented a "paradigmatic convergence between China and the leftist governments in Latin America" (Fernández Jilberto and Hogenboom 2010b, 191).

Chinese commentators steer clear of advocating any ideological convergence with Latin America, at least in *China–Latin America Relations: Review and Analysis* (2012), a characteristically dutiful volume edited by the Latin Americanist He Shuangrong of the Chinese Academy of Social Sciences. The book's twelve authors appear in order of descending rank, dwelling on officially sanctioned concepts like mutual benefit, collaborative development, and food and energy security. Although some of the book's arguments resemble (and may well have informed) official policies, others elucidate Chinese perspectives on less-publicized topics, such as whether China is complicating security arrangements in the Western Hemisphere and anxieties that China's rise may stir among Western analysts. Lin Hua's chapter on overseas Chinese communities offers a glimpse into Beijing's efforts to advance foreign policy goals through Latin America's Chinese diaspora, which the author argues is "the most direct source to carry forward and spread Chinese traditional culture" and to "promote the development of China–Latin America trade relations" (2012, 115 and 116).

Two volumes have explored Sino–Latin American interactions on the ground. *China Engages Latin America*, which José Luis León-Manríquez and I edited (Hearn and León-Manríquez 2011), combines cross-regional analysis with country studies that examine how political ideologies, domestic histories, and informal social ties are embedded in official relations with China. And *From the Great Wall to the New World*, edited by Julia C. Strauss and Ariel C. Armony (2012), presents ten essays that illustrate how Chinese relations with Latin America have moved beyond trade and investment into the political and social spheres of sustainable urbanization, media (print and online), understandings of hegemonic challenge, and engagement with Chinese diasporic communities. The editors argue that this "thickening" of Sino-Latin American interactions invites researchers to formulate new empirical approaches that "recast the ways in which we think about contemporary processes of globalization" (Armony and Strauss 2012, 17).

The following chapters take up Armony and Strauss's invitation by exploring China's impact on the intersection of international engagement, domestic industrial relations, and community development. Researching these connections is as much a methodological challenge as a theoretical one, owing to a persisting academic division of labor that does not favor concurrent attention to macro and micro perspectives. The book draws inspiration from the pioneering cross-disciplinary work of Michael Burawoy (2000), George Marcus (1995), and Aihwa Ong and Stephen Collier (2004), which established a two-way street between global economic systems and local initiative.

No single methodology can fully apprehend Chinese transnationalism, but a combination of historical and anthropological analysis can illuminate the articulation of international relations with social process over time. Multisited ethnography is well suited to explore transnational phenomena because, as Marcus writes, it opens the possibility of "tracing a cultural formation across and within multiple sites of activity" (1995, 96). Setting out with this orientation, the book traces the cultural formation of trust, first as a principle for formulating China's political interactions with—and within—Cuba and Mexico (chapters 1 and 2) and then as a catalyst for purposeful solidarity among Chinese communities in the two countries (chapters 3 and 4). The goal is to generate insight into how top-down policies and bottom-up proposals at times converge and at other times diverge in response to China's rise, and how trust shapes these critical junctures.

To see beyond official statements and statistics on China's engagement with Latin America requires time on the ground. Time, though, is a dwindling resource for twenty-first-century researchers. University budgets are shrinking, teaching loads are growing, and publications are increasingly assessed for their short-term impact. Graduate students in the social sciences—anthropology, in particular—are probably the last remaining group expected (and, if lucky, funded) to leave campus for extended periods to gather data. They can therefore contribute much to the future study of Chinese–Latin American relations, and established scholars stand to deepen their knowledge by seeking out and supervising them.

I have been fortunate to secure a series of grants and fellowships to sustain fifteen years of full-time research and writing on Cuba, China, and Mexico. From 2000 until 2002 I lived in Havana and Santiago de Cuba to learn how Afro-Cuban religious associations were filling new civic spaces to compensate for underresourced government services (Hearn 2008a). These insights provided conceptual orientation for my subsequent work in Barrio Chino, where Chinese associations were also reaching out. Like their Afro-Cuban counterparts, they were consolidating their internal strengths, building bridges to other grassroots associations, and selectively participating in government programs that might empower them. Other neighborhood groups were also emerging at the time, with varying degrees of autonomy, to advocate women's rights, Christian welfare projects, self-employment, and other civic agendas. To document this "rise of the local," as it was becoming known among Cuban observers, I worked with Ernel Mastrapa and María Teresa Montes de Oca Choy at the University of Havana to convene fifteen researchers from Havana, Santiago de Cuba, and Camagüey to share their insights in a workshop and a book (Hearn 2008b).

Shortly after President Hu Jintao's celebrated visit to Cuba in 2004, I returned to Havana for eight months to see Barrio Chino becoming a mass-mediated stop for visiting Chinese diplomats. Its street markets were bustling with local and foreign clients, and its rich cultural heritage was reemerging into public view. The dawn *wushu* tai chi sessions long conducted privately in the Chinese associations were expanding into vacant lots and public parks. Small votive statues of the Chinese deity Guan Gong (关公, known locally as San Fan Con) were appearing in Barrio Chino's informal markets and on ecumenical home altars around Havana. The Chinese associations were welcoming tourists into their flourishing restaurants and in-house museums.

Studying these issues over time inevitably drew me into local politics, reminding me of a lesson from undergraduate anthropology: it is impossible to be a fly on the wall. On several occasions I failed to appreciate how this theory works in practice, only to recognize in hindsight the consequences of my actions. In 2013 Barrio Chino's local government set about renovating a traditional Chinese pharmacy and asked my help to find a Chinese source of homeopathic products (see chapter 3). I saw no harm in this, and with the assistance of colleagues in Beijing, had the government's proposal translated and presented to a supplier we identified. Subsequent discussions in Barrio Chino revealed a broader agenda: a Chinese association was already importing these items formally and informally from China, generating unwanted competition for the government. My matchmaking may have unwittingly undermined this competition and compromised exchanges that over time could have benefited Havana's Chinese community. On reflection I was reminded that participant observation is never an innocent endeavor, a point I have tried to incorporate into this book by including occasional excerpts from my research diary.

As China's engagement with Latin America deepened, conferences on the topic identified a need for closer dialogue with Chinese researchers. I shared this concern, and in 2007 I relocated to Beijing for one year to study Mandarin and explore the development of Latin American studies in Chinese universities and research institutes. I presented the preliminary arguments of this book at the Chinese Academy of Social Sciences, Fudan University, Nankai University, Jinan University, and the China Center for Contemporary World Studies. Ensuing debates opened my eyes to the multiple opinions, agendas, and political pressures conditioning Chinese interactions with Latin America. These exchanges were the starting point for a series of workshops at the University of Sydney; the University of California, Berkeley; the Inter-American Dialogue; and the University of Chicago. Support from the Open Society Institute, the Australian Research Council, the Latin American Studies Association, and the Worldwide Universities Network enabled Chinese scholars such as Jiang Shixue, Sun Hongbo, Yang Zhimin, Wang Ping, Zhang Jianhua, and Zhang Xuegang to participate in these events, in turn generating a series of publications (Hearn 2010; Jiang 2011; Mao, Hearn, and Liu 2015; P. Wang 2013; also see Strauss and Armony 2012).

Working with Chinese scholars revealed the controversial place of Mexico in China's foreign relations and sparked my curiosity about how China was perceived in Mexico. In 2008 I took up a lecturing position at the Autonomous University of Baja California (UABC) in Tijuana, home to one of Mexico's largest Chinese diasporic communities. Classroom debates about the impact of Chinese manufactured exports on the city's small businesses provided me with valuable leads for follow-up research, and the UABC historian Catalina Velázquez Morales shared her extensive archives on Chinese settlement in the region. The Chinese consul general had recently gone on record condemning violence against Tijuana's Chinese community and accepted an invitation to participate in a public debate on Chinese-Mexican relations at the UABC. He introduced me to Chinese business and cultural leaders, who in turn arranged meetings for me at the Chinese associations of Tijuana and Mexicali between 2008 and 2011. The China-Mexico Research Center at the National Autonomous University of Mexico also became a focal point for me to consult with researchers and Chinese entrepreneurs in Mexico City between 2010 and 2014.

Countless people contributed sensitive personal and political insights to enrich this book. I have tried to convey their perspectives as faithfully as possible and to build the book's conceptual analysis on their ideas. My attempt to mediate bottom-up experiences of China's impact with top-down analysis of state-society relations has involved compromises, which I hope will validate the trust of the many people who shared their knowledge with me. The mediations pursued by governments, companies, and community associations in their quest for effective responses to China's rise have also required compromise. How diaspora and trust condition these interactions is the question to which we now turn.

Miguel, better known as Chino, gestured enthusiastically toward his new armchair. A carpenter by trade, he had always made his own furniture, but this was a piece to be proud of. It contained the best available fabric and timber, affordable thanks to his new job. Since 2011 he had been working in a nearby marketplace, selling pipes, valves, and spare parts for home plumbing repairs. Chino took me to the small courtyard where his concrete cubicle stood alongside ten or so others, which sold everything from ground coconut to T-shirts (figure 1.1). A promotional sign indicated his professional versatility: "Se realiza todo tipo de trabajo a domicilio y en el puesto, gracias" (I provide every kind of service in-house and in-store, thank you).

Over the bustle of animated negotiations, Chino explained that he had acquired about half of the items on sale in his cubicle through official government-licensed suppliers, and the rest illegally through a network of friends working in state factories. Everybody in the courtyard, he said, relied on the black market for about half of their supplies because "otherwise none of this would be possible. Unfortunately our system is broken, because it only works if you steal things. The newspaper says Raúl [Castro, Cuba's president since 2008] is going to create a wholesale market . . . that's why he went to China again to find suppliers." I had known Chino for a decade, but I had never previously encountered him with money

FIGURE 1.1 Chino and his wares, Havana. Photo by the author.

in his pocket and optimistic about the future. In the absence of a legal supply chain, though, he would continue to operate under the table and under the threat of surprise inspections.

Chino's uncertainty about the trajectory of Cuba's development and China's role in it is shared by observers around the world. Critics argue that in contrast to China's economic liberalization over the past three decades, Cuba's commitment to "updating the socialist system" constitutes a justification for maintaining the fifty-year-old status quo, and that "nothing much will change" (Azel 2011). Others perceive real change under Raúl Castro, describing the suite of reforms announced by his government in 2011 as "a significant realignment of the paternalistic relationship that has existed between the State and its citizenry since the revolutionary period began in 1959" (Laverty 2011, 4). Even Freedom House, which has long doubted the sincerity of the Cuban government's policies, finds that "the opening of a private sector, while still limited, is driving genuine change in Cuba" (Moreno and Calingaert 2011, 25).

The global financial crisis deepened efforts to shift the contours of Cuba's post–Fidel Castro economic landscape, its impact transmitted through the island's sensitivity to foreign credit, export earnings (particularly from nickel), remittances, and tourism (Mesa-Lago and Vidal-Alejandro 2010, 690–91). Cuba's response was unveiled in the April 2011 Communist Party Congress: a series of 313 reforms called the *Lineamientos de la política económica y social del partido y la revolución* (Economic and social policy guidelines of the party and revolution; República de Cuba 2011).

A prominent feature of the *Lineamientos* is an attempt to build synergies between large state enterprises, small private actors like Chino, and suppliers for both. As in China, the goal is not to replace the state with the market, but to create a more liberal blend of state authority and market incentives capable of integrating aspiring entrepreneurs into existing hegemonic structures. Through this process the Cuban government hopes to scale back its share of spending from 95 percent of gross domestic product (GDP) to around 40 percent by 2017 (Frank 2012). This optimistic goal resonates with the advice of Chinese policy researchers in a recent issue of the Cuban journal *Temas*, who argue that the optimal developmental path is one that prioritizes gradual opening under the "supreme guidance of the state" (J. Yan 2011, 13; also see Shi 2011). China is not simply an example for Cuba, but an active player in the reformulation of the Cuban system. China helped Cuba survive the collapse of the Soviet Union and upgrade basic industrial infrastructure, and by 2014 Cuba's GDP (in purchasing power parity) had rebounded to $234 billion (World Bank 2015b). As noted in the introduction, China is now Cuba's second largest trading partner, with annual bilateral trade reaching $1.39 billion in 2014. The dollar amount has fluctuated considerably since reaching a peak of $2.3 billion in 2008, but it is up from just $314 million in 2000 (figure 1.2; United Nations Commodity Trade Statistics Database 2015). Commercial agreements have been accompanied by advice about trade and investment liberalization, conveyed repeatedly to Cuban officials by their Chinese counterparts ever since Fidel Castro's 1995 meeting with Chinese Premier Li Peng in Beijing (Y. Cheng 2007a and 2007b; Jiang 2009). As Chino indicated above, Cuba's emerging entrepreneurs continue to rely on the black market, a problem their government hopes to address in part through inbound supply of Chinese consumer products for the wholesale market.

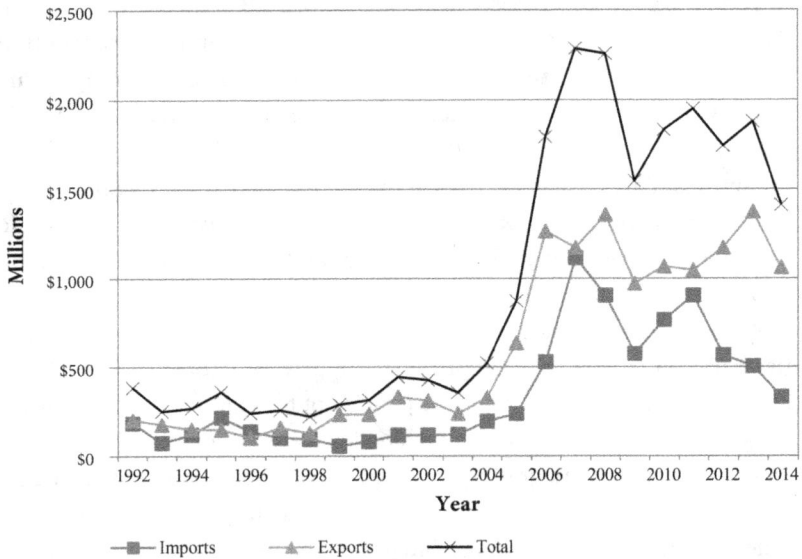

FIGURE 1.2 China's trade with Cuba, 1992–2014. Source: United Nations Commodity Trade Statistics Database 2015.

Ideological affinity is no longer the prime mover of Sino-Cuban engagement. As a former Cuban diplomat in Beijing noted, "we can no longer knock on China's door and ask for favors the way we used to. Political trust is still important in our relationship, but now it's a matter of pragmatism, because the Chinese insist that the numbers have to add up" (Omar Pereira Hernández, interview, May 28, 2012). Cuba's de facto ambassador to China during the Cultural Revolution, Mauro García Triana, described the situation this way: "The Chinese are very clear about one thing: they're not going to be benefactors for Cuba like the Soviets were. I was once told in no uncertain terms by a Chinese diplomat: 'Our relations with Cuba have to be mutually beneficial or they will not work'" (interview, January 11, 2007).

Political solidarity continues to shape the contours of Sino-Cuban cooperation, but the ideological foundations of the relationship are shifting away from doctrines of top-down control. This shift reflects a common development trajectory: centralized governance once sought to command economic development and the social interactions it entails. As Lenin put it, "trust is good, but control is better." More recently, appropriately regulated private sectors have been gaining credibility in both nations as experimental policies open new ground for small businesses and the independent exchanges they require. China and Cuba are grappling with this transformation in their own ways, in the process redefining the balance of vertical and horizontal power that underpins their domestic development and bilateral relations.

This chapter's first section outlines the changing nature of Sino-Cuban cooperation since the establishment of diplomatic relations in 1960, from state-to-state deals premised on political ideology to strategies for expanding the private sector. It then considers bilateral cooperation in oil production, electronics manufacturing, transportation, and education. State management has enabled a high degree of coordination among these sectors, but unrealistic expectations of political solidarity on the part of Cuban negotiators have also produced tensions with increasingly market-oriented Chinese negotiators. The chapter's final section examines the reforms proposed by Cuba's 2011 *Lineamientos*, particularly their approach to decentralization, employment, and the informal sector. While China's earlier liberalization has provided inspiration and insight for this process, the chapter concludes that an important next step will be to permit cooperation between independent Chinese and Cuban citizens. This will require both governments to acknowledge that, in spite of Lenin, trust is sometimes better than control.

THE CHANGING BASIS OF SINO-CUBAN RELATIONS

Political affinities between Cuba and China date back to the early years of the Cuban Revolution. On September 2, 1960, Fidel Castro declared that Cuba would sever ties with Taiwan; this was done on September 28, making Cuba the first Latin American country to establish diplomatic relations with the People's Republic of China. In the first half of the 1960s, China provided economic and military aid to Cuba, supporting its repelling of the Bay of Pigs invasion (People's Republic of China Ministry of Foreign Affairs 1987, 365–66). In return, Cuba supported China's bid to restore its status in the United Nations. Bilateral trade was initiated and regulated through a noncash system of annual quotas, codified in 1960 in the first five-year trade and payment agreement. The agreement was eminently political, with Premier Zhou Enlai proposing that China would buy one million tons of sugar from Cuba (at the inflated price of $100 million) and pay for it with industrial equipment. Ernesto "Che" Guevara recognized the added value of Zhou's offer: "This [proposal] is not tenable from the economic point of view, but we raised it from the political point of view" (Ministry of Foreign Affairs of Cuba 1960, 5).

Ideological differences and rivalry between the communist parties of China and the Soviet Union (known as the Sino-Soviet split) produced tensions—though never a rupture—in Sino-Cuban relations from the middle of the 1960s to the early 1980s (Zhu, Mao, and Li 2002, 319). To remain economically viable in the face of pressure from the United States, Cuba sided with the Soviet Union, and in 1967 the Chinese ambassador was recalled from Havana after Castro called Mao Zedong "a senile idiot" (Garcia Triana, Eng Herrera, and Benton 2009, xxi). The 1975 war in Angola, in which Cuba and China backed opposing factions, and China's invasion of Vietnam in 1979 further strained bilateral relations. At the time of the invasion Castro called Deng Xiaoping a "caricature of Hitler" (ibid., xxi) and denounced China's aggression during a speech in Havana's Plaza de la Revolución, prompting the Chinese delegates to stand up in unison and leave.

As China ceased its policy of antagonism toward countries aligned with Moscow in the early 1980s, a confluence of political and economic interests motivated Beijing's rapprochement with Havana. In 1983 Cuba's minister of foreign trade, Ricardo Cabrisas, visited Beijing to negotiate an agreement enabling Chinese students, diplomats, and military officials to visit Havana (signed in 1984) and to expand the 1960 trade and payment agreement to accommodate the exchange of 100,000 tons of Cuban sugar for Chinese manufactured products (signed in 1988). Chinese leaders recognized that a key problem for Cuba was its dependency on oil imports. In 1985 Cuban oil output was 870,000 tons, enough to meet only 10 percent of domestic demand; the rest was provided at a heavily subsidized rate by the Soviet Union. The disintegration of the Soviet Union forced Cuba to start paying market prices for oil, which seriously hampered its economic growth and drained its foreign purchasing capacity. An exchange of Cuban and Chinese foreign ministers in 1989 focused on initiating cooperation in oil production, a goal that—as discussed below—remains a bilateral priority.

Cuban officials watched with trepidation as Eastern European citizens rose up at the end of the 1980s to challenge the Soviet system. Against all odds, the Castro government survived the so-called end of history, though with severe economic casualties. The withdrawal of Soviet support and the evaporation of trade with the Soviet bloc precipitated a 75 percent reduction in Cuba's import capacity and a 35 percent decline in GDP. China played an important but little-known role in seeing Cuba through this tumultuous period. The Chinese Communist Party had also come under domestic pressure for change at this time, but it emerged intact in part through its 1989 crackdown in Tiananmen Square and in part through a decade of sincere commitment to opening the economy, improving living standards, and creating jobs.

Arriving in Havana in June 1989, just days after the Tiananmen Square incident, Chinese Foreign Minister Qian Qichen was warmly received by Castro. The gesture was deeply appreciated in Beijing, since every other country on Qian's itinerary had canceled his visit. As Cheng Yinghong notes, China's relationship with Cuba became "one of the most important Sino-foreign relations in the eyes of the post-Tiananmen Chinese leaders" (2007b, 727). The show of solidarity was mutually beneficial: in 1993, a time when most of the world believed the downfall of the Cuban Revolution was imminent, Chinese President Jiang Zemin broke the island's isolation with a state visit and an offer of financial assistance. According to a Chinese diplomat I interviewed in Beijing (who requested anonymity), Jiang conducted the visit to "save Cuba's revolutionary project," expressly against the advice of China's increasingly pragmatic Communist Party.

The basis for Sino-Cuban cooperation was shifting in step with global change. Without Soviet support Cuba could not sustain its 1988 accord with China to exchange sugar for manufactured products or the encompassing trade and payment agreement that for three decades had underpinned bilateral barter transactions. As Castro discovered during his first visit to Beijing in 1995, ideology would no longer trump economics. Inadequately briefed by Cuban diplomats in Beijing, he found Chinese officials to be far more pragmatic than he had expected. Publicly, communist ideology was heralded as an enduring linchpin of bilateral relations, but privately Premier Li Peng advised him to liberalize the Cuban economy. Jiang tellingly arranged meetings with Castro both in Beijing and in the

Shenzhen Special Economic Zone, the heartland of China's liberalized export economy. Shortly after, on January 1, 1996, China ended the trade and payment agreement with Cuba.

As Cuba's vice president, Raúl Castro showed more interest than his brother in effecting domestic economic reforms and in building a pragmatic relationship with China. According to a former employee of the Cuban embassy in Beijing, Raúl's 1997 "week-long learning trip" to China actually consisted of a month of research into Chinese approaches to industrial reform, privatization, and urban development. As the evidence collected by Hal Klepak (2010) shows, the military institutions Raúl crafted on his return to manage operations in tourism and agriculture were subjected to essentially the same pressures as Chinese firms: to produce, be accountable, and make a profit. Raúl's efforts to this end were assisted by visiting Chinese advisors, such as a specialist appointed by Zhu Rongji, the future premier, to share insights into China's experience with foreign investment and outreach to expatriates (Y. Cheng 2007b, 729). Another visitor was Mao Xianglin, a special envoy of the Central Committee of the Chinese Communist Party, who developed action plans for expanding Cuban consumer markets. This involved the establishment in 1997 of a bicycle factory with Chinese capital and technical expertise and a facility for producing electric fans and household consumer goods. Mao described this strategy as an incremental process:

I would hesitate to say that our Cuban manufacturing operations are entirely commercial, because what we're doing is broader than that. We're trying to help Cuba to incrementally upgrade its technical ability. If our products prove popular and useful then we assist by setting up factories. . . . It is interesting that China learned from the United States how to manage its economy, and now Latin America looks to China as a teacher of socialism. Today we are a global village, but for the village to be harmonious there has to be mutual understanding and respect. That is why we are helping Cuba to reach its goals. . . . Using Chinese expertise Cuba could come to produce electronic goods for sale to Latin America. (interview, December 14, 2007)

The mutual understanding pursued by Mao in Cuba was based not on orchestrated quotas and artificial prices, as had been the case until 1996, but on the goal of modernizing Cuba's infrastructure to enable the country's integration into international markets. To this end, Jiang visited again in 2001, providing a loan of $200 million to update Cuban telecommunications with Chinese products and a $150 million line of credit to buy Chinese televisions (Erikson and Minson 2006). He also pledged to support Cuban production of rice, soy, sorghum, maize, and sugar for sale to the Chinese state, but the slow pace of Cuban land reforms limited this prospect. Cuba's sugar exports to China nevertheless had grown from $91 million in 2001 to $210 million in 2014 (United Nations Commodity Trade Statistics Database 2015).

The Chinese Communist Party elite was privately less enthusiastic about Cuba than Jiang was, not least because the slow recovery of the Cuban economy had delayed the repayment of loans. In 2003 Fidel Castro made a second visit to Beijing to explain. Together with Jiang, he prepared a schedule of monthly payments from the National Bank of Cuba and a series of strict fiscal requirements to be imposed on Cuban enterprises. The plan's strength was its diplomatic timing. In the context of China's looming leadership transition, it provided Jiang and his allies with a tool to advocate continued support to Cuba. The Cuba lobby was further strengthened by Castro's symbolic power: long revered in China as a revolutionary icon, his public praise of the Chinese system provided relief to a government facing growing concerns about its ability to deal with domestic inequality and advance the socialist cause. Jiang, General Secretary Hu Jintao, incoming Premier Wen Jiabao, Zhu, and other key figures all publicly expressed their solidarity with Castro (*People's Daily* 2003a and 2003b).

The reelection of U.S. President George W. Bush in November 2004 generated diplomatic common ground for Cuba and China. Having become China's president in March 2003, Hu visited Havana the same month that Bush was reelected. Bush's hard-line position on Cuba led to media commentary that for Castro there was "no better time for the visit" (Reuters Havana 2004). Hu affirmed the bilateral relationship with a thinly veiled reference to the United States, stating that China and Cuba "are fraternal brothers . . . passing the test of changing and adverse international circumstances" (quoted in Lam 2004, 3; also see Murray 2004). The visit yielded agreements in education, public health, biotechnology, telecommunications, earthquake detection, solar energy research, cancer treatment, vaccine production, nickel mining, and oil exploration. China pledged to invest \$500 million in Cuba's nickel sector, and although Venezuela emerged as the leading financier of the Las Camariocas ferro-nickel plant near the city of Moa, by 2014 China had consumed \$3.8 billion worth of Cuban nickel—nearly all that had been produced since 2004 (United Nations Commodity Trade Statistics Database 2015). The visit also indicated a shift in economic thinking: Chinese electronic products imported by Cuba such as washing machines, televisions, rice cookers, air conditioners, and refrigerators would now be assembled on the island (see below).

Visiting Cuba again in November 2008, Hu offered extensions on the repayment of previous loans, a donation of \$8 million for hurricane relief, and a credit line of \$70 million for health infrastructure (*Granma* 2008). In another apparent reference to the United States, he stated that "the Chinese people will, as always, support the just struggle of the Cuban people in safeguarding state sovereignty and opposing outside interference" (quoted in *Xinhua* 2008). According to a member of Hu's delegation, China offered thirty-seven investment projects on the understanding that Chinese technicians, investors, and their families would take up residence in Cuba (interview, November 21, 2008). Whether such an influx of Chinese employees would be viewed favorably by Cubans or provoke hostile reactions as it has elsewhere in Latin America would remain unknown, since only a small number of the projects was approved.

In June 2011 Xi Jinping, China's vice president, and Jiang Jiemin, president of the China National Petroleum Corporation (CNPC), visited Cuba to sign thirteen agreements ranging from investment in oil and gas to banking and finance. Underpinning the first Five-Year Plan for Sino-Cuban cooperation, the accords demonstrated China's long-term commitment to assisting Cuba through its reforms. As the economist Richard Feinberg noted at the time, "some observers opine, albeit with some exaggeration, that China has become Cuba's IMF [International Monetary Fund]!" (2011, 42). The director of the Latin America Institute of the Chinese Academy of International Relations, Wu Hongyin, had this to say of Xi's visit: "The deepening of reform in Cuba and the broadening of liberalization measures will call more attention among Chinese companies. This, in turn, will increase Chinese-Cuban economic cooperation, and create more opportunities for both nations in important economic sectors such as agriculture, telecommunications, infrastructure, services, energy, among others. Future economic relations will be closer" (quoted in *Cuba Standard* 2011).

Just as Fidel Castro had traveled to Beijing to meet incoming President Hu and Premier Wen in 2003, Raúl Castro went to China to meet incoming President Xi Jinping and Premier Li Keqiang in July 2012. The visit secured agreements that the Chinese government would boost tourism to Cuba and provide digital television and telecommunications technology, financial and banking services, infrastructure, and equipment for the health sector. It also consolidated cooperation in agriculture through Chinese provision of fertilizers, tractors, and irrigation equipment. Export contracts are a common feature of Chinese bilateral agreements, but as was the case during Fidel Castro's 2003 visit, the deeper value for the incoming government was the Cuban leader's ringing public endorsement of China's scientific progress, humanitarianism, economic stability, and faithful pursuit of socialism. As Cheng writes, "Cuba has been perceived as the most unyielding and thus the most admirable anti-American hero who, as the Chinese government has introduced to its people, sets an example of the defiance of 'international pressures' and of survival against all odds. In this way the image of Cuba has facilitated China's newly emerging nationalism. The hardliners, old Maoists and new leftists have looked upon Cuba as the example of the socialism purer than China's" (2007b, 728; also see Y. Cheng 2012).

Political solidarity continues to serve a diplomatic purpose in Sino-Cuban relations as was evident during Xi's 2014 visit to the island, which he commended for "persisting on the socialist path, firmly safeguarding the sovereignty of the state" (quoted in Pérez 2014). The comment was accompanied by a commitment from China Minmetals Corporation to purchase $600 million of Cuban nickel, illustrating pragmatic substance beneath the diplomacy.

For over three decades ideology permeated Sino-Cuban relations, starting with grandiose commitments such as the 1960 trade and payment agreement and Zhou Enlai's willingness to buy overpriced Cuban sugar. Political solidarity continued to prevail through the doctrinal disputes of the Sino-Soviet split and rapprochement, marked by centrally planned bartering of sugar for manufactured products. Castro's support for China through the Tiananmen crisis and Jiang's endeavor to "save" the Cuban Revolution after the Soviet collapse demonstrated the depth of trust between the two countries. The nature of bilateral relations began to change in the mid-1990s, when China terminated the trade and payment agreement and began advising Cuba to pursue economic reforms. For two decades this advice has focused on the gradual liberalization of markets and the empowerment of private actors to stimulate productivity and reduce the burden on the state. It is only since Raúl Castro assumed the presidency in 2008 that Cuba has shown genuine interest in implementing these suggestions.

Although liberalization implies a greater role for the private sector and civil society, Cuban interactions with China remain notably devoid of contact between nonstate actors. All aspects of formal engagement are designed and managed through governmental accords, limiting the potential for cooperation between the two nations to keep pace with developments within them. Interactions between emerging Cuban small businesses, cooperatives, and nongovernmental organizations and their more established Chinese counterparts would provide a broader basis for building trade, understanding, and trust. The formulation of legal guidelines for regulating such exchanges would also enable both sides to more effectively contain informal connections between the two (a point discussed in chapter 3).

A prerequisite for the emergence of more heterogeneous forms of Sino-Cuban engagement is legal authorization—particularly from the Cuban side—to develop autonomous partnerships, conduct trade, and hold independent conferences and forums. As the Cuban private sector gains strength, to forbid such activities is to invite unregistered trade, clandestine negotiations, and political dissent born of oppositional solidarity. Esteban Lazo Hernández, a member of Cuba's Politburo, predicts that the growth of private initiatives between 2012 and 2017 will see the state's share of GDP production cut in half from its current level of 95 percent (Frank 2012). The Cuban government will tread a dangerous path if it does not permit civil liberties to keep pace with this shift. For the time being, cooperation with China in everything from oil to education remains the preserve of the state.

The rapid development of the Chinese economy has provoked a global quest for oil. Sino-Cuban onshore oil cooperation was first envisioned in 1989, several years before oil and natural gas fields were identified in a 112,000-square-kilometer maritime area under Cuban jurisdiction in the Gulf of Mexico. Quickly attracting international interest, the offshore area was designated as an exclusive economic zone (EEZ) and divided into fifty (later fifty-nine) blocks, each spanning approximately 2,000 square kilometers. Foreign capital and technology were introduced through joint venture contracts in seventeen (later thirty) of the blocks.

In 2004 fuel imports cost Cuba $1.31 billion, a significant figure considering that at the time Cuba's GDP amounted to $32 billion (Economist Intelligence Unit 2008, 48–50). That year, ahead of President Hu's visit, the Chinese enterprise Sinopec signed a "Memorandum on Blocks No. 1, 2, 3 and 4" of the EEZ with the National Petroleum Company of Cuba (CUPET), and in January 2005 the Shengli Oilfield Administration Bureau (a division of Sinopec) signed a product-sharing contract for prospecting in a further three blocks. Hu's visit paved the way for the Great Wall Drilling Company, a subsidiary of CNPC, to commence onshore operations in Varadero in 2005, producing thirteen million barrels of oil over the subsequent seven years. During Hu's second visit, in 2008, CNPC and CUPET expanded their projects in oil and gas field development, engineering and technical services, and the export of Chinese equipment to Cuba (China National Petroleum Corporation 2008).

The U.S. Geological Survey estimates that Cuba's Gulf of Mexico fields contain 4.6 billion barrels of crude oil and 9.8 trillion cubic feet of natural gas (USGS 2005). Cuban sources have estimated that the island's maritime oil reserves exceed 20 billion barrels (compared to Mexico's 11.7 billion), and that the exploitation of these reserves will place it within the top twenty oil-producing nations ("Cuba Claims Massive Oil Reserves" 2008). In June 2011, during Xi and Jiang's visit to Havana, CUPET and CNPC signed a new framework agreement granting the latter five blocks at the western edge of the EEZ (numbers 19–22 and 30), adjacent to the maritime border with Mexico (China National Petroleum Corporation 2008). Exploratory drilling in the EEZ by the Spanish firm Repsol commenced in January 2012, despite U.S. security and environmental concerns (Council on Hemispheric Affairs 2011; Hutchinson-Jafar 2011; Piñón 2011, 24).

The successful extraction of Cuban oil would significantly redirect the island's development trajectory. As a BBC report put it in early 2012, "this is a key moment for Cuba. . . . Substantial deposits of oil, and most likely gas, would transform this struggling economy into an energy exporter" (Rainsford 2012). Pressure to end the U.S. trade embargo, or at least adjust it to permit cooperation in the oil sector, would mount, since "the United States would find it difficult to accept being sidelined without a piece of the pie, especially with regard to gas reserves that could reduce energy costs in some southern states" (Ravsberg 2012).

At the end of 2011 the Chinese-built (and Italian-owned) Scarabeo-9 Ultra-Deepwater Rig arrived in the EEZ, designed specifically to comply with U.S. trade sanctions against Cuba that limited components to less than 10 percent U.S.-made. Repsol (Spain), Petronas (Malaysia), Gazpromneft (Russia), and Petróleos de Venezuela (Venezuela) each leased Scarabeo-9 to drill in the EEZ. All failed to achieve results, citing the compact nature of the underlying rock as unsuitable for oil and gas extraction. In November 2012 the Scarabeo-9 departed Cuba but was immediately replaced by the Songa Mercur, a Soviet-built platform owned by Songa Offshore of Norway and leased for one year to the Russian oil giant Zarubezhneft for $88 million. Refitted in Trinidad and Tobago to replace its U.S.-made components (including five generators from Caterpillar, mud pump motors from General Electric, and cementing equipment from Halliburton), the platform commenced drilling off the coast of Ciego de Avila and Villa Clara Provinces.

Zarubezhneft continues to prospect in the EEZ with the support of another Russian state enterprise, Rosneft, which has agreed to build a base at the Port of Mariel to relay equipment and personnel to offshore rigs (Gibson 2014). Should Zarubezhneft or any other company strike oil, China's CNPC has positioned itself to take advantage of the event. Anticipating an eventual discovery, CNPC subsidiary Huanqiu Contracting and Engineering Corporation has entered a joint venture with the Cuban-Venezuelan enterprise Cuvenpetrol and an Italian subsidiary of the French oil engineering company Technip to upgrade a refinery in Cienfuegos. The renovated facility will be capable of increasing production from 65,000 barrels per day to 150,000. Using Venezuelan reserves as collateral, Huanqiu is the main financier of the $5.5 billion project, which also involves building a gasification plant to process Venezuelan—and potentially Cuban—liquid natural gas (*Cuba Standard* 2011).

As shale gas becomes globally available and the Organization of Petroleum Exporting Countries (OPEC) tries to compete by oversupplying the world with crude oil, energy prices have declined by nearly half to their lowest point since 2009—and with them Cuba's dreams of becoming an oil giant. In January 2015 Venezuelan President Nicolás Maduro visited Saudi Arabia to request that OPEC reduce its production ceiling of thirty million barrels per day because oil revenue subsidizes his government's hallmark social programs. It also underpins Venezuela's Petrocaribe oil distribution program, whose supply to Cuba diminished from 100,000 barrels per day in 2013 to around 70,000 at the end of 2014 (Pitts 2014). Cuba's oil supply is protected to an extent by its reciprocal provision of some thirty thousand health-care workers to Venezuela, but Maduro's opponents have pledged to rescind the oil-for-doctors program if elected. To manage this risk the Cuban government is once again reevaluating its foreign relations, including with the United States. The diplomatic rapprochement announced by Presidents Barack Obama and Raúl Castro in 2014 is likely to stimulate a growing presence of U.S. firms in Cuba, including in the oil sector. There they will find Chinese counterparts whose state-backed trade and investment activities will pose competitive challenges.

The Cuban and Chinese governments view their oil cooperation as national priorities and manage it entirely through state enterprises. This is logical considering the required capital outlays, which private firms even in China would have trouble raising, but state control of core industries also reflects a political strategy. As Joshua Kurlantzick writes, "The Chinese government wants to control the entire process, from taking commodities out of the ground to shipping them back to China, because it does not trust world markets to ensure continuous supplies of key resources. It is purchasing stakes in important oil and gas firms abroad, constructing the infrastructure necessary to get those industries' resources to port, and building close relations with refiners and shippers" (2008, 200). By linking distinct sectors into an integrated system, the Chinese government has attained a high degree of control over production chains around the world (Ellis 2005, 193–212; Hira 2007, 87–96). As the next section shows, this approach is evident in Sino-Cuban projects that connect electronics manufacturing with the education and transportation sectors. Coordinating these initiatives has involved a high degree of top-down oversight but also some hard lessons for Cuban negotiators, whose faith in ideological solidarity has been shaken by the pragmatism of their Chinese counterparts.

THE SUM OF THEIR PARTS: ELECTRONICS, TRANSPORTATION, AND EDUCATION

The diversity of Chinese projects in Cuba distinguishes them from Spanish and other foreign investments, which have focused on enclave sectors like hotel construction and tourism services. Recent Chinese projects include a marsh gas extraction facility, a sheep-rearing farm, a reservoir fishery, a sugar biofuel power station, and three pesticide production plants. The China specialist Arsenio Alemán notes that Chinese initiatives in Cuba are designed to complement each other across sectors. For instance, Chinese light manufacturing, transportation upgrading, and port redevelopment projects are designed to function as a unified system of domestic production, shipping, and prospective export to Latin American and Caribbean members of the Bolivarian Alliance for the Americas (interview, January 10, 2012; also see Frank 2006).

Cuba's capacity for foreign trade will grow significantly with the renovation and expansion of the Port of Mariel. Expected to become the largest shipping hub in the Caribbean, the port will handle more than two million cargo containers annually and accommodate the "post-panamax" (extra large) vessels that will pass through the Panama Canal when it has been widened. Mariel's first phase was completed in January 2014 and inaugurated by Castro and Brazilian President Dilma Rousseff, whose government loaned Cuba $682 million for the $950 million project. Cuban Foreign Trade and Investment Minister Rodrigo Malmierca has spoken of Mariel's significance for Chinese exporters, which he anticipates will use it as a distribution hub for markets in the Caribbean, Central America, and Mexico, none of which can accommodate post-panamax cargo ships.

A special economic zone adjacent to the revamped Mariel Port could also become a focal point of Chinese activity. In September 2013 Castro signed a decree permitting foreign firms to import goods duty free into the zone, and to remain exempt from taxation on profits for ten years. Unlike previous regulations that have required foreign investors to form joint ventures with the Cuban state, the new framework permits investors 100 percent ownership and contracts of up to fifty years. The decree served as a basis for the 2014 revision of Cuba's general Foreign Investment Law (last updated in 1995), which now protects investors against the nationalization of their assets, exempts them from personal income and labor taxes, and guarantees a profits tax ceiling of 15 percent preceded by an eight-year grace period. In the Chinese pavilion at the 2013 Havana International Trade Fair, Malmierca told representatives from sixty-five Chinese enterprises that "the Chinese companies that today produce in China and bring their goods here could produce here in Cuba, in this special zone . . . with many incentives" (quoted in "Cuba Seeks Chinese Investment" 2013).

The Havana fair has long attracted Chinese firms interested in Latin American markets. Since the early 2000s, Chinese state enterprises such as Haier and ZTE have dominated the fair's electronics exhibits. The kiosk of one regular exhibitor, China Putian Corporation, has for several years been adorned with a banner that confidently outlines a regional strategy: "China Putian Corporation was founded in 1980. It is an extralarge state-owned enterprise directly under the management of [the] Chinese central government. . . . China Putian Corporation will regard Cuba as a platform so as to develop its business in Latin America." The ambition of state enterprises like China Putian to conquer Cuban markets and then use them as a springboard into Latin America is characteristically optimistic but, for the time being, uncharacteristically impractical. For one thing, Cubans have yet to embrace Chinese brands. In the absence of affordable alternatives, they have become familiar with Chinese televisions, rice cookers, and other appliances, but these products live notoriously short lives under local conditions. The extensive circulation of spare parts expertly recovered from antique Russian and U.S. models has done little to service the sleek, energy-efficient, but incompatible Chinese versions.

A longer-term hurdle for China's industrial ambitions in Cuba is the inability of the latter's markets and service sectors to provide capital goods, technical support, and capable employees. Aware of these deficiencies—

and emerging opportunities to address them—in 2004 President Hu delivered his main Cuban speech at the leading information technology training facility, the Universidad de Ciencias Informáticas (University of Information Science). Proposing to link Cuba's higher education system with existing Chinese projects, he declared that thousands of the computers on campus had come from China and been bought at subsidized prices, and that Cuba's growing expertise in information technology should feed into electronics manufacturing. This goal soon took concrete form in a three-story assembly plant for the production of rice cookers and television sets carrying the Chinese brand Panda. The project proved successful, stimulating an agreement during Hu's second visit, in 2008, to establish a joint venture (signed in 2009) between the Grupo de la Electrónica (of the Cuban Ministry of Information and Communication) and the Chinese electronics firm Haier to manufacture electro-domestic products (refrigerators, air conditioners, etc.), and computer equipment in Cuba (Cubaencuentro 2009).

The Grupo's director, Ramiro Valdés Menéndez, had been Cuba's minister of information, and in 2009 was appointed by Raúl Castro as one of several vice presidents. He is a committed advocate of cooperation with China, and through his efforts, electronics has become a key nexus of bilateral collaboration. However, the management of resulting projects exclusively through state channels, and Valdés's blend of political and commercial responsibilities, have generated suspicions about the rationale for Sino-Cuban electronics cooperation. The Cuban-American communications consultant Manuel Cereijo argues that "there are three main areas of concern for us in the new and dangerous axis formed by China and Cuba: radio frequency weapons, computer technology, missile capabilities. The problem with the Chinese Cuban rapprochment [sic] is that it is driven by . . . mutual hostility towards the United States" (2001).

Cereijo (2010) asserts that China has set up Cuban listening posts in the towns of Bejucal and Lourdes to monitor U.S. telecommunications. Similarly, the Association of Former Intelligence Officers alleges that the Chinese government is operating a former Soviet facility at Lourdes to engage in "cyber warfare" against the United States (2006). The evidence for this, though, is circumstantial and easily exaggerated. An image published by Cereijo of "golf ball-shaped radar domes: Bejucal base Cuba" drew international attention in the early 2000s, but on closer inspection the image turned out to be of the Echelon surveillance station operated by the U.S. National Security Agency at Menwith Hill in England (Ratliff 2006).

Less newsworthy but more verifiable is Chinese involvement in Cuban transportation and logistics. Cooperation in these sectors is often praised in both countries, but below the surface, differing expectations about state management, ideological solidarity, and the role of the market have caused headaches. In 2006 the China Export and Credit Insurance Corporation (Sinosure) provided a $1.8 billion revolving credit line to upgrade Cuban transportation infrastructure, and the same year the Cuban government announced that contracts totaling more than $2 billion had been signed to improve the island's road and rail networks. Five hundred Chinese freight and passenger train cars were ordered for the rail fleet, with twenty-one locomotives entering service in 2009. By this time, over 1,500 fuel-efficient cars from the Chinese manufacturer Geely had been shipped to Cuba, largely for use by the police and security services (Pérez Pizarro 2009b).

The most significant development in this sector was Cuba's 2008 bulk purchase of 1,000 energy-efficient Chinese buses, adding to an initial fleet of 400 purchased in 2005 (figures 1.3–1.6). Rather than deliver complete vehicles, the Chinese state enterprise Yutong shipped components from its factory in Zhengzhou for assembly in Havana. This reduced the shipping costs by around 15 percent and promoted skills transfer through the training of Cuban personnel by a team of thirty visiting Chinese technicians (Pérez Pizarro 2009a). Two hundred of the buses were in circulation by midyear and the other 800 several months later. In late 2008 Rosa Oliveras of the Group of the Integrated Development of the Capital noted the positive impact: "When the Special Period [in Time of Peace] hit us, the vehicles and spare parts we had imported from the Soviet bloc fell out of production, and our transport system was so damaged that the mobility of Havana's citizens was reduced to between 20 and 30 percent. Until recently people had to wait at bus stops for two or three hours and were forced to work half days, and sometimes not at all. We couldn't have carried on like this. The Chinese buses have saved our city, and actually the whole country, from a very grave situation" (interview, November 18, 2008).

FIGURES 1.3, 1.4, 1.5, AND 1.6 Over the hump: Chinese-made Yutong buses and their predecessors, known as the "camellos" (camels). Photos by the author.

En route from Havana to Santiago de Cuba I experienced the impact of the Chinese buses firsthand, and I recorded the episode in my research diary:

NO DEJES EL CAMINO POR VEREDA (DON'T TAKE SHORTCUTS)

An hour after it was supposed to depart, we're told the train to Santiago de Cuba has technical problems and is out of service. The transport officer blares at us (two hundred or so) through a megaphone: we'll be taking a bus instead. People chatter and laugh: "Better call to say we'll get there late . . . at least we'll get there . . . coño maybe it's one of those new buses . . ." We're led out of the station and around the corner to see a gleaming Yutong bus, and the scramble for seats begins. Those who fight their way in first sit near the front, looking happy with themselves and commenting that the blue seats are soft and good for sleeping. I get one near the back and settle in. I'm woken by bumps. It's 2:15 AM so we've been going four hours. The bumps are getting worse, more like flying through a storm than driving on a road, and it's too dark outside to see what's going on. The man sitting next to me, probably in his sixties, can see I'm perplexed and offers an explanation: "Looks like we're taking a shortcut." I ask him what he thinks of the new buses, and now he looks perplexed too: "They're well built, though the seats are too small . . . must have been made for Chinese passengers. These bumps are nothing compared to last time. Cuban roads are in very bad condition, especially when you get off the highway."

—En route to Santiago de Cuba, February 27, 2006

The Chinese buses enabled Cuba to stay mobile, but in 2011 the initiative hit an ideological roadblock. Having entered service en masse in 2008, the buses were subjected to relentless use, often on unpaved roads, which caused many to break down simultaneously in 2010. According to an official close to the project, Cuban negotiators incorrectly assumed that political solidarity at the ministerial level would materialize in complimentary maintenance and replacement parts for the Cuban fleet. Their Chinese counterparts, meanwhile, felt that they had shown sufficient solidarity by providing Cuba with a loan to buy the buses in the first place. The setback was a stark reminder of the point conveyed to Fidel Castro by Li Peng in 1995: political trust would no longer subsume economic pragmatism.

As ideology becomes subordinated to pragmatism, Cuba and China have developed new projects to maintain common ground. People-to-people ties have become more important, propelled by high-level agreements in education and health. Academic exchanges between China and Cuba date back to the early 1960s, when 150 Chinese students were sent to Cuba to study Spanish. The program was suspended in the mid-1960s when relations became strained and reinitiated on a small scale in 1984, following the landmark visit of Foreign Minister Ricardo Cabrisas to Beijing. Two decades later, during President Hu's November 2004 visit to Cuba, the two countries announced a program of annual scholarships for thirty Cuban students to visit China and twenty Chinese students to reciprocate. In 2006 the program was expanded to a hundred scholarships each way, plus a special initiative to host a thousand high-school graduates from central and western China to learn about Cuba's medical system. Li Jianmin, the deputy secretary general of the China Scholarships Council, which funded many of these students, described China's approach: "Look where the students come from: overwhelmingly from the western provinces of China, because that's where our central government is trying to develop infrastructure and social programs. So these [newly trained] doctors will return from Cuba to western China and fill an important need. In the meantime, a significant number of Cuban doctors are in western China, filling the need for the short term" (interview, July 5, 2007).

Educational exchanges with Cuba, particularly in medical fields, give the Chinese government access to high-quality training and services at low cost. They also create a strong human bond between the two nations, evident in Premier Wen's emotional praise for the Cuban doctors who responded to the Wenchuan earthquake in May 2008. Cuba's medical activities in China extend into the training of local technicians to manufacture biopharmaceutical products in Beijing (anticancer drugs), Changchun (interferon), and Xinjiang and Shandong (drugs for blood diseases). These initiatives have resulted in the sale of jointly produced, owned, and marketed pharmaceuticals in both countries. A Cuban-Chinese anticancer vaccine, Cimavax, was approved for European and Asian clinical trials in early 2012, marking a key prospective return on this joint investment ("China and Cuba Co-develop New Anti-cancer Vaccine" 2012).

During his 2008 visit to Cuba, President Hu spoke at the Tarará Student City, where some three thousand Chinese students of medicine, tourism, and Spanish were residing. His speech confirmed China's intention to see five thousand Chinese students graduate from the program by the end of 2011, with the aim of building a human platform for long-term cooperation. The goal was met and surpassed: by 2014, over nine thousand Chinese students had graduated. The number of Cuban students in China has been smaller, totaling around 130 in 2014. However, the University of Havana's Confucius Institute has helped increase the numbers, preparing 535 students to sit the Chinese government's *Hanyu Shuiping Kaoshi* (汉语水平考试) International Chinese Proficiency Test in 2012. Most of the students are from Cuban state enterprises that have projects in China, such as a rice cultivation initiative financed by the Cuban Ministry of Agriculture. As well as training the students in Chinese, the institute teaches them how shared cultural and political values have underpinned the history of Sino-Cuban cooperation. The institute's director, Arsenio Alemán, notes that students learn about the changing nature of the Sino-Cuban relationship, including its growing reliance on concrete economic outcomes (interview, January 10, 2012).

Implicit in the institute's curriculum is the message that trust between Cuba and China requires more than political ideology. It also requires pragmatism, as became evident in the misunderstanding over spare parts for the Yutong buses, and in Malmierca's recognition that the best way to draw Chinese investors into the Mariel project is through tax concessions and operating incentives. The Cuban government has become more pragmatic, articulating a reform agenda that draws on insights both from China's successful economic transition and from a somewhat less successful experience at home. The next section considers how these insights are informing recent efforts to decentralize economic management, generate employment, and contain the informal sector. These long-neglected problems are integral to a key goal of the *Lineamientos*: to foster commercial linkages between large state enterprises and emerging private actors. Their resolution implies a new balance of state and market forces, and policies that encourage rather than erode trust.

BALANCING THE FORCES: DECENTRALIZATION, EMPLOYMENT, AND THE INFORMAL SECTOR

When Ricardo Alarcón—then president of Cuba's National Assembly—visited Beijing in 2010, he publicly recognized the relevance of China's economic evolution to Cuba's development. Raúl Castro had already expressed this sentiment during his visits in 1997, 2005, and 2012, which focused on labor market reform, the integration of state and private enterprises, and the expansion of domestic markets. In China's experience, particularly since joining the World Trade Organization in 2001, these transformations were achieved through state oversight of market reform, an approach that Chinese officials have persistently advocated to their Cuban counterparts.

Under the stewardship of Deng Xiaoping in the late 1970s, the Chinese government implemented pilot programs to introduce market structures into the planned economy (Devlin 2008, 129). Reforms were "incremental and gradual, with national policies decided only after evaluating the results of local experiments" (Dickson and Chao 2001, 6). Contrasting with Fidel Castro's dictum "not to create individual millionaires but to make the citizenry as a whole into millionaires," Deng Xiaoping pledged to "let one part of the populace become rich first" (quoted in Y. Cheng 2007b, 729). Differences over this sensitive issue have long been buried beneath a shared commitment to what both countries call "socialism with local characteristics," but the Cuban government now acknowledges that China's controlled introduction of private initiative provides useful insights.

As U.S. and European markets falter, President Xi Jinping has identified nationally led growth as imperative for maintaining employment and social stability in China. However, his administration's attempt to shift the drivers of growth toward internal consumption is hindered by large, export-oriented state enterprises, which enjoy preferential access to rebates, loans, and subsidies. In contrast, small private firms face restrictions on acquiring credit and employing workers. The result is a high level of employment in state enterprises, whose health and pension benefits make them widely attractive to employees but economically unproductive. In comparison, small companies that could provide products and services that add value to the economy currently have little capacity to attract, employ, and maintain staff. To address this problem the Chinese government is ramping up spending on dedicated health and welfare facilities, freeing up consumer credit, and promoting the provision of paid vacation to employees, all of which will enable citizens to become less dependent on state enterprises, seek more productive jobs, and generate disposable income. The Chinese government predicts that as private investment grows, its own level of investment (particularly in infrastructure and heavy industry) will decline from 45 percent to 25 percent of GDP. Calling for "reform and opening up," the reduction of "undue emphasis on formality and bureaucracy," and the eradication of "corruption and bribe-taking" (quoted in "China Confirms Leadership Change" 2012), Xi's November 2012 presidential acceptance speech might just as well have been delivered in Havana as in Beijing. Cuba is also attempting to streamline its overburdened public sector, expand domestic markets, contain the black market, and as noted above, reduce the state's current virtual monopoly of GDP. Consultation with China on these issues has become a focal point of bilateral dialogue, for instance through the regular summit meetings of Cuba's Ministry of Science, Technology, and Environment (CITMA) and the Chinese Academy of Social Sciences. According to a senior CITMA official, these meetings have increasingly focused on strategies for reducing citizens' dependence on the state (Juan Luís Martín, interview, November 16, 2012).

Among the insights that Cuba has derived from China—with varying degrees of attentiveness—are the gradual sequencing of reforms under the management of a state-appointed reform commission (Laverty 2011, 65; Lopez-Levy 2011a, 9, and 2011b, 43–44), the adaptation of socialist principles to national conditions (Mao et al. 2011, 199), the military management of commercial activities (Klepak 2010), the attraction of investment from emigrants (Ratliff 2004, 21–22), and the testing of liberalization in target territories prior to wider implementation (Hearn and Alfonso 2012).

The Cuban private sector is growing in size and capacity, particularly through the 2014 opening of the housing and automobile markets and through the 2012 authorization of independent cooperatives in transportation, construction, fishing, restaurants, and repair services. A critical ingredient in this process is the confidence of citizens that their work will be rewarded, and that any benefits generated by partnerships with state-owned enterprises will be shared. Cuban policy makers have observed China's approach to building public faith in the reform process, as outlined in the state newspaper *China Daily*: "Market discipline and incentives drive labor productivity improvements, while a government 'helping hand' protects labor welfare via job creation and higher wages. . . . Ensuring a 'win-win' situation—which, among other positives, should help assuage worker resistance to the privatization phenomenon—is important for any government wanting to create vested interests that support an agenda of reform" (Amess, Du, and Girma 2011).

The Cuban government's attentiveness to China's experience was sharpened by the global financial crisis and by spikes in international food and oil prices in 2008 and 2011. Its strategy was initially published in the draft *Lineamientos* in November 2010, which was debated during the following six months and reissued in revised form following the sixth Communist Party Congress in April 2011. The resulting 313 recommendations show growing, albeit tentative, acceptance of market forces to complement Cuba's state-dominated system of trade and investment. Reflecting both external pressures and the more liberal approach of President Raúl Castro, the final document states that private property, long considered antithetical to socialism, would now be permitted on the condition that it is not "concentrated" (República de Cuba 2011, 5 and 11).

While China has provided Cuba with useful insights, the *Lineamientos* also draw heavily on domestic experience. As the political scientist Rafael Hernández notes, "many of the concepts and proposals in the document cover themes that were already being debated" (Hernández et al. 2011, 27). For instance, new provisions entitling small farmers and agricultural cooperatives to greater autonomy in selecting crops, managing budgets, and sourcing inputs (*Lineamientos* numbers 178–84) build on legislation passed in the early 1990s that permitted farmers to sell their produce in designated urban marketplaces. Similarly, the reformist ethos of the Special Period, evident in the authorization of private taxis, home restaurants (*paladares*), and small trading in clothing and artisanal goods, has reemerged in the *Lineamientos'* endorsement of self-employment (*cuentapropismo*).

Much of the legislation authorized by Fidel Castro in the early 1990s to diminish the impact of the Soviet collapse were later deemed excessive and rescinded. Two decades later, though, Raúl Castro has strong support in the National Assembly and appears determined to leave behind a legacy of profitable economic management (Ritter 2011). The resilience of the current strategy is bolstered by the involvement of the Revolutionary Armed Forces in key sectors of the economy, leading Eusebio Mujal-León to conclude that "these reforms could reduce the weight of the state and create conditions for the emergence of private property and a 'social market' economy" (2011, 159). To achieve this outcome, the *Lineamientos* attempt to confront the long-standing challenges of decentralization, employment, and the black market.

Decentralization is critical for leveraging the range of potentials offered by Cuba's diverse socioeconomic geography. This geography is now set to diversify further, requiring locally appropriate policies to address growing inequalities and maximize human capacities (Torres Pérez 2011). The *Lineamientos* advocate local solutions to national problems, employing the words "territory," "territorial," "local," or "municipal" no fewer than thirty-four times (Hernández et al. 2011, 29). The document's introduction, for instance, identifies the need to "effectively promote the initiative harbored by the territories to empower, in a sustainable way, their own economic development" (República de Cuba 2011, 8).

Talk of decentralization in Cuba has long evoked suspicions of corruption, since the delegation of resources inevitably multiplies opportunities for abuse. Previous moves to devolve executive authority—such as the constitutional reforms of 1992 and Decree Law 91 in 2000, which divided Havana into ninety-three (subsequently 105) Popular Councils—were therefore not accompanied by the devolution of economic resources (Fernández Soriano 1999). The 2011 proposals do not recommend the dissolution or retrenchment of the state, but they go a step further than previous reforms by postulating more adequately resourced local governments. A combination of political and economic decentralization, they suggest, will enable local governments to more effectively serve citizens' interests.

Few citizens' interests are as urgent for Cuban policy makers as employment. Recognizing that a greater degree of economic liberalization holds the best promise for providing jobs, the *Lineamientos* establish the legitimacy of private initiative: "socialism signifies equal rights and opportunities for all citizens, but not egalitarianism" (República de Cuba 2011, 5). The 1974 constitution provides a legal basis for this assertion, guaranteeing access to employment for all Cubans without specifying the public or private status of their work. *Lineamientos* numbers 31 and 32 therefore face no legal obstacle in shifting the burden of responsibility for employment away from the public sector: "The quantity of subsidized entities will be reduced to the minimum number necessary to guarantee the fulfillment of assigned functions. . . . Subsidized entities that are capable of covering their own expenses with their earnings and generating profits will become self-financing entities, without neglecting their assigned functions and attributes, or will assume, with prior approval, the status of companies" (13).

Critical to this process is greater interdependence between state enterprises and small businesses operating in their vicinities, which could provide staff, intermediate inputs, and services. The Politburo member responsible for reforming inefficient state-owned enterprises, Marino Murillo, has described the strategy this way: "If an institution has . . . $200 million to import, and a local producer can produce what it plans to import, this body can directly pay that local producer with the approved funds" (quoted in Frank 2013). Rigid centralized supply and demand quotas have long impeded the formation of such vertical synergies. This has been the case not only for heavy industry enterprises, such as Cubaniquel in the nickel sector and CUPET in oil, but also in more dynamic industries like tourism. The hotels and clubs lining the beaches of Varadero, for instance, "have become enclave economies, whose linkage to their surrounding territory is negligible, and the the spillover effects of these investments, and the dynamics of their growth, barely register in the territory" (Hernández et al. 2011, 33).

Tourism will continue to underpin Cuba's development, and therefore represents a key opportunity to build state-society synergies. Two decades ago, in the wake of the Soviet collapse, Andrés Oppenheimer summed up the political trauma associated with the sector's growth: "The Revolution's ideological principles were bent every which way in the bid for new tourist dollars" (1992, 286). In the words of a tour operator in Havana, "the Cuban government calls the Special Period a cancer, for which tourism is the chemotherapy: it can work, they say, if it doesn't kill us!" (interview, April 25, 2003). Ideological trauma yielded economic results, and in 2002 Eusebio Leal Spengler, director of the Office of the Historian of the City of Havana, stated that "for every person employed in tourism, ten people live from their income" (interview, April 29, 2002).

Tourist arrivals in Cuba shot from 300,000 in 1990 to 1.77 million in 2000, and to 2.85 million in 2013 (figure 1.7). The sector has attracted interest from the Chinese government, which approved Cuba as an ideologically sound destination for its citizens (the first country in Latin America to achieve this status) during Fidel Castro's 2003 visit to Beijing. Cuba soon established a tourism office dedicated to China and in 2007 signed an "Operational Plan for Chinese Group Tourists Visiting Cuba." That year, for the first time, the number of Chinese tourist arrivals in Cuba exceeded 10,000 (growing to 22,218 arrivals in 2013; Oficina Nacional de Estadísticas e Información 2014). According to Omar Pereira Hernández, former director of tourism at the Cuban Embassy in Beijing, the tourism office has focused on Chinese package tours to Cuba, which are growing in size and frequency and will grow further if direct flights are established. China Suntime International holds a 49 percent stake in a $150 million tourism development project on Havana's Marina Hemingway, and community leaders in Havana's Barrio Chino have proposed the construction of a hotel to cater to tourists from China's growing middle class (see chapter 3). Conversely, the Gran Meliá Shanghai hotel, featuring Cuban artwork and the Havana Night Cuban Cabaret, was recently completed with Cuban investment (amounting to 51 percent own-

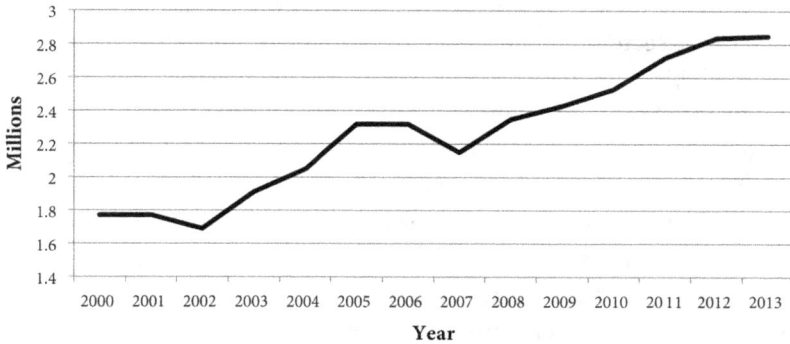

FIGURE 1.7 Tourist arrivals in Cuba, 2000–2013. Source: Oficina Nacional de Estadísticas e Información 2014.

ership), targeting Asian travelers wishing to experience a taste of Cuba close to home.

To more effectively link tourism (and other sectors) to Cuba's emerging private sector, the *Lineamientos* stipulate greater flexibility for state enterprises to select suppliers and for small businesses to cater to their needs. *Lineamientos* numbers 262–66 note that tourism could generate new jobs and tax revenue in lodging and restaurant services, and that policy makers will "study mechanisms for supplying tourist facilities that take advantage of local productive forces" (República de Cuba 2011, 33–34). For this strategy to succeed, the list of 178 private occupations approved in early 2011 (and expanded to 199 in late 2013) will need to be further extended to accommodate the skills and capacities of Cuban employees. Lodging and restaurant services may be a logical starting point, but they are a far cry from the skills accrued by graduates of specialist institutions like the Colegio Universitario San Gerónimo in heritage management and urban development (discussed below). As the economist Juan Triana argues, "It would be a strategic mistake to limit, in the name of development, the growth of the nonstate sector to jobs or occupations that produce products or generate services of low added value. This would undermine an important part of the considerable investment made by our country in human development over more than fifty years" (Hernández et al. 2011, 33).

By mid-2014 approximately 470,000 Cubans were registered as self-employed or working for a self-employed individual, compared with

150,000 in 2010. Most self-employed Cubans occupy positions in the basic services sector and improvised retail markets, their rise up the value chain inhibited not only by the narrow selection of authorized jobs, but also by the absence of an affordable and reliable supply chain. One component of the supply problem is a lack of financing available to private businesses for purchasing raw materials and inputs. The appearance of the word "credit" eleven times in the *Lineamientos* signals the state's recognition of this obstacle. Cubans have been permitted to take out bank loans since 2011, but until recently they were required to provide liquid collateral, such as a guarantor with sufficient savings to cover the loan amount. Poor public uptake of the loans led the government to relax this condition in December 2013, decreasing the minimum amount from 3,000 to 1,000 pesos ($67) and permitting the use of jewelry, works of art, and even livestock as collateral. Foreign banks such as Canada's Bank of Nova Scotia are exploring opportunities in the Cuban credits and loans market but have been discouraged by the limited growth capacity of small businesses (Simon 2011).

Cuba's underdeveloped credit market has hindered the expansion of small businesses and their supply chains, but a more encompassing obstacle is ideological antagonism toward the accrual of private property (Mesa-Lago 2013). Policy adjustments under Raúl Castro favor greater entrepreneurship and self-sufficiency, but the *Lineamientos* do not specify the extent to which private actors will be permitted to stock their back rooms and expand their activities. Instead, *Lineamiento* number 3 offers a general principle of conduct: "in the nonstate system, the concentration of property will not be permitted" (República de Cuba 2011, 11). This tension is borne out in Cuba's new tax code, which introduces a long overdue graduated system of sales, personal income, public service, and payroll taxes but maintains tight deductibility limits and crippling overall rates. As a recent report from the Center for Democracy in the Americas observes, "taxes are a delicate issue within the Communist Party. Conservative party members demand maximum wealth distribution and measures to avoid inequality, whereas moderates are more inclined to listen to economists and *cuentapropistas* [self-employed people] who argue excessive taxes will stymie growth in the non-state sector. With several adjustments made thus far, it appears Raúl Castro's government is searching for the middle ground on the issue" (Laverty 2011, 40).

Functional supply chains are essential not only for the viability of private businesses and the creation of jobs, but—as Chino demonstrated at the beginning of the chapter—for containing the black market. It is difficult to distinguish among investments, gifts, and remittances as opportunities for private enterprise expand in Cuba, generating an acute need for start-up capital and supplies. Authorized by the Obama administration to travel and send remittances to relatives, Cuban Americans are thought to have financed over half of *cuentapropia* activities in 2010 (Meo 2011). According to an International Monetary Fund economist Rafael Romeu, "The renewed visits of Cuban Americans have come at a critical time for the Cuban economy, because these are not traditional tourists—they have strong linkages to the real economy. They are assumed to be financing an important part of the investment necessary to start Cuba's budding microenterprises through visits to Cuba and remittances. The latter are estimated to be at least $500 million, and perhaps exceed $1 billion annually" (Romeu 2012, 66).

Alongside remittances and gifts, undeclared investments and resources—from cash to computer hardware—are also streaming steadily into Cuba. The official response has been to limit the pace of liberalization through heavy taxation on remittances and the prohibition of unlicensed reselling of clothing and other consumer goods brought into the country by Cuban American and other visitors. Seen from the top down, the strategy is to study the impact of liberalization on the flow of goods and services and adjust policies accordingly. From the bottom up, though, time is money. The prolonged absence of legal supplies has forced Cuba's new entrepreneurs to rely on finances and inputs acquired illegally either from family overseas or from *socios* (well-placed business partners) in state factories. In this environment, broader legalization of frontline retail activities—a move often advocated by foreign commentators—might be counterproductive, as it could deepen the underlying illicit wholesale market.

Functional supply chains would diminish the appeal of the black market, but tight capital controls have inhibited foreign investors from supporting this process. The former Cuban diplomat Carlos Alzugaray Treto notes that the European Union (EU) has long been willing to get involved: "As Cuba's ambassador to the EU I often heard that as soon as the Cuban government is ready to support the expansion of small businesses, the EU will be ready to provide credit for everything from small private loans to large logistics projects. This is still the case, but now the Chinese are filling that space on more favorable economic terms. . . . The Chinese are [also] less insistent about political conditions" (interview, November 25, 2012).

Furnishing Cuba with credits to finance the purchase of Chinese exports was an approach promoted by Jiang Zemin during his 2001 visit to Cuba. Credits and loans have since enabled Cuba to acquire Chinese products ranging from home appliances to farm machinery at low cost. Demand for Chinese supplies will increase as Cuban private businesses expand, a point Cuba's Vice President Miguel Díaz-Canel discussed with his Chinese counterpart Li Yuanchao in Beijing in June 2013. Díaz-Canel's visit secured an unspecified Chinese "donation" and interest-free credit for the purchase of Chinese agricultural equipment.

As Jiang discovered, the repayment of the credits that enable Chinese sales to Cuba will require the latter's economic diversification and growth. However, the state-centric solutions that characterize Sino-Cuban cooperation may hinder—rather than help—the development of Cuba's private sector. Chinese trade credits enable the Cuban state to act as a surrogate for the market, distributing tractors to farmers, buses to the Ministry of Transport, and refrigerators to the masses according to centrally governed supply quotas. In this controlled environment, the prospect of greater enterprise autonomy, interdependence between emerging businesses, private credit, GDP growth in the nonstate sector, and loan repayments to China will remain limited.

State-centric cooperation with China may nonetheless be a necessary first step for subsequent liberalization, as it could help to set Cuba's nascent private businesses on a legally sustainable course. Retail and services with formal channels of supply, such as those established with China, are more amenable to regulation and auditing for tax compliance and can therefore be more easily demarcated and extracted from the black market. As frontline retailers become less dependent on informal sources of supply, these sectors are more likely to be authorized for private management. The periodic extension of the Cuban government's list of approved professions reflects this strategy of controlled economic opening. According to José Barreiro, an official in the Labor Ministry, the list's expansion to 199 occupations in September 2013 resulted from the government's ability to securely supply equipment and basic inputs (A. García 2013).

Chinese suppliers have been closely involved in Cuba's sequential economic opening. Following Hu Jintao's 2004 visit, Chinese mobile phones, DVD players, computers, and other appliances were approved for sale through Cuban government outlets to authorized individuals. By 2008 the chain of supply from Chinese factories to Cuban retailers was well established, enabling Raúl Castro to mark Hu's second presidential visit by authorizing the unrestricted sale of these products to the Cuban public. Similarly, since 2009 the Chinese automobile manufacturer Geely has supplied the Cuban police and security services and is now expanding into Cuba's newly liberalized automobile market. The establishment of regulated supply chains with Chinese support is enabling the controlled opening of sectors that would otherwise remain stocked largely by the black market.

The liberalization of sectors conducive to Chinese exports serves the interests of both governments. For Cuba it provides a secure mechanism for stocking the nation's wholesale warehouses for the emerging private sector. For China it opens new export markets and an opportunity to recover unpaid loans. A businessman accompanying Hu's 2008 delegation put it this way: "We are hoping to see new opportunities for trade and investment in Cuba. . . . If some market factors can be added to the Cuban economy, Chinese enterprises will have more business opportunities" (interview, November 21, 2008). To expand the range of goods and services they provide to Cuba, Chinese exporters clearly wish to see Cuba's private sector grow.

Chinese support for market-oriented policies in Cuba contrasts with the centralized development programs that once underpinned bilateral cooperation. The history of Sino-Cuban relations nevertheless shows that state and market approaches can sometimes complement each other, and that China's creation of a mixed economy over the past three decades can provide useful insights. Cuba's *Lineamientos* indicate an official disposition to allow greater autonomy and empowerment at the grass roots, but it is not yet clear if this disposition will influence the way bilateral cooperation is structured. To complement existing state-led programs with more heterogeneous, nonstate forms of interaction would first require the Cuban and Chinese governments to trust their private sectors to focus their interactions strictly on commercial pursuits and steer clear of politics. Experiments along these lines have previously been conducted—for instance, in the mid-1990s, when small-scale trade was authorized between autonomous Cuban importers and Chinese exporters to service the stores and restaurants of Havana's Barrio Chino. As chapter 3 shows, Cuba's Chinese associations have since drawn inspiration from that early experience to foment contemporary partnerships with Chinese investors. However, they are still a long way from gaining the trust and leeway they seek from the Ministry of Justice and the other government institutions that are responsible for them.

Whether through microsocial connections or macroeconomic agreements, the gradual shift away from top-down management envisioned by the *Lineamientos* will shape the contours of Sino-Cuban interactions. Greater space for free enterprise does not imply the erosion of the Cuban state, which is taking great care to embed the island's budding entrepreneurs in its hegemonic structures. The likely result is a hybrid system of small private businesses that are more vertically integrated with large state enterprises, stricter (and clearer) regulation of supply chains, and a less pervasive black market. China's development will continue to generate insights for Cuba, not least as the Xi administration attempts to open domestic markets, stimulate internal consumption, and scale back the power of large state enterprises. The slow process of exploring, deciphering, and operationalizing insights from China may test the patience of ordinary Cubans, but they are more likely to trust their government's judgment if they can sit back, like Chino, in self-made comfort.

CONCLUSION

The pros and cons of Cuba's reform agenda are currently being debated throughout Cuba, in civil society publications like *Temas* and *Espacio Laical* and in organizations like the Association for the Study of the Cuban Economy. Differences of opinion abound, but there is consensus that a more mixed economy is in the making and that its consolidation will require new approaches to decentralization, employment, and containment of the informal sector. In practical terms this means broader capacities for economic governance at the provincial and municipal levels, a wider range of authorized private occupations, and supporting structures of commercial wholesale activities that respect what *Lineamiento* number 12 calls "the absolute observance of legality" (República de Cuba 2011, 11).

Among the stakeholders with a vested interest in Cuba's reforms is the Chinese government, which negotiated the first Five-Year Plan for Sino-Cuban cooperation in 2011. With considerable economic and political incentives conditioning the bilateral relationship, Fidel and Raúl Castro, Ricardo Alarcón, and numerous other past and present Cuban leaders have publicly recognized the appeal of China's approach to reform. Gradualism, experimentation, and the incorporation of market forces into state structures of authority are principles that sit well with the Cuban leadership. It must be noted, though, that the aspirations of Cuban people to fill more sophisticated jobs may ultimately test their willingness to follow China's lead. Any attempt to emulate the low-skilled manufacturing that provided the basis for China's remarkable growth may prove to be at odds with these aspirations. As the Cuban anthropologist Yenisel Rodríguez writes, "we are not so economically desperate that a *maquiladora* can bring us the taste of liberation" (Hernández et al. 2011, 39). These words may soon be put to the test in the Mariel Free Trade Zone, and Chinese investors will be watching.

How China will influence the trajectory of private initiative on the island is a key question for the future. On the one hand, state-centric accords with China enable the Cuban government to supplant the market by controlling access to wholesale activities. On the other, the tight regulation and stability of Chinese supply chains has enabled the insulation of some sectors from the black market—a precondition for their subsequent deregulation. In this sense, integration with China is helping Cuba to create the necessary conditions for economic opening.

Implementing policies that support rather than impede the emergence of private initiative is a challenge faced as much by district-level administrators as by national lawmakers. Unless overarching policies create opportunities for employment and improved livelihoods, commercial regulations will fail to earn the trust and compliance of citizens. Until recently this has been the case in Cuba, which is evident in the existence of an informal sector that pervades most aspects of daily economic life. As Chino showed at the beginning of the chapter, citizens are willing and able to "provide every kind of service in-house and in-store." There is no shortage of work ethic, but to entice Chino and his network of suppliers out of the black market will require more sophisticated jobs, supply chains, and development policies.

Cuba's emerging entrepreneurs want to shape their own futures, and this desire is becoming especially acute in the Chinese diasporic community. Commercial networking has long been one of the community's strengths, but the informal connections and trust that underpin its networks are creating unprecedented policy dilemmas. As these networks extend across the Pacific, the need for improved state-society communication is nowhere more pressing than in the Chinatowns of Cuba and Mexico. Chapters 3 and 4 will consider recent attempts in both countries to harness the expanding economic connections and capacities of resident Chinese communities. First, though, chapter 2 examines how China's impact is forcing the Mexican government to rethink the role that large elite enterprises and small businesses play in national development. As in Cuba, there is a growing awareness in Mexico that industrial policies must build trust from the bottom up.

In 1974, two years after Mexico became the fourth Latin American country to establish diplomatic relations with the People's Republic of China
(after Cuba, Chile, and Peru), its first ambassador to Beijing, Eugenio
Anguiano Roch, was working hard to build trust. An exhibition of Aztec
artifacts, meticulously coordinated by Anguiano, had drawn interest at
museums in Beijing and Shanghai. Selected episodes of Mexican TV soap
operas, first screened at the embassy and later released on public television, had generated enthusiastic curiosity among the Chinese public. The
breakthrough, though, was a Mexican movie about the 1938 nationalization of Mexico's oil industry under President Lázaro Cárdenas (1934–40).
Anguiano recalls: "They loved it! The Communist Party organized enormous crowds of thousands of people. Chinese audiences had never seen
Mexican movies, and this one fit perfectly with their political thinking
at the time. They began to see us as comrades!" (interview, June 9, 2010).

Forty years later the comradeship has, as Marx might say, melted into
air. In 2014 Mexico reported that its bilateral trade with China had grown
to the impressive sum of $72.24 billion, but also that it sustained a bilat-
eral deficit of $60.28 billion (United Nations Commodity Trade Statistics
Database 2015). Mexico's oil sector still provokes animated discussions
in Beijing, but rather than praising Mexico's defense of its sovereignty,
Chinese officials bemoan the ongoing impediments to deregulation in

Mexico. Xu Shicheng, a senior Latin America analyst from the Chinese Academy of Social Sciences, argues that Chinese investment would boost Mexican oil sales to China, thereby reducing the chronic trade imbalance (interview, November 23, 2009). This is an uncertain prospect even under Mexico's promarket President Enrique Peña Nieto, a member of the Partido Revolucionario Institucional (Institutional Revolutionary Party, or PRI) who took office in December 2012. One year into his term, Peña Nieto secured the necessary two-thirds of congressional votes (353 votes to 134) to amend article 27 of the 1917 constitution, which proclaimed governmental ownership of minerals and energy resources. Despite its historical significance, this maneuver will not abrogate a 1939 decree guaranteeing the sole stewardship of the state enterprise Petróleos Mexicanos (PEMEX) over untapped oil reserves (Ely 1961, 10).

Peña Nieto's oil reforms permit private contracts for exploration, drilling, and reservation of subterraneous oil, which remain government property until extraction. Multinational companies such as Exxon Mobil, Chevron, Royal Dutch Shell, and ConocoPhillips will have priority access, thanks to the 2013 U.S.-Mexico Transboundary Hydrocarbons Agreement. The Mexican government favors these established firms over emerging Chinese rivals, for both conventional and shale activities (S. Hall 2013). Xu's proposed injection of Chinese finance is still a long way from reality.

With oil cooperation yet to bear fruit and efforts to collaborate in copper mining, automobile production, and information technology repeatedly delayed, Sino-Mexican relations have little traction. As the rest of Latin America scrambles to balance competition from Chinese consumer products by exporting ever-larger quantities of natural resources, Mexico has yet to formulate a China strategy. "Compared to the other Latin American countries," writes Roberto Hernández Hernández, "Mexico is the most vulnerable, with 97 percent of its manufacturing exports—which represent 71 percent of the national export base—under threat from China" (2012, 76). The problem is as much cultural as economic, underpinned by a history of overreliance on the United States and of intense ambivalence toward China. It is also political, owing to a steadfast skepticism of state-guided industrial policies among Mexico's political and economic elites since the early 1980s (Cypher and Delgado 2010, 86).

Despite its hands-off approach, the Mexican government has provided federal funding, tax concessions, and personal advocacy to selected sectors. As discussed below, large enterprises in the automotive and agriculture industries have been recent beneficiaries and have used this support to develop new products and build partnerships in China. There has also been some input from state-level governments, such as funding for universities to establish internship programs that build Mexicans' familiarity with the Chinese market. In these cases, government support has generated new partnerships, fomented cooperation, and strengthened bilateral trust.

The problem with these instances of successful public-private engagement is that they are rare. Mexican analysts lament the track record of the federal government, particularly the Ministry of the Economy and its foreign trade division, ProMéxico, in withholding its support from vulnerable sectors. Industries from handicrafts to textiles have struggled both at home and overseas owing to their poor access to finance and official advocacy and their inability to upgrade. As Chinese manufactured goods displace Mexican products in national and foreign markets, sectoral advocacy groups such as the Cámara Nacional de la Industria del Vestido (National Chamber of the Clothing Industry, or CNIV) and the Confederación de Cámaras Industriales (Confederation of Industrial Chambers, or CONCAMIN) have spearheaded calls for the government to take firmer measures to mitigate the so-called China threat. Reluctant to commit to assertive industrial policies but eager to placate voters, politicians have resorted to trade barriers on Chinese products. This has provided short-term respite but—as discussed below—has also encouraged smuggling and informal retail, undermining the prospects for trust between state and society in Mexico, within the Mexican economy, and between Mexico and China.

Although they are rare and overly focused on big business, instances of synergy between the Mexican public and private sectors offer useful insights into Sino-Mexican relations. They suggest the need, articulated by the economist José Luis Calva, for more systematic policies of national economic empowerment: "it is necessary to launch a genuine industrial policy characterized by long-term strategic planning, which includes support mechanisms for sectoral development, without undermining horizontal mechanisms of general economic development" (2012, 19).

Developing modes of cooperation that simultaneously cultivate vertical public-private synergies and horizontal commercial linkages is key to Mexico's formulation of a China strategy. For the time being, though, this process has been derailed by a political riddle: what comes first—trust or policy?

TRUST AND POLICY: CHICKEN AND EGG

China's impact is felt from the big business of Mexican industrial manufacturing to the small kiosks of the nation's rampant informal sector. The emerging superpower encroached on traditional handicrafts in the early 2000s, then on textiles and shoes in the middle of the decade, and is now provoking trepidation in the automotive industry (Dussel Peters and Ortiz Velázquez 2012, 22–24). The consequences of China's rise became clear between 2001 and 2003, when the export-oriented manufacturing sector saw the loss of over 25,000 jobs—many through the transfer of maquiladoras to China—and when China displaced Mexico as the second largest exporter to the U.S. market. The informal sector is woven closely into these indicators, as 60 percent of clothing sold in Mexico is thought to consist of contraband, most of which is from China (Mayoral Jiménez 2011; Rodríguez 2011). By themselves, top-down directives from the state will not overcome the much-heralded China threat, but neither will unsupported initiatives from the private sector and civil society. Solutions will more likely emerge from a framework of engagement between the two. However, a contentious question must first be answered: can industrial policies set in motion a virtuous circle of economic growth and trust, or does state intervention inevitably throw the circle into a tailspin?

The latter view has reigned supreme in Mexico ever since the presidency of Miguel de la Madrid (1982–88). His administration sought to rebuild the credibility of the PRI in the face of the enormous foreign debt accrued through social programs and infrastructure spending during Mexico's oil boom (1976–81). The boom had begun with the discovery of the Cantarell oil field, but it ended just as abruptly when the U.S. Federal Reserve increased interest rates to stem domestic inflation, prompting capital flight from Mexico and other indebted nations. As Calva explains, "instead of correcting the failures of macroeconomic management and redefining the industrial strategy . . . the new governing group opted to apply an adjustment program of severe macroeconomic contraction and to dismantle industrial policy" (2012, 15). De la Madrid oversaw Mexico's 1986 accession to the General Agreement on Trade and Tariffs, but there was also a decline in real wages by 30 percent, a rise in unemployment to 25 percent, and a spike in inflation to 159 percent (United Nations Development Program 1990, 35).

Mexico's deteriorating situation prior to the 1988 election saw the PRI facing possible defeat for the first time since its founding in 1929. Challenged by the left-leaning Frente Democrático Nacional—led by Cuauhtémoc Cárdenas, son of the legendary President Lázaro Cárdenas—the PRI's candidate Carlos Salinas de Gortari (1988–94) prevailed after the suspicious malfunction of a newly installed electronic voting system. Continuing de la Madrid's hands-off economic policy, Salinas negotiated Mexico's entry into the North American Free Trade Agreement (NAFTA), but his fervent pursuit of privatization generated popular discomfort with the country's conservative adherence to the Washington Consensus. Salinas's minister of commerce and industrial development, Jaime Serra Puche, epitomized this approach, famously stating that "the best industrial policy is no industrial policy" (quoted in Boltvinik 2003, 387).

Appointed by Salinas to direct the Ministry of Finance (Secretaría de Hacienda), Pedro Aspe assured citizens that free market economics was working in Mexico except for one detail: the country's population of eighty-five million people was fourteen million too many. Some interpreted this as an insinuation that 15 percent of Mexicans—the number living below the poverty line at the time—were an economic burden and would do everybody a favor if they left. However, as Alexandra Délano has shown, the Salinas administration generally tried to "delink" migration from trade and investment to strengthen Mexico's negotiating position vis-à-vis the United States (2011, 139). Telling citizens that his government would "export goods, not people" (quoted in García Zamora 2009, 79), Salinas tried to keep migration off the NAFTA agenda to avoid having to trade Mexican oil for U.S. immigration permits. U.S. demand for labor was growing at the time, propelled by a combination of decreasing fertility and economic growth. Encouraged by a U.S. Immigration and Naturalization Service amnesty for 2.3 million undocumented Mexicans, legal emigration from Mexico to the United States reached a historic annual peak of 946,167 in 1991, slightly fewer than the estimated number of illegal entries the same year (Durand, Massey, and Zenteno 2001; U.S. Immigration and Naturalization Service 2002, 27).

Among NAFTA's side effects for Mexico were the loss of jobs in traditional agriculture and a resulting displacement of rural workers, creating a pool of economic emigrants. Their resettlement in the United States would pay off for Mexico: remittances grew from $2.5 billion in 1990 to a high of $26 billion in 2007 prior to the global financial crisis (Iliff 2009; Mark Lopez, Livingstone, and Kochhar 2009, 9; Zamora 2005, 4). Despite its deleterious impact on social integration and national pride, emigration is a convenient alternative to industrial policy for the Mexican government: it involves neither investment nor political risk.

Mexico's so-called lost decade under de la Madrid and Salinas generated ambivalent reactions to the country's free market trajectory both among citizens and in the PRI, resulting in the nomination of Luis Donaldo Colosio as the party's candidate in the 1994 elections. Early in his campaign Colosio enjoyed the support of Salinas and the party machine, but he soon showed progressive leanings, proposing new state industrial investments and social programs to be financed with property taxes. Colosio's increasing advocacy of a "redistributive" state, his support for assertive industrial policies, and his conciliatory stance on the Zapatista insurgency suggested that as president he would depart from the Salinas model (Marquez 1994). These gestures, summarized in his public statement that Mexico was "hungry and thirsty for justice," augmented his popularity, but they may have ultimately gone too far. During a campaign rally on March 24, 1994, Colosio was assassinated, the first Mexican politician of such status to meet a violent end since 1928.

Whether or not the gunman acted alone is still unknown. The opposition alleged that he was linked to Salinas, who encouraged his protégé Ernesto Zedillo (1994–2000) to campaign for office on the platform of continuity with the country's free market trajectory. Unfortunately for Zedillo, continuity brought with it the repercussions of the preceding months. Within days of his victory, foreign investors nervous about the potentially destabilizing impact of Colosio's murder and an invigorated Zapatista uprising in Chiapas withdrew portfolio capital and sold foreign debt instruments they had bought on unrealistically favorable terms under Salinas. To compensate for the central bank's dwindling foreign reserves, Zedillo, a Yale-trained economist, reversed several macroeconomic policies inherited from Salinas, such as a commitment to minimizing inflation by pegging the peso's exchange rate to the U.S. dollar. During Zedillo's first year in office, the free-floating peso lost 55 percent of its value (from 3.4 pesos per dollar in December 1994 to 7.6 pesos per dollar in December 1995), bringing on a rapid increase in the price of goods and services. Zedillo attempted—with some success—to offset rising living costs by implementing the progresa program of cash subsidies to Mexico's poorest households, 2.5 million of which had registered in the initiative by 2000 (Bate 2004).

The crisis had a negative impact on other Latin American economies (a process termed the "tequila effect"), leading President Bill Clinton's administration to negotiate a bailout for Mexico's banking sector in 1995. Critics argue that this maneuver served mainly to protect the capital—both financial and social—of the U.S. investment bank Goldman Sachs, whose former cochairman Robert Rubin had become Clinton's treasury secretary. A financial analyst explained it this way: "Goldman Sachs has steered billions of dollars of its clients' money into Mexico. The bank's clients, partners and reputation all stand to suffer large losses in Mexico unless a successful bailout can be engineered. Heavy losses could encourage lawsuits from disgruntled clients" (Wheat 1995). Zedillo's policies were economically coherent, but their reliance on U.S. investment and his unequivocal commitment to NAFTA were a continuing source of disillusion for advocates of industrial diversification.

The latter would find no respite under Mexico's next leader (and former president of Coca-Cola Mexico) Vicente Fox (2000–2006). The first non-PRI president in seventy-one years, Fox promised Mexican auto and textile manufacturers that his incoming Partido Acción Nacional (National Action Party, or PAN) would secure them a greater share of the U.S. market under NAFTA. His pursuit of closer economic integration between Mexico and the United States reflected his commitment to Washington's push for market reforms across Latin America. This liberal-democratic orientation also characterized his broader foreign policy, which became clear when, in 2002, Mexico voted with the United States for the first time against Cuba at the UN Human Rights Commission. Fidel Castro described Mexico's decision as evidence of Fox's subservience to U.S. interests, and to prove it Castro released the transcript of his telephone conversation with Fox a month earlier. The transcript revealed that Castro had abruptly left the 2002 UN Summit on Development Financing in Monterrey because Fox had asked him to, and that despite the Mexican government's insistence to the contrary, the request had come from George W. Bush. Fox's political embarrassment drew attention to a broader divergence of Mexican and Cuban political ideology, the former marked by an intensifying commitment to U.S.-led market liberalization and the latter by an enduring devotion to socialist planning.

Fox's promise to take advantage of the opportunities presented by NAFTA was a credible pursuit, but its regrettable corollary was a further narrowing of Mexico's productive capacities to manufacturing industries dependent on specific niches in the U.S. market. Less fortunate still was the subjection of these industries to intensifying competition with China. In 2001 China joined the World Trade Organization, and by 2002 Chinese exports to the United States had surpassed those of Mexico, causing the loss of over 672,000 Mexican jobs across twelve industrial sectors. The export-processing maquiladora sector was particularly hard hit: by 2003 Sony, NEC (Nippon Electric Company), V Tech, and Kodak, together with 85 percent of shoe manufacturers in Mexico, closed their Mexican operations and moved to China (Comisión Económica para América Latina 2004; Domínguez et al. 2006, 38–39). Textile producers were similarly affected, and even the auto parts sector registered growing Chinese competition in the U.S. market (Álvarez Medina 2007; Watkins 2013). All the while, Mexico's annual trade deficit with China was growing to enormous proportions: from $2.6 billion in 2000 to $22.8 billion by the end of Fox's administration in 2006 (United Nations Commodity Trade Statistics Database 2015). Between 2000 and 2009, Mexico exhibited an extreme degree of export competition with China (figure 2.1).

China's impact revealed the need for Mexico to upgrade and diversify its industrial sector, but instead of guiding manufacturers through this process, the Fox administration simply advised them to divert production away from competing sectors. Fox hoped that by creating the Mexico-China Bi-National Commission in 2004, key problems could be delineated and addressed in the private sector, but the commission's most noteworthy finding was that Mexico's chronic trade imbalance with China resulted largely from inadequate state support to industry and lack

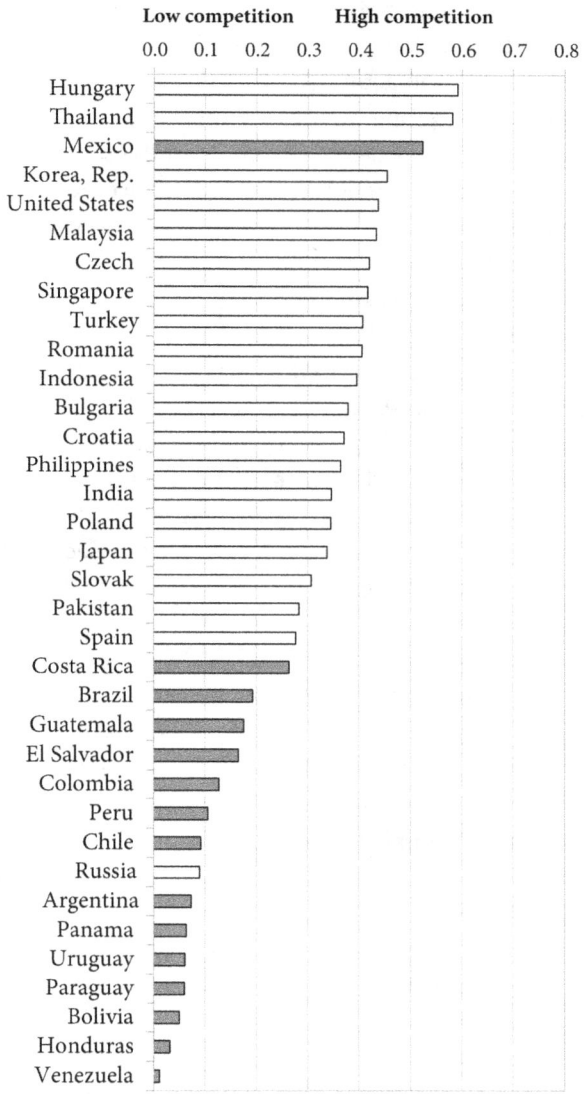

FIGURE 2.1 Selected countries' export competition with China, 2000–2009: Average coefficients of specialization and conformity (Latin American countries shaded). Source: Santiso and Avendaño 2011, 79.

of dialogue with the Chinese government. Rather than address these issues, Fox focused on building domestic credibility by aligning himself with angry Mexican manufacturers, attributing the blame for Mexico's predicament to unfair competition from China. His political discourse targeted the lack of civic values in China, which he said had produced an authoritarian labor system, low wages, and anticompetitive exports (León-Manríquez 2011, 168–69). More assertive industrial guidance from the Mexican government was not on the agenda, much less collaboration with Chinese authorities. Seeking popular support for his conservative PAN in the coming elections, Fox cautioned voters about the ideological track record of the opposition PRI, which he said had deceived Mexicans "as if we were vile Chinese when they were selling their grandiose ideas, populism and demagoguery" (quoted in Canseco 2006).

Serving as Mexico's president from 2006–12, Felipe Calderón was elected by a razor-thin margin to succeed Fox for the PAN, prompting millions to protest in the streets that he had stolen the election. Calderón demonstrated a more conciliatory approach to China early in his tenure, signing seven agreements in Beijing in 2008 and assuring Mexican manufacturers that cooperation with China would create new opportunities for inter-industry collaboration. Just as the bilateral relationship seemed to be improving, in April 2009 the first cases of swine flu (AH1N1) were announced in Mexico. With memories of the 2003 outbreak of severe acute respiratory syndrome (SARS) fresh in the minds of Chinese officials, their government immediately quarantined more than fifty healthy Mexican citizens without consulting Mexico City. In a veiled criticism of China, Calderón stated in a televised intervention that "some countries and places are taking repressive and discriminatory measures because of ignorance and disinformation" (quoted in Branigan, Borger, and Tuckman 2009).

Swine flu could not have struck at a worse time for Mexico. The impact of the global financial crisis, after a series of optimistic evaluations by the Mexican government, was by then becoming painfully evident. In February 2008, Minister of Finance Agustín Carstens had distinguished the crisis from previous downturns, stating that for Mexico it signified "a slight cold and not pneumonia as before" (*El Universal* 2008). Optimistic that the crisis would soon recede, the Mexican Ministry of Finance predicted growth of 3 percent in gross domestic product (GDP) for 2009

(Secretaría de Hacienda y Crédito Público 2009, 13). To mitigate the impact, Calderón announced a stimulus package in October to finance the construction of a new refinery for the state oil company PEMEX, a special program to support small and medium-sized enterprises (SMEs), and further deregulation of trade (Calderón 2008). These measures, combined with the Finance Ministry's forecast, seemed to validate the "slight cold" thesis.

But the global financial crisis turned out to be more akin to pneumonia, manifested in shrinking oil prices, declining exports to the United States, diminishing remittances from U.S.-based Mexican workers, and a contraction of domestic demand. In January 2009 the Ministry of Finance downgraded its growth estimate to 0 percent, imposing emergency measures that included a freeze in the prices of gasoline and electricity and credit disbursements of some $150 million for industries hit by credit restrictions. In mid-2009 the World Bank forecasted that Mexican growth would plunge to −6 percent, while the International Monetary Fund predicted −7.3 percent. The economy ultimately registered growth of −6.5 percent, the worst contraction since the so-called tequila crisis of 1994−95, and arguably the most serious since the 1920s. Overly confident in the health of their economy, Calderón's ministers had implemented the much-touted stimulus measures only half-heartedly at best, and of Mexico's 106 million citizens, the number in poverty soared from 14 to 20 million (Cortés 2009).

While governments around the world fended off the global financial crisis with assertive countercyclical strategies and stimulus packages, Mexico's official response was characteristically hands-off. Some federal funds were employed to prevent further devaluation of the peso against the dollar, but the country's reserves, which in July 2008 approached $87 billion, remained virtually untouched. In November 2009 the prominent economist Joseph Stiglitz stated that Mexico's performance in handling the crisis had been among the worst in the world, adding that the Calderón administration had not adequately supported the capacities of SMEs to engage in international trade (Lombera 2009). Stiglitz suggested that Mexico consider new pathways to revitalization, such as government investment in technology, education, and infrastructure. In response, Ernesto Cordero, minister of social development (and later minister of finance), declared: "I believe that Stiglitz does not know in detail the countercyclical policies implemented by the Mexican government; he does not know the reality of Mexican public finances. I think he should read a little more about Mexico" (quoted in Ramos Pérez 2009). Apparently overlooking Stiglitz's observation that "the only real source of growth is in Asia," Mexico's response to the crisis was in keeping with history: wait for the United States to recover. In 1990, 70.2 percent of Mexican exports went to the United States, and by 2009 the figure had increased to 80.7 percent (Economic Commission for Latin America and the Caribbean 2010).

Integration with the United States has favored some sectors of the Mexican economy, such as the automotive industry, but it has also narrowed the nation's industrial base and produced an overconcentration of within-sector output since the mid-1980s (Organisation for Economic Co-Operation and Development 2009, 104). The country's twelve free trade agreements (with forty-four countries, including the European Union and Japan) harbor the potential to reverse this trend, but a macroeconomic strategy for generating exports, rewarding up-and-coming companies, and incentivizing the diversification of trade has yet to be articulated. As José Luis León-Manríquez puts it,

> In contrast to China and other East Asian countries, the expression "industrial policy" has become almost taboo in the discourse of Mexican economic officials, even in the midst of a recalcitrant economic crisis that saw national GDP plunge to −6.55 percent by the end of 2009. Mexico's development banking, led by Nacional Financiera (NAFINSA), appears to be heading toward extinction; commercial banking does not support large industrial and exporting projects; investments in applied research and development by Mexican firms are virtually nil; and subsidies to production in the secondary sector have long exhibited levels below the average in member countries of the Organization for Economic Cooperation and Development. (2011, 170)

As Mexico's trade deficit with China grows, vote-conscious politicians have come under pressure to formulate a response. Following a series of street protests in the early 2000s demanding protection from the so-called China threat, the Ministry of the Economy agreed to maintain commercial tariffs on products imported from China. This quelled the anger of the textile, toy, electronics, and other labor-intensive sectors, but it did not resolve the underlying problems of overreliance on the U.S. market and poor competitiveness.

Rejecting the argument that their problems result from excessive state protection, industry advocates ask why the subsidies, tax breaks, seed funding, and diplomatic support that have sustained the competitiveness of big business are not extended to them (Cámara Nacional de la Industria Textil 2006; Dussel Peters 2011a, 98). Their grievances resonate with the World Economic Forum's *Global Competitiveness Report 2011–2012*, which lists "access to financing" as one of the most serious problems facing businesses in Mexico, alongside violence and corruption (2012, 258). To make matters worse, what gains in efficiency have been achieved in recent years have resulted largely from the downsizing of the labor force (Calva 2012, 18–19). According to a survey by Vanderbilt University's Latin American Public Opinion Project, 40 percent of Mexican households had a member who lost his or her job between 2009 and 2010, the highest figure in Latin America (Parás García, López Olmedo, and Vargas 2011, 25). The survey also found that 65 percent of Mexicans do not trust their political parties to govern, and that this distrust is associated "primarily with the management of the economic crisis and government budgets" (2011, 110).

Distrust permeates Mexican political culture, limiting citizens' willingness to engage in collective action. A 2014 study by Mexico's National Electoral Institute found that 73 percent of citizens did not trust "most people" and that less than one in ten respondents had ever signed a petition. According to the report, widespread suspicion of politicians, political parties, police, and judges constitutes a profound "distrust and disconnect among citizens, and between the population and the government" (Saldierna 2014). This environment of weak horizontal and vertical trust reflects the civic apathy produced by seven decades of de facto one-party rule and corruption in the twentieth century (Morris 2001; Morris and Klesner 2010, 1259–60). The trend is fortified by a series of more recent electoral disputes, such as the infamous computer malfunction of 1988 that installed Salinas as president, the 1994 assassination of Colosio, and the allegations of fraud that tainted Calderón's 2006 victory.

The prevailing "distrust and disconnect" has been deepened by the continuing diffusion of criminal violence under the Peña Nieto administration. The alleged June 2014 execution of twenty-two criminal gang members by Mexican police in a warehouse in Ttatlaya, Mexico State, has deepened public perceptions of impunity for corrupt officers. The case is complicated by conflicting accounts, including by three women apparently rescued from the warehouse and subsequently accused of being members of the gang. The protracted trial has provoked allegations of government corruption on the one hand, and street protests in Mexico City for the human rights of the twenty-five accused police officers on the other hand (*La Jornada* 2015).

Even more damaging to the government's credibility is the September 2014 disappearance and murder of forty-three students from a rural teachers' college in Ayotzinapa, in Guerrero State. An official investigation has found that the students were detained by police in the nearby city of Iguala while protesting preferential government funding for urban colleges. An operative of the Guerreros Unidos crime syndicate states that Iguala police handed the students over to him, and believing they were involved in a rival gang, he ordered their incineration in a municipal landfill. Iguala's mayor and his wife fled after the incident but were apprehended in Mexico City, while the Iguala chief of police remains at large. The governor of Guerrero subsequently resigned in the face of mounting accusations of collusion between crime syndicates, police, and government agencies. As Ángel Calderon writes, "the killing fundamentally shakes the pillars of trust between individuals and institutions and highlights lack of accountability in the lines of command" (2015).

Public trust in government has been further shaken by Peña Nieto's personal indiscretion. Following a 2013 interview with the president's wife, Angélica Rivera, in the glossy magazine *Hola*, journalists found that she was in the process of buying a $7 million mansion (dubbed the Casa Blanca, or White House) from a subsidiary of the public works contractor Grupo Higa. In 2014 another of the company's subsidiaries was contracted to build the Mexico City–Querétaro high-speed rail link as part of a Chinese-led consortium. The conflict of interest became a liability in September 2014, when Peña Nieto visited New York to assume the presidency of the Alliance for Open Government, promising to "ensure that transparency and accountability are daily practices among all government offices and bureaus of member countries" (quoted in Reséndiz 2014). Facing allegations that he had not declared the purchase of the mansion as required by law, in November 2014 the president canceled the high-speed rail contract over concerns that the selection of the Chinese-led group did not demonstrate "absolute clarity, legitimacy and transparency" (quoted in Webber and Mitchell 2014).

The Casa Blanca debacle damaged Peña Nieto's credibility at home and in China, since the $3.6 billion high-speed rail project depended on $2.9 billion from the China Railway Construction Corporation (85 percent of which would have been financed by the Chinese government's Export-Import Bank). Days after he rescinded the contract, Peña Nieto visited Beijing for the Asia-Pacific Economic Cooperation summit, where Premier Li Keqiang implored him to treat Chinese companies "fairly" (quoted in *Global Times* 2014). Mexico's director of rail transport, Pablo Suárez Coello, anticipated a new tender application led by China Railway within weeks, but in February 2015 the Mexican government shelved the project, together with other public works, owing to the falling price of oil (Tan 2015).

The Peña Nieto administration has attempted to rebuild public trust mainly through economic reforms. The president describes his goal of attracting $250 billion of private capital into the oil sector as "the centerpiece" of his tenure, and as *Bloomberg* reports, foreign investors appear to believe it:

> Investors anticipate that President Enrique Peña Nieto will deliver on his promises for economic growth. Their conviction stems from the constitutional changes pushed through by the 48-year-old president. . . . In his first two years in office, Peña Nieto pushed through the biggest economic overhaul since the North American Free Trade Agreement took effect in 1994. The government estimates that allowing companies including Exxon Corp. and Chevron Corp. to produce crude [oil] on their own for the first time since the 1930s will help lift annual growth to above 5 percent, a level not seen since 2010, by the end of Peña Nieto's six-year term in 2018. (Bain and Martin 2014)

The achievement of these goals would enhance the PRI's stature as a party governing with a comprehensive industrial plan ranging from trade tariffs to structural reform, but optimism has been tempered by the declining price of oil. Investors are unlikely to plunge into the energy sector unless the price recovers, an uncertain prospect as shale gas production increases in the United States, Europe, and Australia. When the oil price fell below $50 per barrel in early 2015, PEMEX canceled contracts in Campeche, one of its most important production zones, leaving 10,000 subcontractors out of work. The government simultaneously announced that it would cut spending by $8.57 billion owing to oil's poor long-term outlook. Carstens, now governor of Mexico's central bank, told legislators: "We no longer have those revenues, especially when it appears that the drop [in oil prices] is pretty durable and we can say it is going to be a question of years, not months" (quoted in EFE 2015). One month later the Mexican president bucked concerns over the future of oil, travelling to London to accept a $1 billion loan from U.K. Export Finance to purchase British oil technology. Questions about presidential integrity followed Peña Nieto to Buckingham Palace as Mexican social media circulated photographs of his wife and daughter "on tour" in London wearing a $3,000 gown and a $7,000 dress, and of his wife carrying a $7,000 handbag ("Indigna en redes" 2015).

The only solace Mexico can derive from the declining price of oil is the cheaper energy it affords manufacturers, whose total production costs in 2014 were 5 percent below those of China (Sirkin, Zinser, and Rose 2014). Hopes of bringing back industries that abandoned Mexico for China during the PAN's tenure (2000–2012) are becoming more realistic, especially given the inflation of Chinese wages by more than 400 percent since 2004.

The Peña Nieto administration's reforms have focused on macroeconomic conditions and foreign investment, but they also have important implications for small businesses. This is evident in the 2014 budget, which pledged to work with lenders to loosen credit for small enterprises, noting that lending in Mexico amounts to only 16 percent of GDP (compared to 50 percent in most of Latin America). The government has also promised to reduce the inordinate cost of mobile phone services, one of the most pernicious daily barriers to the success of small businesses. To this end, the government has ordered Carlos Slim's América Móvil telecommunications monopoly to divest so that smaller firms might introduce lower-cost services into the market. A potentially less popular measure is a 2014 tax (of one peso per liter) on drinks with high sugar content, generating much-needed revenue for government programs but increasing the price of this Mexican staple by 14 percent. Peña Nieto's budget also envisions a 10 percent tax on personal profits from stock sales and dividends, while sparing food and medicine from an anticipated value-added tax because, he said, this would hurt Mexican families (Cattan and Martin 2013).

Tax reform is long overdue in Mexico, both because of the narrow taxation base and because evasion has seen the government's tax take decline to the lowest among the thirty-four members of the Organisation for Economic Co-Operation and Development. In 2014 the Mexican Tax Administration Service responded by initiating investigations into seven large multinational firms in the automotive, mining, and retail sectors. This has generated popular approval for the government but may fall short of formal audits into ingrained evasion practices, such as shifting profits to countries with lower taxes. Nevertheless, the above measures constitute tentative steps toward a more diverse economy that is less reliant on large enterprises and more likely to generate economic activity at the grass roots.

Broader opportunities for small businesses are critical for generating public trust in government, for—as Kenneth Newton puts it—"the relationship is likely to be reciprocal . . . winners tend to be trusting" (2001, 207; also see Armony 2004, 28; Freitag 2003). Mexico demonstrates better than most countries that collective action and the trust it generates are strongest in sectors that benefit from political and economic conditions. "Big business in Mexico," writes Ben Schneider, "invests far more time and money in voluntary encompassing associations than do the business sectors in other countries in the region" (2002, 78). For instance, major industry associations like the Consejo Coordinador Empresarial (Council for Business Coordination, or CCE) and its affiliate the Consejo Mexicano de Hombres de Negocios (Mexican Council of Businessmen, or CMHN) maintain symbiotic relationships with government institutions and funding bodies like the National Council of Science and Technology. Consensus and trust among the members of these associations have advanced their ability to influence policies and win state support, from tax breaks to subsidies for research and development. For Mexico's political and economic elites, targeted industrial policies and trust have reinforced each other. It remains to be seen whether or not Peña Nieto's policies will extend the radius of this virtuous circle beyond elite enterprises to smaller actors.

As Chinese exports encroach on Mexican markets in progressively higher value–adding sectors, including automobiles, economic diversification will become increasingly necessary. The next section illustrates why customs duties on Chinese products are no substitute for industrial policy. On the contrary, tariffs have encouraged the expansion of smuggling, eroding rather than fomenting trust among the state, businesses, and citizens.

IMPORTING FROM CHINA: EVADING THE GREAT WALL OF MEXICO

Until the mid-1980s Mexico stood out as an industrialization success story. Despite its limited export capacity, 85 percent of its foreign sales were manufactured goods such as textiles, household appliances, and automobile parts. While consolidating this industrial agenda in the 1970s, President Luis Echevarría developed cordial relations with the Chinese government, supporting its position on Taiwan and making Mexico China's leading trade partner in Latin America. But at that time China was laying the institutional foundations that would underpin its transition to market socialism, a transition whose enormous commercial output has now undercut Mexico's industrial achievements.

Mexican newspapers have made much of the dangers posed by untrustworthy Chinese products such as disintegrating automobile tires; contaminated pet food; seafood containing high levels of antibiotics to prevent infections from the industrial waste of China's eastern shores; and toothpaste and cough medicine containing lethal quantities of diethylene glycol, a cheap substitute for glycerine. An article reprinted in the Mexican newspaper *El Mural* concludes: "There was a time when the words 'made in China' evoked an immediate perception of 'bad quality.' These days many North Americans and Europeans perceive 'danger'" (Martin 2007). Chinese media have responded by accusing commercial competitors of overreporting such incidents to spread distrust of Chinese products and fuel perceptions of a China threat (French 2007).

Almost all Mexican industries, from traditional handicrafts and textiles to the export-oriented assembly sectors, have complained to the Mexican government about the lack of protection against the flood of low-priced products arriving from China and the loss of employment due to low wages in Chinese factories (Páramo 2008). To quell public anger, Calderón declared at the 2007 General Assembly of the CNIV: "it is necessary to take action to reduce the notable unjust disadvantages that are crippling the textile industry vis-à-vis those of other countries, particularly China" (quoted in *Epoch Times* 2007). In a country where 55 percent of people described China's economic development as a threat—the highest figure in Latin America, according to the Pew Research Center (2007)—Calderón's statement resonated with concerns within and beyond the textile sector. His call for action, though, was never developed into a coherent strategy. Instead, the Mexican government adopted a politically safe solution: commercial tariffs on products imported from China.

Trade barriers have not significantly staved off Chinese competition; nor have they fomented horizontal cooperation between Mexican businesses or vertical cooperation with the state. On the contrary, they have eroded trust between state and society as basic manufacturing industries, offered little support to advance and upgrade, have fallen further behind foreign competitors. Furthermore, tariffs on Chinese products have fueled the growth of the informal sector by providing a disincentive to declare trade.

Mexican protectionism against Chinese products became politically controversial with China's 2001 entry into the World Trade Organization. Unable to derail China's bid to join the group, Mexico negotiated a six-year grace period during which import tariffs would apply in 953 product categories, allowing its national industries time to upgrade their technologies, enhance efficiency, develop new strategies for inserting themselves into global production chains, and generally become more competitive. As the expiration date approached in November 2007, Mexican manufacturers successfully lobbied the Ministry of the Economy to seek an extension. The 2007 Transition Trade Agreement on Compensatory Fees established a period of four more years for Mexican industrial sectors likely to be affected by the elimination of the tariffs. Duties had previously ranged from 100 percent to 1,105 percent; under the agreement they would be 60–360 percent in the first year and 35–250 percent in the last (Hernández Hernández 2012, 83–84).

When the four-year extension expired in December 2011, tariffs in the 204 most sensitive sectors (such as clothing, shoes, bicycles, and baby strollers) were reduced to 35 percent. Although this figure was still fifty-nine times greater than Mexico's average general import duty, CONCAMIN opposed the tariff's reduction and the government's plan to progressively phase it out. According to CONCAMIN, for every two manufactured products exported by Mexico, ten were entering the country from China, and consequently, by 2011 between 900,000 and a million workers had lost their jobs (*El Mural* 2011). Together with other sectoral advocates, CONCAMIN continued to lobby the Ministry of the Economy to reinstate tariffs at their previous levels.

Industry pressure prevailed in August 2014, when Peña Nieto's minister of finance, Luis Videgaray, announced a new tax on imported footwear and potentially other items, based on benchmark value (estimated market price) rather than declared customs value. Videgaray argued that the tax, levied at 25–30 percent, would correct the previous government's negligence: "We [the previous government] eliminated benchmark prices and decided unilaterally to begin reducing tariffs, and for industry, from the perspective of industrial policy, that essentially amounted to wishing them good luck" (quoted in EFE 2014). The minister's attempt to improve the "luck" of embattled manufacturers may temporarily alleviate their anxiety about Chinese imports, but if history is any guide, tariffs will not overcome their competitive woes.

One negative but logical consequence of Mexico's successive barriers against Chinese imports is that suppliers and retailers have found creative ways to circumvent them. According to the 2007 Inquiry into Antidumping Quotas against Imports of Chinese Origin, undertaken by the Mexican consultancy IQOM Trade Intelligence, Mexican firms have habitually arranged legal loopholes and exceptions to antidumping quotas for their Chinese suppliers (M. García 2007). Interviews I conducted between 2008 and 2014 indicated that illegal methods are even more common, particularly bribery of customs officials. It is well known, for instance, that shipping containers entering the ports of Manzanillo and Lázaro Cárdenas frequently pass through customs without their contents ever being reviewed.

A related practice known as technical smuggling involves the classification of goods under an incorrect harmonized tariff schedule code that receives a smaller tax. Informally known as the *salto arrancelario* (tariff jump), this enables new T-shirts to enter Mexico as used T-shirts, petroleum engines as diesel engines, and so on. Textile products such as suits, underwear, and curtains are falsely classified as containing no cotton or other inputs that are also produced in Mexico. Should they choose to inspect a shipping container, customs officials often lack the necessary training to discern an item's true composition or function. An erroneous approval by customs agents—whether honest or subsidized—can therefore be explained to meticulous supervisors, if necessary, as an *error de dedo* (literally, an error of the finger). Technical smuggling first emerged as a serious concern between 2003 and 2005, when the Ministry of the Economy recorded that imported textiles classified as used clothing increased from 6,500 to 17,500 tons (Dussel Peters 2009, 304). Customs officials acknowledge the problem but argue that they cannot overcome it because most of these products arrive from China, where they have no authority to conduct investigations (López 2006b).

Another form of tariff avoidance underlying Sino-Mexican commerce is illegal transshipment, known in Mexico as *triangulación* (triangulation). Chinese exports enter the United States, Guatemala, and Belize free of duty as temporary imports destined for a third country. While the merchandise is held in storage, criminal accomplices acting as inspectors replace "made in China" shipping papers and package labels on the merchandise with documents stating "made in USA." Under NAFTA these products then enter Mexico free of duty. They are sold in street markets around the country at prices that are impossibly low for products genuinely manufactured in the United States. The yarn-textile-garment chain has been particularly hard hit by triangulation, and studies show that between 2006 and 2011, 60–65 percent of Mexican retail in clothing consisted of illegal imports from China (Dussel Peters 2009, 304; I. Rodríguez 2011). As Mexico's ambassador to China from 2001 to 2006, Sergio Ley witnessed the diplomatic fallout firsthand: "When I was working in Beijing, a Mexican official gave a public speech here in Mexico City, declaring that China was responsible for the influx of contraband. Today this is still the dominant perception. But a Chinese friend of mine told me, 'How can we be responsible? We don't control Mexican customs!' He was absolutely right, and I'll tell you the real culprit: the enormous quotas against Chinese products, which are higher than the Great Wall! With these quotas it becomes logical to 'pagar la mordida' [literally, pay the bite—meaning to offer a bribe]" (interview, June 15, 2010).

Ley has good reason to oppose tariffs on imports from China. As chairman of the Asia-Pacific section of the Mexican Business Council for Foreign Trade, Investment and Technology, he dedicates himself to promoting Sino-Mexican trade. His family, of Chinese origin, owns several baseball teams and the successful Casa Ley department store chain, which retails the popular Ley brand of jeans. Although Casa Ley is known to import from China, and although Sergio and his brother are widely known as Los Chinos Ley for their Chinese heritage, these connections have not damaged their sales. "The important thing," Sergio insists, "is that we have the lowest prices."

The same can be said of imported Chinese products generally, which retail not only in stores like Casa Ley but also in informal street markets. Studies conducted in 2012 found that 53 percent of Mexicans aged 16–25 habitually purchase contraband, and that the informal sector constituted 15 percent of GDP that year ("La economía informal representa 15% del PIB" 2012). Statistics from the Instituto Nacional de Estadística y Geografía (National Institute of Statistics and Geography) suggest that informality is likely to be more widespread: between 2007 and 2012, 7.2 million Mexicans entered the workforce and 2.4 million jobs (including both permanent and temporary jobs) were created, implying that only a third of new workers entered formal employment (figures cited in Dussel Peters and Ortiz Velázquez 2012, 15). Labor Minister Alfonso Navarrete has acknowledged that some 60 percent of Mexicans do not pay taxes and have no social security benefits, and that economic opportunities at the grassroots are critical for turning the situation around: "If there are no real incentives to make it attractive for informal workers to turn formal . . . it's difficult to get this group to migrate" (quoted in Hughes 2013). A popular Mexican saying confirms the point: "For every ten people who lose their jobs, eight will go to the informal sector."

Mexico's most famous outlet for unregistered consumer goods is Tepito, an expansive informal marketplace on the eastern perimeter of Mexico City's historic center (discussed in chapter 4). Customers are drawn to the district by its famous slogan: "dress yourself for 100 pesos [approximately $8]." One of Tepito's innumerable suppliers is Ángel, a twenty-three-year-old from Harbin, north of Beijing, who has a master's in business administration and moved to Mexico City in 2009 to join his older sister. In 2003 she had opened a women's clothing store, but over the next two years it was robbed three times. On each occasion the police ignored her reports, leading her to abandon her legitimate business for underground trading in counterfeit shoes, jackets, and handbags from China. Soon after arriving in Mexico, Ángel established a new product line of Chinese-made watches and office equipment. Unlike his sister, he chose to import items that are not also produced in Mexico and that therefore have relatively small tariffs. According to Ángel,

> In five days I can get any brand of watch you want shipped over by UPS [United Parcel Service]. My suppliers in China write lower prices on the papers to reduce the tariff, but even without their help the tariff is smaller than for jackets and shoes. Jackets are charged [a tariff of] 50 percent in Mexico because they make jackets here, but only around 15 percent in Guatemala, so my sister ships them by boat [from China to Guatemala] and sends a van to pick them up. People working at the Guatemala border are easy to bribe, so getting the products into Mexico is easy. Most of our customers are Mexicans who sell the products in street plazas and markets like Tepito, and in Guadalajara. . . . It's dangerous. Even when my sister started [her legally registered business] the police couldn't be trusted. We're Chinese, and if there's a problem we can't rely on the police, so we call the Chinese embassy instead. (interview, June 17, 2010)

The niche that Ángel and his sister fill results from the high import tariffs on products that compete with those made in Mexico, combined with easy access to inexpensive alternatives from China. Employing a range of strategies to circumvent these tariffs, Ángel and his associates operate outside the law. The fact that they turn to the Chinese embassy rather than the police for protection indicates their precarious and marginal status in Mexico. This is to be expected considering the illicit nature of their trade, but it was a lack of trust in the police on the part of Ángel's sister that led her (and by extension him) into the black market to begin with. Distrust of official authorities is common in Mexico's Chinese communities, whose members typically turn to ethnic associations and informal support structures rather than the police when their businesses are robbed or vandalized (see chapter 4). The result for Ángel has been diversion away from registered forms of Sino-Mexican exchange and assimilation into a tight-knit underground network of smugglers.

The case of Ángel bears out Michael Woolcock's observation that tightly integrated illicit networks with thin linkages to the public sphere impede inclusive development and broader societal cohesion (1998, 172–77). When such instances of what Woolcock calls "integration without linkage" grow to the extent that Mexico's informal sector has, the capacity of governments to enforce the rule of law and for societies to "get ahead collectively"—in Albert Hirschman's (1984) sense—is powerfully undermined. Instead, reliance on "informal institutions" (O'Donnell 2006) engender what Alejandro Portes calls "downward leveling norms" (1998, 15) that ingrain expectations of illegality and preclude the formation of extragroup relationships (Hilgers 2008). The only viable pathway to vertical cooperation under these conditions is to draw government officials into covert networks, as has recently been alleged in Mexico City's historic center (see chapter 4).

Weak state-society ties also undermine the formation of horizontal cooperation at the grass roots. As unchecked rival networks vie for political and geographic hegemony, loyalties become sharply defined and trust is limited to immediate associates. It is a far cry from the "spontaneous sociability" that conservative theorists argue should flourish as the state scales back its interventions to unleash society's entrepreneurial initiative (Fukuyama 1995, 27).

Vertical disengagement in Mexico since the 1980s has impeded legally compliant forms of cooperation not only among informal networks, but also among registered small businesses. The latter have had to fend for themselves, often in bitter competition with each other, envious of the support reserved for a narrow band of large enterprises. Outside of major representative bodies like the CCE and CMHN, private-sector coordination, cooperation, and trust are remote prospects in this fragmented context, and consequently, so is Mexico's ability to compete with China. The problem is deepened by excessive import tariffs, which may have generated short-term political capital for officials seeking the trust (and votes) of workers, but have not empowered national industries to explore new markets, develop technologies, and expand formal employment. Despite these difficult circumstances, as the next section shows, there have been cases of successful cooperation between the public and private sectors, and they offer useful lessons for improving Sino-Mexican relations.

EXPORTING TO CHINA: IN SEARCH OF PUBLIC-PRIVATE BALANCE

In November 2013 the Confederation of Chinese Associations of Mexico (CACHIMEX) sponsored the fifth annual Expo China trade fair. Held in the city of San Luis Potosí, the fair hosted some fifty Mexican companies alongside their counterparts from China, Peru, and Vietnam. Hoping to extend their reach into Chinese markets, participants secured export contracts for Mexican fruits, vegetables, and shellfish. Since Expo China's establishment in Mexico City in 2009, its organizers have presented it as an initiative that serves Mexican interests. According to CACHIMEX's Secretary General Jimmy Li, "by promoting exports to China we hope to reduce the perception that our fairs are all about bringing 'made in China' products into Mexico" (interview, June 11, 2010).

Ricardo Chang, public relations manager for CACHIMEX, says he wants to distance Expo China from accusations that Chinese businesses are perpetrating a trans-Pacific invasion of cheap textiles, shoes, toys, and steel products, voiced on Mexican websites like "Pinche Chinos" (Damn Chinese) and "Ten Reasons Not to Buy Chinese Products This Christmas." Using Expo China to import Chinese products would only deepen this perception and, according to Chang, undermine the long-term networking strategy of Chinese exporters: "Chinese manufacturers have become interested in the Expo, but not to sell their products. What they want is to raise awareness of Chinese brands and build distribution networks. Just look what they sent to the last Expo: buses made by Yutong and a submarine! No one's going to buy these things, but they might be impressed by them and start to trust their makers. In the end CACHIMEX is about building international networks, and that means building confidence in products" (interview, May 27, 2014).

Politicians and business executives have been reluctant to endorse events like Expo China for fear of popular criticism. Although Chang has found the PRI more receptive than the PAN to working with CACHIMEX, "it's still an uphill battle . . . some local governments now let us use their logos, but not much more than that" (interview, May 27, 2014). Expo China's vertical ties to government are therefore weak, a predicament that the economist Enrique Dussel Peters believes has undermined its ability to advance Mexican interests: "The Mexican government—and even the Chinese government—won't get involved because it's too sensitive, so Expo China is run 100 percent by the business community. This won't work because it results in a focus on importing over exporting and leaves no space for policy strategies that could turn this around" (interview, June 16, 2010). For Li, the first step to turning the situation around is simple: "We'd like some high-ranking officials to come to the opening ceremony and cut a ribbon or something" (interview, June 11, 2010).

Endorsement from above will be critical if Expo China and similar trade fairs are ever to place more than fruit, vegetables, and shellfish in Chinese markets. Expo China's organizers believe that Mexico would find ready consumers in China for everything from tequila and abalone to ground-up rubber from used tires, but owing to a lack of official sponsorship, national suppliers are either unaware of the event or have little faith in its legitimacy. Sponsorship would help build public confidence and encourage new domestic linkages between Mexican producers and exporters. In Li's words, "culture and commerce are like two hands of the same person . . . as we say in China, first make friends, and then do business" (interview, June 11, 2010). While the Ministry of the Economy's Fondo para Pequeñas y Medianas Empresas (Small and Medium Enterprise Fund) has financed the participation of several Mexican companies in an Expo-related marketing mission to Chengdu and Fuzhou, the annual event has been set back by "the lack of government support for selling to China" (Tai 2012, 367, 370).

Expo China is not unique in the lack of support it receives. As noted above, SMEs have little access to subsidies and tax breaks and have therefore been unable to compete in domestic markets or through Mexico's twelve free trade agreements (León-Manríquez 2011, 169–70). Although SMEs comprise 52 percent of GDP and 72 percent of formal employment, they contribute almost nothing to Mexico's exports ("Importancia de las Pymes" 2011). For a country that scores well on the World Economic Forum's indices of market size (11th out of 142 countries), time required to start a small business (35th), and gross national savings (40th), Mexico's ranking of 92nd in ease of access to loans is an aberration (World Economic Forum 2011, 259). Such scant financial support for SMEs is far from ideal in a global environment that rewards the diversification of exports, particularly for a country whose output does not include a heavy concentration of primary products.

The Organisation for Economic Co-Operation and Development recommends that Mexico adopt a long-term approach to export competitiveness by investing in education and technical training (2009, 114–16; also see Santiso and Avendaño 2011, 88). The federal government has been slow to follow this advice, but in 2005 nine state governments jointly formed the Program for Mexico-China Business Formation under the Asociación de Secretarios de Desarrollo Económico (Association of Mexican Secretaries of Economic Development, or AMSDE) to fund Mexican students at the master's and doctoral levels to undertake internships in China, learn Chinese, and research opportunities for technology transfer and bilateral trade. Eloy Vargas Arreola, former secretary of economic development of the state of Michoacán, argued that the initiative was a critical factor in building familiarity with China and overcoming the existing commercial imbalance (Wu 2006). Having sent over 200 students to China, the AMSDE program was suspended in 2008 amid reports that grants had been awarded to friends and relatives of politicians and influential businesspeople with little interest in advancing bilateral cooperation.

The China-Mexico Research Center (CECHIMEX) at the National Autonomous University of Mexico has established a more successful grant program. Funded by Mexico City's government, the program placed 46 students in Chinese internship and research programs between 2007 and 2015. As well as studying the development of technical linkages between Chinese universities and industrial parks, grantees have designed strategies for boosting Chinese tourism to Mexico, establishing a high-level Spanish-Mandarin interpretation service, harmonizing Mexican and Chinese professional and academic qualifications, convening a bilateral commission on agricultural biotechnology, and duplicating a Chinese plastic injection molding facility in Mexico City (Trápaga Delfín, Dussel Peters, and Martínez 2012). The Asia Pacific Institute of the Tecnológico de Monterrey has also leveraged state-level funding to develop a strategic plan for China, working with its permanent staff members in Beijing and Shanghai to coordinate activities with the Mexican embassy in China. Over 500 students have passed through its programs in Beijing, Shanghai, Guangzhou, and Harbin, where the Tecnológico offers placements in engineering, international relations, business, and language through student visits to embassies, factories, and work centers.

Despite these achievements, state funding has sometimes been awarded to advance political agendas instead of genuine outcomes. One program in Hangzhou hosts eighty Mexican government-funded students annually to live together in an on-campus residence hall, where their level of interaction with Chinese society—even academic society—

is very low. Familiarity with Chinese culture is apparently not an objective of the local coordinator (a former Mexican bureaucrat whose program has never been formally audited), who has set up a taco restaurant at the gates of the university. Interviewees in Mexico and China reported that such programs are not unusual; while they ostensibly focus on language and business training, they function largely as propaganda for Mexican politicians eager to convince their electorates that they are dealing with the so-called China threat. As a former student of one such program put it, "I think it's good that the Mexican government is trying to do something about China, but I feel very angry that the money is so often misused, and with no consequences!" (interview, November 3, 2007).

Mexico's state-sponsored travel grants have generated information and opportunities for national exporters, but the political scientist Laura Rubio of the Instituto Tecnológico Autónomo de México (Autonomous Technological Institute of Mexico) notes a lack of follow-through once initial strategies have been drawn up. One student, she reports, designed a project to export tequila to China and soon identified a Mexican provider and a Chinese buyer and distributor. Chinese consumers responded enthusiastically, but the Mexican provider was unable to meet their demand. The project soon collapsed because the provider, having secured phytosanitary certification from Chinese customs, was unable to secure seed investment to expand production and develop partnerships with other Mexican producers. As Rubio notes, "it's precisely the kind of company the government should support" (personal communication, October 8, 2010).

These cases illustrate the considerable potential of state-backed educational and research programs to advance cultural and commercial engagement with China. Implementation, though, has been undermined by a lack of strategic and financial follow-through. Frustrated by this state of affairs, in 2008 Dussel Peters founded the Mexico-China Working Group, which has published a set of twenty-nine proposals for commercial engagement with China. The Working Group recommends that the Ministry of the Economy and its international division, ProMéxico, urgently "undertake an exhaustive campaign" to promote the export of Mexican primary products, auto parts, electronics, food, and drink to China; attract Chinese tourists to Mexico; and secure Chinese investment in the mining, infrastructure, alternative energy, textile, and automotive sectors (quoted in Dussel Peters 2011b, 5). The reluctance of Mexican political and commercial elites to engage with China is reflected in poor investment figures: according to the Economic Commission for Latin America and the Caribbean, between 1990 and 2011 Chinese firms invested $19.7 billion in Brazil, $9.2 billion in Argentina, and $718 million in Costa Rica, but only $132 million in Mexico (Mingramm 2012, 101).

The Working Group also calls on ProMéxico to reopen its offices in Shanghai and Hong Kong, and on the Ministry of the Economy's undersecretary of SMEs to ensure that Mexican products appear in Chinese trade fairs (Dussel Peters 2011b, 6–7). Furthermore, it suggests fully reinstating Mexico's tourism office in China (which was closed in 2010 to cut costs and reopened in 2011 with only one staff member) to increase Mexico's share of China's fifty million annual outbound tourists from its current base of 0.1 percent, and running a series of educational courses in the Mexican Ministries of Foreign Affairs and Migration to "improve knowledge about China and its culture, and especially to eradicate prejudices" (Dussel Peters 2011b, 6).[1] These recommendations have since been elaborated into the *Agenda Estratégica México-China* (Mexico-China strategic agenda), a compilation of over eighty proposals presented to President Peña Nieto under the auspices of the newly formed think tank AgendAsia (AgendAsia 2012).

State support will be a critical factor in Mexico's ability to compete with China, but as Mexican business consultant Rafael Valdez Mingramm has argued, national companies must also become more proactive: "The responsibility does not lie exclusively with the state. The Mexican private sector also needs to modify its agenda with China, to look beyond particular or group interests, and take advantage of our country's wide range of offerings and comparative advantages. . . . All that's needed is to stop focusing exclusively on the North American market and reestablish the strategic relationship that we constructed with China over the past 500 years" (2012, 103 and 105).

Mexican firms that have done well in China are large enterprises with global reach. A good example is Nemak, the world's leading producer of aluminum engine blocks, cylinder heads, and transmission parts for automotive applications. The company has close to fifteen thousand employees in thirteen countries, including China, and has established research and development partnerships and joint ventures with a range of original equipment manufacturers (OEMs) (Santiso and Avendaño 2011, 83). A key factor in Nemak's success has been the establishment since 2000 of overseas factories, in anticipation of Chinese competition, to fill specific niches in the automotive chain. Although these niches do not occupy the highest value–adding segments of the production process, Nemak has demonstrated design and technology innovation through its lightweight aluminum engine blocks, or monoblocks, which are suitable for a range of OEMs. Exporting to China since 1995, Nemak does not control the production process, but it is one of only a handful of Latin American companies working in close partnership with long-term clients like Ford, General Motors, Chrysler, Hyundai, and BMW. It is also one of the few Latin American firms to invest heavily in China, acquiring a plant from Fiat-Teksid in Nanjing in 2007 for $18.1 million and constructing a new facility in Chongqing in 2012 for $42 million to service its China-based customers (Dussel Peters 2012, 10).

Nemak stands out as an exceptional example of private initiative, but it also demonstrates the importance of long-term strategic support from the state. The company would probably not exist at all had the Mexican government not awarded its parent company, Alfa Group, 12 billion pesos ($480 million) in 1981 to get it through the oil crisis. Five federal decrees between the 1960s and the signing of NAFTA in 1994 ensured the health of the automotive sector, and a series of tax breaks and research grants has since supported Nemak's expansion. Alfa Group is a prominent member of CMHN, and in 2007 Nemak was the primary beneficiary of an investment of 142 million pesos ($13 million) awarded jointly by the state government of Nuevo León and the National Council of Science and Technology (P. González 2007). Foreign governments have also provided Nemak with concessions to generate jobs in their territories, such as a $3 million tax break to establish an engine block production plant in Windsor, Ontario, in 2010 (Macaluso 2010). Similarly, energy and land use incentives provided by the Chongqing city government were critical in attracting Nemak's investment (Dussel Peters, personal communication, December 27, 2012).

High-level diplomatic support from Mexican officials has been important in securing outcomes for Nemak and other large-scale operations. Patricia Espinosa, Mexico's secretary of foreign affairs, demonstrated this when she visited Beijing to meet Chinese President Xi Jinping and Foreign Minister Yang Jiechi in 2012. Reflecting the Calderón administration's more conciliatory approach to China, her personal advocacy overcame five years of impasse to secure official Chinese endorsement of Mexican pork imports (Bermúdez Liévano 2012). However, as anybody who has worked in China knows, cooperation is forged over time, and Espinosa's efforts will not produce economic outcomes without diplomatic follow-up. The current challenge is to steer pork and other Mexican products such as beef, poultry, mangos, and avocados through China's inevitably political quarantine regime. By 2014 Chinese inspectors had assessed and approved six of nine pork processing facilities in Mexico, and further delays will be averted only through a combination of high-level advocacy and improved coordination between private-sector producers and government trade representatives.

China's growth has created new opportunities for large Mexican firms like Nemak, but it is also generating unforeseen competition for the automobile, agriculture, and manufacturing sectors, particularly in the U.S. market. For the time being, federal assistance is supporting the viability of Mexico's automotive and agriculture sectors, but the future of manufacturing and small business is more precarious. Over the past decade, numerous studies have advocated measures that the government should adopt to strengthen the long-term competitiveness of these sectors. It remains to be seen if these studies are reaching and influencing the relevant officials in the Peña Nieto administration.

CONCLUSION

Strategies for building the competitiveness of Mexican businesses have been slow to emerge, in part because of overreliance on the U.S. market (deepened by NAFTA), and in part because "the expression 'industrial policy' has become almost taboo in the discourse of Mexican economic officials" (León-Manríquez 2011, 170). As discussed above, conservative thinkers have provided a rationale for this policy orientation, arguing that intrusive regulations, reporting requirements, and unnecessary costs incurred by state intervention undermine the trust necessary for economic cooperation and growth. The recent history of Mexico's trade relations with China does not support the view that intervention is a "substitute for trust" (Fukuyama 1995, 27); on the contrary, instances of targeted state support have stimulated a range of partnerships and associations.

In the absence of a coherent industrial policy, import tariffs have become an ad hoc response to Chinese competition. While the political mileage generated by trade barriers cannot last forever, there is strong popular support for maintaining them, as demonstrated by the protests of industry groups discussed above.

As a substitute for more sophisticated and proactive measures, import tariffs have generated opportunities for informal traders. Tax evasion and smuggling are too difficult to resist for thousands of people like Ángel, the Tepito supplier whose illicit dealings and tight networks demonstrate the toll that "integration without linkage" takes on social cohesion, the rule of law, and trust. The informal sector will grow further unless opportunities at the grass roots entice people like Ángel into registered, tax-paying occupations. Assertive industrial policies may therefore be Mexico's best defense against the black market, especially since the influx of Chinese manufactured goods shows no sign of slowing down. The fact that the otherwise conservative Peña Nieto administration should publicly identify a need to diversify the Mexican economy through credit and tax breaks for small businesses indicates its awareness that inadequate formal opportunities are driving the black market's growth.

There is a growing consensus that genuine solutions to the Sino-Mexican trade imbalance could be achieved through greater efforts from the Ministry of the Economy, ProMéxico, and other state institutions whose mandates include coordinating and promoting trade and development. These efforts could focus on establishing vertical synergies for industrial upgrading through public-private partnerships and encouraging horizontal linkages among suppliers, exporters, and importers. Without these connections, small entrepreneurs who have identified and begun to exploit niches for Mexican products in the Chinese market, as was the case with tequila, have been unable to acquire start-up grants, logistical support, and official endorsement. The Expo China trade fair, founded in 2009 to promote exchange between Mexican and Chinese small businesses, is well placed as a hub for such connections. Its organizers lament, though, that politicians and businesspeople have been too wary of criticism on the sensitive issue of Chinese competition to endorse and promote their efforts. In the absence of sponsorship, Mexican producers and exporters have remained unaware that they could use Expo China to develop partnerships with each other and potential Chinese customers.

In spite of Mexico's competitive woes, there have been several illuminating examples of success. The automotive parts producer Nemak has identified niches for its specialized engine blocks in China, which since 2009 has produced and consumed more automobiles than any other country. Nemak's exemplary performance is underpinned by a combination of private business acumen and government support in the form of research and development funding and incentives. Such awards would yield more broadly shared benefits if extended across Mexican businesses, particularly to SMEs. Results have also been achieved for Mexican farmers, who can take comfort in China's April 2012 commitment to opening markets initially to large-scale pork producers and potentially also to smaller beef, poultry, fruit, and vegetable suppliers. Markets do not open by themselves, but rather as a result of assertive high-level diplomatic engagement and personal advocacy, in this case under the leadership of Espinosa.

At the level of small businesses, state governments have been more active than federal institutions in building relationships and pursuing emerging opportunities. The Mexico City government, for instance, has provided research grants enabling CECHIMEX to establish a systematic program of student placements in internships in China. The project has generated detailed proposals, publicly available on the CECHIMEX website, for building commercial partnerships and familiarity with the Chinese market. This and the other cases analyzed in this chapter suggest that Mexico's problems with China will not be solved simply through more government, but they may diminish through more sophisticated and assertive policies of domestic and foreign engagement.

Chapter 4 will describe another positive case of vertical synergy, driven by the state government of Baja California—where, despite potentially debilitating anti-Chinese popular sentiments, local officials have developed trusting relationships with the resident Chinese community. Long-term cooperation built on legislation to facilitate commerce and migration has enabled a range of initiatives, from registered street markets to high-level visits from Chinese trade and investment delegations. Before examining microlevel developments in Mexico, we first return to

Cuba, where the Chinese diasporic community has also come to perform an important diplomatic function between China and Cuba. The capacity of governments to build nationally beneficial relations with China depends not only on vertical state-society relationships, but also on robust horizontal linkages in civil society and the private sector. The activities of members of the Chinese diaspora illuminate the formation of such horizontal linkages, and how their effectiveness is integrally tied to the delicate project of building vertical trust with the state.

FACING THE FUTURE

The 120th anniversary celebration of the legal registration of the Casino Chung Wah marks a return to prominence for the coordinating body of Cuba's Chinese community and its seventeen nationwide sub-associations. Four smartly dressed waiters—employees of the Casino—are serving green tea and black coffee during an intermission in the speeches. Nearby a well-meaning European scholar is firing pointed questions at Juan Eng, the Casino's president: "In other countries Chinese associations are pushing business relationships with China like never before . . . what's holding you back?" The renowned Chinese Cuban artist Flora Fong unveils her latest work: a photographic tapestry chronicling Chinese Cuban faces past and present, mounted on a six-foot-tall sculpture of her signature icon 人 [*ren*, meaning person]. Eng sips his tea and answers as well as possible: "We've been waiting patiently for a long time, and now things are starting to change."

—Havana, May 20, 2013

The question put to Eng had long been on my mind, though it had seemed to me better not to ask. It is a question suited to observation and exploration over time, and it raises many others. Among them: Since Cubans can now legally buy and sell houses and cars, are Chinese associations filling the niche of informal commercial brokers? As Cubans take advantage of permission to establish small businesses, are the thick social networks of the Chinese community once again coalescing—as they did a century ago—into networks of supply, distribution, and retail? As Cubans increasingly travel overseas, to what extent are Chinese community leaders connecting with friends and relatives in China to develop independent lines of supply and investment? To answer these questions requires sensitivity to the legacies of history. They are, after all, questions about relationships, social capital, and trust, all of which take time to build.

Barrio Chino is less endogamous than other overseas Chinese communities—for instance, those in Indonesia and Malaysia, where strong ethnic affinities and inward loyalties provoked anti-Chinese riots in 1965 and 1969 (Heryanto 1998; Yahuda 1985, 222–23). In Cuba, first-generation Chinese immigrants have been declining in number ever since their businesses were nationalized in the 1960s. Jorge Chao Chiu, secretary general of the Casino Chung Wah, reported in 2011 that the Casino registered only 171 surviving first-generation Chinese immigrants on the island (interview, February 23, 2011). By mid-2013 the number had fallen to 141 (table 3.1).

To breathe life back into Cuba's seventeen remaining Chinese associations (twelve of which are in Havana), in 1986 the Casino Chung Wah advised them to open their membership to second- and third-generation Chinese Cubans. In the early 1990s most did so, and by 2013 the associations together reported 2,223 members. Unlike their first-generation predecessors, the descendants driving this revival hold Cuban rather than Chinese citizenship, and they are more culturally and genetically integrated into Cuban society. Chinese descendants have demonstrated a strong interest in the associations and now occupy senior (though not the highest) posts in the most important of these, including the Casino Chung Wah.

Since the turbulent post-Soviet decade of the 1990s, Barrio Chino has been at the forefront of Cuba's economic evolution. In 1994 a group of descendants of Chinese immigrants successfully lobbied the government for permission to establish Cuba's first freely operating markets and stores since 1959 and to import products directly from China. Today the district's restaurants are among the most popular and profitable in Cuba, and their success has provided a point of formal and informal entry for Chinese suppliers. As the government rolls out its plan to promote heri-

TABLE 3.1 Members of the Casino Chung Wah in May 2013

PROVINCE	FIRST-GENERATION CHINESE IMMIGRANTS		SECOND- AND THIRD-GENERATION CHINESE	
	Chinese citizens	Cuban citizens	Descendants	Total
Pinar del Río	0	1	6	7
Isla de la Juventud	0	0	8	8
Artemisa	1	2	16	19
Mayabeque	3	1	38	43
Havana	35	43	1,397	1,475
Matanzas	7	2	66	75
Villa Clara	4	4	104	112
Cienfuegos	6	1	58	65
Sancti Spíritus	1	1	4	6
Ciego de Ávila	5	3	23	31
Camagüey	3	1	41	45
Las Tunas	0	1	21	22
Granma	2	0	15	17
Holguín	1	2	38	41
Santiago de Cuba	9	1	216	31
Guantánamo	0	0	31	31
Total	77	64	2,082	2,223

SOURCE: COURTESY OF MARÍA TERESA MONTES DE OCA CHOY.

tage tourism in Barrio Chino, a steady stream of visiting Chinese officials and investors has expressed interest in supplying the required goods and services, including Chinese-themed hotels and supermarkets.

Its emerging public profile imbues Barrio Chino with diplomatic appeal. Combining the allure of what Rosalie Schwartz (1997) calls the "pleasure island" with growing international interest in China and its diaspora, the district carries the credentials of an up-and-coming national icon. It showcases a relatively underrepresented feature of Cuban cultural heritage at a time when the Cuban and Chinese governments are emphasizing their historical ties. As bilateral trade and investment accelerate, leaders from both countries habitually invoke these ties to draw attention to the human link that has long connected their nations.

In November 2008, during his second state visit to Cuba in four years, Chinese President Hu Jintao proclaimed: "Even though the physical distance that separates China and Cuba is great, friendship between both people goes back a long way" (quoted in Weissert 2008). The sentiment was symbolically enacted in media coverage of Hu's delegation taking a guided tour of Barrio Chino.

High-level diplomatic exchanges inevitably make headlines, but more common are quiet visits from small entrepreneurs exploring potential new openings for their products, including in Barrio Chino's informal sector. The innumerable retail kiosks and stalls that have sprung up across Cuba under Raúl Castro peddle everything from kitchen items and clothing to home appliances and DVD players, often supplied on the black market. In Barrio Chino undeclared exchange of goods and services has long been a way of life, in part because of a legacy of protective associations predisposed to discreet business conducted through extended mutual aid networks. Webs of informal cooperation infused with interpersonal trust have historically underpinned the local economy and have now begun to accommodate encounters between Chinese Cubans and visitors from mainland China. Conscious of the political ramifications of these exchanges, district administrators have attempted to bring them under control through stricter bookkeeping requirements, heavier taxation, and programs to strengthen state-society engagement. In this respect too Barrio Chino reflects the broader regulatory challenges facing Cuba, and the attempts of the state to meet them.

As a cultural and diplomatic bridge between Cuba and China, a potentially profitable site for tourism development, but also a hub of unregistered commerce, Barrio Chino concentrates a variety of nationally pertinent threats and opportunities into twenty-three city blocks. Seen from the bottom up, two encompassing challenges are shaping the rules of the game. The first is the task of carving out civic spaces that enable a broader range of small business activities and autonomous commercial relationships with partners in China. The efforts of Raúl Castro's administration to stimulate independent entrepreneurship and local self-sufficiency have inspired confidence that these outcomes will soon be within reach, though important legal steps remain unresolved. Second is the task of defining a development agenda for Barrio Chino that balances unity of purpose with diversity of voices. Meeting this challenge is arguably a prerequisite for exerting upward pressure on the state and achieving greater local leeway, but two decades of calls for unity from community leaders suggest that there is no easy pathway toward grassroots solidarity.

The support of Barrio Chino's residents is crucial for the state's capacity to elicit compliance and boost tourism in the district. Administrators have therefore tried to consolidate their authority to govern by reaching out to community leaders. But Barrio Chino's budding entrepreneurs argue that trust must be earned. Stable supply chains, the relaxation of commercial restrictions, approval of would-be investors, and less crippling taxation would stimulate goodwill, they say, more than the statues of Confucius and exotic tourist attractions appearing around them. They also point out that trust takes time to build, and that bitter memories of the 1960s—when the state nationalized Barrio Chino's thriving businesses—are yet to fade away. Even more deep-seated are historical narratives of crimes committed by successive colonial and republican Cuban governments against their ancestors.

This chapter's first section examines the arrival and settlement of Chinese contract laborers in the late nineteenth and early twentieth centuries, a turbulent process that laid the foundations of Barrio Chino's contemporary governance challenges. To protect themselves from the conditions of de facto slavery, Chinese immigrants established mutual aid networks that over time evolved into thick networks of informal exchange. For Chinese newcomers, the trust and cooperation fomented by the ethnic associations were a matter of survival, but colonial commentators seized on the apparent refusal of Chinese Cubans to integrate into mainstream social and economic life. Interracial unions were common, but Barrio Chino nevertheless became disarticulated from its civic and legal surroundings. By the mid-twentieth century, tourism from the United States cemented the district's infamy as a hub of gambling, drug activity, and organized crime.

The second section considers Barrio Chino's predicament after the rebel movement led by Fidel Castro seized political power in 1959. Early strategies to bring the district into the revolutionary fold included a neighborhood campaign staged by a Chinese Cuban division of the National Revolutionary Militia and the nationalization of Chinese businesses during the 1968 Great Revolutionary Offensive. The disruption of local life was compounded by the deterioration of Cuba's diplomatic relations with China during the Sino-Soviet split (see chapter 1), leading Barrio Chino into two decades of stasis and neglect. As China reached out to former Soviet allies in the 1990s, a team of entrepreneurial Chinese Cubans set up the Grupo Promotor de Barrio Chino (the Barrio Chino promotion group) to develop commercial partnerships in China and simultaneously build fresh ties with the Cuban state. The project showed early signs of success, but the task of mediating local, national, and foreign interests became increasingly difficult as bottom-up community demands came into conflict with top-down government directives. The team learned the hard way that strong bonds of inward-looking trust can easily be characterized by competitors as nepotism and by municipal regulators as corruption. Their plight reflects a known sociological paradox: allegiances are often most effective when they are weak.

Barrio Chino's entrenched informal sector has long represented a frontier in the regulatory quests of Cuban governments. The chapter's third section draws on three years of participant observation, conducted between 2000 and 2014, to explore the circles of cooperation underpinning contemporary informality in the district. Propelled by the popularity of its restaurants, Barrio Chino's prominence has generated legal and illegal opportunities for commercial expansion. Newly established state-operated convenience stores and countless improvised private kiosks simultaneously sell registered and unregistered products, from pirate DVDs and contraband clothing brought into Cuba by foreign accomplices to recycled rice cookers and mobile phones. Services are equally vulnerable to informal trade, as Barrio Chino's restaurants demonstrate. Efforts to effectively tax them—whether through national or local strategies—have failed, providing insight into the state's broader battle to enforce the rule of law. The section concludes with an analysis of the more benign informal relationships that emanate from the Cuban School of Wushu. Orchestrating exchanges between visiting Chinese officials, Barrio Chino's residents, and the state, the school's charismatic director is a key broker of consensus. The Cuban government has recognized that working with such individuals offers the best hope of containing informal activities and building vertical trust.

The fourth section looks at recent government attempts to redefine Barrio Chino's development agenda around tourism. On the instructions of Cuba's paramount executive body, the Council of State, in 2006 the Office of the Historian of the City assumed responsibility for Barrio Chino's administration. Drawing on its experience in the neighboring municipality of Old Havana, the Office has attempted to integrate Barrio Chino into a broader scheme of civic governance oriented toward economic growth, stricter transparency requirements, and a public sense that these goals are consistent with local history and culture. This agenda has provoked mixed reactions, ranging from support for the fashionable cafés and cobblestone streets brought by gentrification to resentment that an outside institution should presume to know what is best for the Chinese Cuban community. These polarized responses illustrate the complexity of defining an inclusive neighborhood development agenda, much less one that builds unity of purpose.

The fifth section argues that the dynamics of state-society relations in Barrio Chino have begun to be affected by China's rise. This is the first time since the neighborhood's establishment a century and a half ago that the Chinese Cuban community has been able to draw support from an external superpower. Thickening interactions with mainland Chinese visitors focus largely on informal small investments and supplies for local restaurants and emerging businesses. Unable to contain these expanding nonstate linkages, the Office of the Historian has attempted to diminish their appeal by providing official alternatives. Consensual and responsive governance has long been the Office's stated mission, but as China's reach extends across the Pacific, the Office must now demonstrate its sincerity. With their bargaining power augmented, community leaders have found the Office more responsive than ever before to bottom-up proposals, two of which are discussed in the section. The opportunities generated by this nascent vertical synergy are also making Barrio Chino's diverse actors more willing to work horizontally with each other. There is room for optimism, I conclude, that the historical legacies of distrust are fading.

FROM DECEPTION TO DECEPTION: THE ROOTS OF SELF-EXCLUSION

Cuban and Chinese portrayals of enduring brotherhood are common, especially among the nations' leaders, but historical records reveal that from its inception Chinese immigration to Cuba was neither patriotic nor glorious. Rather, it set in motion a vicious circle of personal sacrifice, racial hostility, objectification, and resistance whose legacy endures to the present day.

The 1843 Treaty of Nanking marked the end of the first Opium War, establishing the British as the dominant traffickers of Chinese labor at the same time that they were abolishing the transatlantic slave trade. Deterred by a British naval embargo, imports of enslaved Africans to Cuba dropped from 10,000 in 1844 to 1,000 in 1847, a 90 percent reduction in just three years that was compensated for by the arrival of Chinese coolies in 1847 (Yun and Laremont 2001, 102). The enterprise was profitable for the British merchants who monopolized this new legal source of labor from eastern China. On January 2, 1847, 300 Chinese indentured workers, or coolies (from the Chinese kuli—苦力—literally, bitter use of strength) boarded the Spanish frigate *Oquendo* in Amoy (now called Xiamen), bound for Cuba. Through contracts with the Manila and Tait Company in London, they had agreed to serve the Spanish Real Junta de Fomento y Colonización (Colonial and Development Office) as laborers for eight years. The 206 coolies who survived the transpacific voyage arrived in Havana's port of Regla on June 3 and were joined ten days later by 365 more coolies who had traveled on the British vessel *The Duke of Argyle*. By 1853 more than 5,000 Chinese had arrived in Cuba, and by 1873 there were an additional 132,453 (Padura Fuentes 1994), initiating a cross-cultural encounter that artist Pedro Eng Herrera has portrayed as a "paradigm between two cultures" (figure 3.1).

Chinese workers arrived in Cuba with the hope of fulfilling their contracts and returning home wealthy, but on four pesos per month, few returned home at all. Transcripts of an 1874 court case analyzed by Lisa Yun (2008) demonstrate that whether or not the coolie trade constituted slavery, the social conditions in which Chinese laborers and enslaved Africans lived were practically the same. The deception of the endeavor is still registered in Cuba through a popular phrase used to denote common cheating: "Lo engañaron como un chino Manila" (he was tricked like a Chinese person from Manila).[1]

The Chinese in Cuba were almost all male, and they mixed with females of similar economic standing, most of whom were African Cuban. This added to the already intricate cultural and biological blend—described by Fernando Ortiz as an "ajiaco" (stew; 1940; [1940] 1995)—already pres-

FIGURE 3.1 *Paradigma Entre las dos Culturas* (Paradigm between two cultures) by Pedro Jesús Eng Herrera, 1999. Courtesy of the artist.

ent in Cuba through European and African mixing.[2] Nevertheless, as Rogelio Coronel writes, "in truth, it is incorrect to imagine a profound process of transculturation between the Chinese and the Spanish, but rather [there are] some indications of a selective intercultural blend" (2008), for instance in Chinese Cuban cuisine. Indeed, accounts of the time, such as the following report from Manuel Villanueva in 1877, suggest that the Chinese community was shunned by Cubans of both European and African origin, and was marginalized to such an extent that it had to depend on criminal activities:

> Induced to abandon their native land through the stimulus of false promises which they begin to suspect they will never see realized within a few days after they embark, separated from their native land by a distance which their imagination exaggerates upon recollection of the immense amount of water crossed during the long voyage, exploited by the rapacity of the ship's crew, placed at tasks foreign to their training, subjected to the discipline of a plantation ruled by

the criterion and traditions of slavery, walking from deception to deception even to seeing in many cases a lack of religious fulfillment of their contracts, excluded from family life because of a lack of women of their own race, despised by the Whites, hated by the Negroes, separated from their master more than are the slaves in proportion as the time of expiration of their contracts approaches and for the same reason treated with less consideration, real pariahs in Cuban society, how can it be questioned that this condition produces crimes and vices? (quoted in Corbitt 1971, 81–82)

Nineteenth-century accounts of Chinese immigrants in Cuba reflected a fundamental paradox of Latin American modernism: a heterogeneous and inclusive national identity must also be narrow enough to permit unity. As Francisco Morán writes, Chinese immigrants—and Chinatowns in particular—did not fit into the nation-building agenda: "The Oriental subject is probably one of the most resistant to any attempt to delimit a sense of 'inside' vs. 'outside.' If Chinatowns can be read as marginal spaces in relation to the national center, then for the same reason they impede the homogenization to which all nationalist imaginaries aspire. . . . The Oriental subject was persistently considered a foreign body within the national body, and decadent in physical and moral constitution. This decadence represented a danger—and it questioned from within—the vigor of the Nation in particular, and Latin America in general" (2005, 385). Writing for an audience in Madrid, in 1864 the prominent Cuban historian José Antonio Saco expressed his conviction that Chinese immigrants were undermining Cuba's already tenuous demographic balance: "If the African race has in recent times threatened Cuba's hopeful future, the Chinese race, which has begun to be introduced, further complicates our situation since instead of the two irreconcilable races we had before, there now joins a third party that can amalgamate with neither, owing to complete differences in language and color, ideas and feelings, functions and customs, and religious opinions" ([1864] 2000, 196). Hostile appraisals and bleak prospects for domestic advancement disposed Chinese Cubans to join the collective national insurgency that culminated in the Ten Years' War (1869–78). The rebel leader Gonzalo de Quesada praised their patriotism with the legendary words: "There was not a single Chinese Cuban traitor; not a single Chinese Cuban deserter."[3]

Their vitality in battle deepened perceptions in Madrid that the Chinese coolies were ungovernable, and on the advice of the Cuban captain general, the Spanish government issued a decree in 1871 outlawing their passage to Cuba (Chou 2002, 50). The Chinese government—informed by its special envoy, Chin Lanpin, in 1874 that its subjects in the towns of Matanzas and Las Villas were being exploited—also banned further contracting of Chinese labor.

The U.S. consul in Matanzas at the time of the Ten Years' War, Captain James William Steele, described his perceptions of the cultural backwardness, yet unparalleled work ethic, of "the Chinaman," concluding that the Chinese "colonists" were inherently inward looking and resistant to integration:

> He is always neat, and his house is always dirty. It is among the contradictions of his character.... If you enter the back room of his store, you will find there enthroned in a red shrine the deity he still believes in, with every appurtenance of his peculiar worship. It is all wrong, and the height of unconverted and unregenerate paganism in a country devoted to the true church.... Whenever, in the time to come, the Chinaman shall have gained over a district of the New World to himself—and he will do it—he will make that district like Canton or Macao, in no way modified save by climate and resources.... There will be no discussions about the government, and all that the community will desire will be to be let alone, and if it should be so left alone, the colony will increase and multiply, and spread by a steady and contiguous growth.... And through all his residence there, the colonist will still think of the flowery kingdom [China], and still intend to go back, and never become a citizen of the country which surrounds his temporary home. (Steele 1885, 96–97 and 100)

Most nineteenth-century reports, like Steele's, portrayed Chinese culture in condescending terms that overlooked patriotism and emphasized instead the "contradiction" of congenial appearances and hidden vices, including a penchant for prostitution and opium. For the Cuban "social hygienist" Benjamín de Céspedes the two misdeeds were intimately linked, finding refuge in the murky corners of Barrio Chino among "a race that is dead to human civilization" (Céspedes 1888, 201–2).

Supplied or withheld by their contractors—often through Chinese middlemen and subcontractors—opium devastated the economic and physical well-being of Chinese laborers (Hu-DeHart 2005a). As early as the 1860s well-organized distribution networks were trafficking the drug between Cuban cities and plantation zones, and by 1936 half of the 2,225 drug addicts ever committed to the Mariel lazaretto (isolation hospital) were Chinese Cubans (Rovner 2004). María Teresa Montes de Oca Choy, director of the University of Havana's Center for the Study of Chinese Immigration to Cuba, and Roberto Vargas Lee describe how the abject predicament of Chinese immigrants drove them not only to opium, but also to social withdrawal: "This [oppression] led to the self-exclusion of the Chinese community and, together with the difficulty of verbal communication, led the coolies to close themselves off for a period of many years, looking almost exclusively within. They became hostile and resistant to any process that implied a loss of culture and the humiliating acceptance of the work regime they were subjected to" (2008, 172–73).

By the end of the nineteenth century the Chinese community had become diverse, incorporating at least 5,000 "Californian" Chinese, described by Juan Pérez de la Riva as "a hybrid mix of American and Oriental, gentlemen in jackets and ties" (2000, 116). When it occupied Cuba in 1899, the U.S. military reported that the Chinese population amounted to just 14,614, but this figure increased between 1919 and 1924 after the governments of China and Cuba (following pressure from sugar producers) lifted bans on labor contracts. Lok Siu (2008, 169) notes the difficulty of accurately determining the number of Chinese arrivals in the early twentieth century, citing a statistical discrepancy in the records of the Cuban Department of Housing (showing 373 arrivals between 1903 and 1916 and 11,311 between 1917 and 1924) and those of the Chinese consulate in Havana (showing 6,258 arrivals between 1903 and 1916, and 17,473 between 1917 and 1924). As Siu suggests, the discrepancy probably results from widespread illegal immigration at the time (c.f. Herrera Jerez and Castillo Santana 2003). Chinese immigrants who arrived in Cuba from the United States were already familiar with discrimination and had developed collective strategies for overcoming adversity: "Barred from factory employment by nativist prejudice and prevented from bringing wives and other family members by the Chinese Exclusion Act, these hapless seekers of the 'Mountain of Gold' had no recourse but to band together in tightly knit communities that were the precursors of today's Chinatowns. . . . Solidarity born out of common adversity is reflected in the 'clannishness' and 'secretiveness' that outsiders were later to attribute to these communities" (Portes and Sensenbrenner 1993, 1328).

Wealthier than the coolies, the "Californian" Chinese consolidated the local economy of Barrio Chino, which since 1858 had grown up around the family restaurant of Chang Li and the fruit market of Laig Siu-Yi. "The creation of Havana's Barrio Chino," reads a Cuban government newsletter, "arose precisely from the need of these migrant people to protect themselves in a hostile, exclusionary, and marginalizing environment" (*Opus Habana* 2013). In the early to mid-twentieth century, interdependent businesses and convenience stores trading in fruits and vegetables, laundry services, artisanry, and restaurants underpinned Barrio Chino's expansion to forty-four city blocks, making it the largest and most important Chinatown in Latin America and the rival of those in San Francisco and New York. Forbidden by law to live within the city center (today's Old Havana), the Chinese community developed Barrio Chino as "an independent sector that sought to be the Cuban extension of the province of Canton" (Fornieles Sánchez 1993, 26).

Local businesses were supported by the Chinese ethnic associations, which were organized according to members' family names (Sociedad Lung Kong Cun Sol, Sociedad Chang Weng Chung Tong, Sociedad Chi Tack Tong, Sociedad Long Sai Li, Sociedad On Teng Tong, Sociedad Sue Yuen Tong, Sociedad Wong Kong Ja Tong, and Sociedad Yee Fung Toy Tong), members' region of origin (Sociedad Chung Shan and Sociedad Kow Kong), and political affiliation (Alianza Socialista China de Cuba and Sociedad Min Chih Tang). Their coordinating body, the Casino Chung Wah, was founded in 1883 and registered as a legal entity in 1893 under the honorary presidency of the Chinese consul general in Cuba, Tam Kin Cho. The associations provided crucial support to local businesses, helping them overcome the legal segregation of the Chinese community by linking suppliers to consumers through networks of mutual aid and ethnic solidarity. They also fostered the development of Chinese restaurants as sources of employment and acculturation for new arrivals, and as social epicenters where community affairs were discussed and deals negotiated. Together, the associations and restaurants epitomized the development of the social economy, relying on informal lines of trade with agricultural producers on the outskirts of Havana for ingredients and supplies. Duvon Corbitt, who worked as a lecturer in Havana in the early 1940s, described the commercial success of Chinese agricultural initiatives: "Today the growing and distribution of green vegetables is largely in Chinese hands; they compete successfully with the Spanish immigrants in the operation of groceries and general stores. . . . So widely distributed is their business that there is scarcely a town or important village in Cuba without some enterprise owned by Orientals. The Chinese have been successful as truck-farmers, and in a few instances have taken to large-scale agriculture" (1944, 131).

Despite their success in agriculture, laundry services, and other niche sectors, wealth eluded most Chinese Cubans, and beyond the economically elite "Californians," it was only those involved in organized gaming and opium trafficking who prospered. Nevertheless, their perceived affluence provoked protests against Chinese businesses in the early 1930s, leading the government of Ramón Grau San Martín (1933–34, 1944–48) to implement laws (as Mexico had done in 1930 and as Panama would do in 1935) requiring them to diversify their workforces to include at least 50 percent (later 80 percent) non-Chinese Cubans. Jealousy and resentment toward the Chinese community is evident in the music of the time, featuring imitated Chinese accents and lyrics about Chinese immigrants and their descendants working multiple jobs, buying up property both locally and in the United States (Pérez Brito 1953), and attracting Cuban women with their wealth (J. López 1942). Corbitt observed that behind the image of harmonious ethnic integration, discrimination was widespread: "The good terms on which almost all Chinese live with their Cuban neighbors, and the relatively numerous marriages between the races, would seem to belie the fact that prejudice exists; nevertheless, close contact with the situation will reveal that the Cubans generally look on the Chinese as social, and even intellectual inferiors (1944, 131)."

By the 1930s Barrio Chino was attracting tourists from the United States, who found abundant facilities and accommodation (by 1915 Cuba boasted seventy-two hotels, a third of them in Havana), and whose desire to mix with the purportedly ungovernable Chinese community was driven in part by Prohibition at home (D. Hall 1992, 109). As Schwartz writes, "guidebooks lured tourists to Havana's Chinese quarter with accounts of murky opium dens and pungent herbs sold in Oriental markets. Newspapers heightened a sense of mystery tinged with danger in reports of tong wars, assassinations, and acts of terrorism perpetrated by political rivals among naturalized Cuban Chinese and immigrant Chinese nationalists. In the popular imagination, the Chinatown 'labyrinth' became an 'exotic, impenetrable, obscure' neighborhood. What an extraordinary accumulation of touristic possibilities! Cuba could embellish its identity and character and invent a distinctive personality to enthrall the most jaded foreigner" (1997, 76). Chinese Cubans and Barrio Chino had again been portrayed for foreign eyes as a community disarticulated from its surroundings and impervious to the law.

Postwar decadence generated mutually reinforcing descriptions, expectations, and experiences as travel writers emphasized those aspects of the district most likely to attract and resonate with audiences back home. A guidebook by Walter Roberts tempted its readers with the tantalizing opportunity to observe Chinese Cubans hopelessly addicted to gambling and, if lucky, to join in: "The Chinese of Cuba cannot be induced to forego [sic] their special games of chance, which they are willing to share under certain conditions with thrill-seeking foreigners" (1953, 224). And thrills there were. Visiting Barrio Chino in the 1950s, the novelist Graham Greene found that the Teatro Shanghai lived up to its notorious reputation: "For one dollar and twenty-five cents one could see a nude cabaret of extreme obscenity with the bluest of blue films in the intervals" (1981, 184).

By the mid-1950s Cuba outpaced Jamaica and other regional competitors as a destination for recreational visitors, 85 percent of whom were from the United States (Villalba Garrido 1993). The mounting wave of tourists found Barrio Chino particularly appealing. As James Pringle notes, it was "the most notorious district in the most notorious city in the Caribbean—a playground for sun and sin-seeking tourists, especially Americans who arrived on $10 flights from Key West, Florida, to drink, gamble and indulge in the pleasures of the flesh" (2003, 53). The Canadian scholar Hal Klepak, who went to school in Havana in the 1950s, reports both that his parents forbade him to visit Barrio Chino for precisely these reasons and that he found their concerns to be justified (personal communication, February 28, 2011). The tendency of outsiders to seek, find, and advertise Barrio Chino's darker corners did not escape Enrique Labrador Ruiz, a prominent Cuban writer of the time who objected to the district's vilification: "It is said that opium is smoked in Chinatown and that there is heavy gambling. Whether or not this is true, such disorders are not visible to the world. The people are sober and honest" (1952, 43).

While there was no shortage of foreign fascination with Barrio Chino's sordid temptations, little external attention was paid to its vibrant artistic qualities. As the Cuban ethnologist María Teresa Linares Savio (2000) reminds us, from the 1870s until the 1930s actors, puppeteers, and singers performed regularly in local theaters such as the Gran China and the Teatro Pacífico. The Afro-Chinese Cuban writer Antonio Chuffat Latour (1927) observed that enthusiasm for the arts made Barrio Chino a regular port of call for visiting Chinese opera companies from Guangdong, Hong Kong, and the United States. Linares Savio notes that these artistic delicacies, including a local Chinese opera troupe, were a pillar of cultural memory for Chinese immigrants and their descendants in Cuba.

By the mid-1950s Barrio Chino's theaters had adapted to the lucrative new market generated by the arrival in Cuba each year of some 380,000 tourists, who provided the second largest foreign currency earnings after sugar (Padilla and McElroy 2007, 651; Sharpley and Knight 2009, 242). Labrador Ruiz described the local transformations brought on by the tourism boom in a 1952 article: "The tourists prefer the new style to the way it used to be. They got very bored, the present theater owners say, with those unendingly tedious outpourings. A horse represented by a tassel of corn, and no women on the stage" (1952, 42). Indeed, Nancy Wonders and Raymond Michalowski point out that most tourists had fixed their gaze on more carnal entertainment: "In the eyes of many potential tourists in the 1950s, the estimated 270 brothels and as many as 100,000 prostitutes who operated there, defined Havana" (2001, 560).

Barrio Chino's moral reputation was at an all-time low, but in truth, as the historian Kathleen López (2013) has documented, Chinese immigrants in Cuba had endured a lack of respect, trust, and honesty since the arrival of the first indentured laborers from Amoy in 1847. From the outset, the contractual conditions underpinning the coolie trade were misleading and did not fully disclose the conditions awaiting the coolies on Cuba's sugar plantations. For at least the rest of the nineteenth century, condescending reports and communiqués described the closeted moral and social vices of Chinese workers, from "unregenerate" pagan religious beliefs to a hopeless addiction to opium. Historians have since argued that the oppression suffered by Chinese immigrants provoked both self-destructive forms of escape (the use of opium and suicide among them) and self-protective forms of collective withdrawal. Chinese ethnic associations institutionalized the latter through a network of informal supply and demand that eventually enabled members to become successful in the formal agricultural and commercial retail sectors. All the while, a growing wave of foreign tourists sought out, and provided incentives for the expansion of, Barrio Chino's reclusive and unregulated underworld. Such were the pressures and opportunities facing the Chinese community at the dawn of the Cuban Revolution.

THE LOCAL IMPACT OF REVOLUTION

Notorious as a shady retreat for unscrupulous foreigners, Barrio Chino epitomized the revolution's grievances against the regime of Fulgencio Batista, particularly its collusion with U.S. gangsters, pimps, and drug dealers (Simoni 2009, 100–106). When Fidel Castro marched into Havana in 1959, the district continued to function as a hub of unregistered commerce, economically and socially disarticulated from its surroundings. On February 17, 1960, a special unit of the National Revolutionary Militia was created and charged with bringing order to Barrio Chino. Named the José Wong Brigade in honor of a young Chinese Cuban communist assassinated in 1930 after founding the illegal newsletter *Grito Obrero Campesino*, the unit launched a campaign against gambling, prostitution, and drug trafficking. Comprised entirely of Chinese Cubans and operating in Cantonese, the brigade was led by Pedro Jesús Eng Herrera (also known as Tai Chao), who has since become a prominent painter of Chinese Cuban cultural history (see figure 3.1). According to him, "an important achievement of the José Wong Brigade was to bring together people of different Chinese ethnic backgrounds, from Hakkas to Californians. These folks were members of different associations and hadn't gotten along with each other until the Brigade forced them to. When the Brigade started working in Barrio Chino, we found that prostitution was rife, though more on the outskirts of the neighborhood than in its center. The exception was the Teatro Shanghai, which was famous in the 1950s for showing pornography and selling adult magazines right in the heart of Barrio Chino" (interview, May 17, 2013).

On Zanja Street, opposite the Teatro Shanghai, the Brigade took control of the Alianza Nueva Democracia de China en Cuba (New China Democratic Alliance in Cuba) and renamed it the Chinese Socialist Alliance of Cuba. It also took over the Casino Chung Wah, which until then had maintained its allegiance to the Taiwan-based Chinese Nationalist Party (Kuomintang, or KMT), with a portrait of Chiang Kai-Shek hanging in its main hall. Alfonso Bu of the local Chinese opera company was asked to sew the flag of the People's Republic of China (PRC) from traditional stage costumes, which the Brigade's second-in-command, Rufino Alay Chang, raised on the Casino's roof. This event occurred on the eleventh anniversary of the founding of the PRC, shortly after Cuba and China established diplomatic relations, but before Fidel Castro declared that his government would adopt a socialist course. Eng Herrera notes that "one of our main objectives was to rid the neighborhood of the KMT, because until then all of the associations were obliged to register with the KMT through the Casino Chung Wah. Not surprisingly, many in Barrio Chino branded me as a communist, so I guess you could say I was a step ahead of Fidel!" (interview, May 17, 2013). In 1961 the Brigade was sent to the Isla de Pinos (now called the Isla de la Juventud) to defend it from a potential U.S. invasion. Eng Herrera reportedly told his troops: "We will fight to the death to impede the conversion of the Isla de Pinos into another Taiwan!" (quoted in A. González 2005).

Despite their apparent ideological affinities, China's relations with Cuba cooled when Fidel allied his government with the Soviet Union in the early 1960s (see chapter 1). At this time the Chinese community in Cuba and its ethnic associations experienced various forms of discrimination, intensified by the nationalization of Chinese small businesses, which began in the early 1960s and culminated in the Great Revolutionary Offensive of 1968. Only those restaurants linked to the Chinese associations remained in community hands. According to Montes de Oca Choy, the combination of geopolitical tension and local frustration sent Barrio Chino on a downward socioeconomic spiral:

I started studying the history of the Chinese presence in Cuba at a difficult time. The Chinese community, and anything to do with it, was discriminated against because of the political problems with China. When Chinese businesses were nationalized in the early 1960s and in the Great Revolutionary Offensive, some felt they had been unfairly targeted and neglected, and so they left Cuba. Others said this would allow the Chinese community to participate more fully in the revolution, and up to a point it did. . . . Many were able to keep their restaurants, but they kept to themselves and quietly bought whatever they needed from their *socios* [informal business partners] in the countryside instead of official suppliers. Effectively, Barrio Chino was forced underground. (interview, February 10, 2006)

The revolution had successfully stemmed the flow of foreign thrill seekers to Barrio Chino, but by nationalizing the district's economic base it also disrupted a century of ethnic entrepreneurship. Facing diminished commercial opportunities as their community had thirty years earlier under Grau San Martín, a large portion of Chinese Cubans left the island, while those who remained turned once more to the informal support networks of the ethnic associations.[4]

The precarious standing of the Chinese Cuban community was compounded by the 1975 war in Angola, in which Cuba and China backed opposing factions, and by China's invasion of Vietnam in 1979. Public activities related to Chinese Cuban heritage, from academic research to artistic performances, practically disappeared from view. Some people in Barrio Chino report feeling disillusioned when Fidel Castro declared in 1975 that Cuba should henceforth be recognized as an Afro-Latin nation, since their own contributions to nationhood had never been openly acknowledged. The anthropologist Jesús Guanche notes the ongoing relevance of this problem: "Our national assembly has always had trouble coming to terms with Cuba's demographic diversity, since it has always prioritized the nation over race" (interview, May 15, 2013).

As Sino-Cuban relations improved in the 1980s, developments in Barrio Chino kept pace. In 1982 the Chinese Socialist Alliance of Cuba worked through the Casino Chung Wah and the Ministry of Culture to organize a public display of traditional Chinese opera costumes at the Provincial Center of Plastic Arts and Design in Havana. Using the 1983 centennial of the Casino as a platform, the associations began rehearsing and reviving the dragon dance, and in 1986 they performed it openly for the first time since 1960 (Hun Calzadilla 2010; Alay Jó and Hun Calzadilla 2015). They also oversaw the production of two short films on Chinese traditional festivals, both of which were shown on national television. To promote understanding of contemporary China, the Chinese Socialist Alliance began hosting regular evenings of Chinese cinema. According to the Chinese Cuban scholar Yrmina Eng Menéndez, these state-endorsed activities were designed to show both the Cuban population and the growing number of Chinese visitors that Barrio Chino had a place in the Cuban Revolution (interview, January 17, 2006).

Chinese President Jiang Zemin's 1993 visit to Cuba and Fidel Castro's reciprocal visit to China in 1995 heralded an era of post-Soviet bilateral cooperation. In 1994 a small group of descendants of Chinese immigrants seized the opportunity created by China's rising public profile by creating a neighborhood advocacy association, the Grupo Promotor de Barrio Chino. Under the leadership of Eng Menéndez, the Grupo lobbied the municipal government of Central Havana for authorization to oversee the creation of a small private sector to supply local Chinese restaurants: "It was something of a magic moment that allowed us to take advantage of the links we'd built to the municipal government and the [Communist] Party. Our main achievement was that through periods of economic opening and closure, we managed to maintain the independent character of the restaurants. For their part they [the restaurants] promised to use the markets and follow the rules" (interview, January 17, 2006).

Another of the Grupo's achievements was to secure permission for the small-scale retail of consumer goods imported from China. Silk sheets, shoes, clothing, lip balm, and specialty cooking items began to appear in neighborhood kiosks and marketplaces. Hosting one of the first legal farmers' markets of the Special Period, Barrio Chino drew the attention of international media eager to report on the way Cuba might implement market reforms to overcome the deepening economic crisis of the time (Strubbe and Wald 1995; *Xinhua* 1994). The 1999 construction of a traditional Chinese archway (*pailou*, 牌楼) at Barrio Chino's entrance symbolized China's deepening engagement with Cuba (figure 3.2). Donated by the Chinese government, designed by a team of Chinese engineers, and crafted with Cuban hands, the pailou represented a convergence of global and local ambitions to revitalize Barrio Chino.

A key political goal framing Barrio Chino's revival was to draw its residents out of the informal sector into a program of regulated market

FIGURE 3.2 The symbolic entrance of Havana's Barrio Chino. Photo by the author.

exchange. Mediating between the municipal government of Central Havana and the Casino Chung Wah, the Grupo was asked to ensure that the reemergence of local commerce—especially its connections with mainland China—remain aboveboard. Unofficial trade had for decades linked the associations and their restaurants with suppliers of meat and vegetables on the outskirts of Havana and had continued to provide an alternative to understocked state outlets (Cheng 2007a, 40; Corbitt 1944).

The Grupo's senior administrators—Yrmina Eng Menéndez, Carlos Alay Jó, and Julio Hun Calzadilla (figure 3.3)—were descendants of Chinese immigrants with a high regard for the grassroots priorities of their community and the official opportunities afforded them by the state. They worked to position the Grupo as an intermediary between the community and the state, but they found that advancing local interests within the broader structures of state authority became increasingly difficult. While the Grupo's affiliation with the Casino Chung Wah afforded it a unique ability to convey government objectives to the Chinese associations and vice versa, its proximity to community concerns generated an increasingly severe conflict of interests. The leadership team refused to

FIGURE 3.3 The founding members of the Grupo with the author, 2011. Left to right: Yrmina Eng Menéndez, Julio Hun Calzadilla, the author, and Carlos Alay Jó.

demand greater financial transparency from informal welfare programs, food and medicine distribution schemes, and elder care initiatives such as those of the Lung Kong Cun Sol and Min Chih Tang associations and their restaurants. According to Carlos Yion Lee, then president of the Min Chih Tang, social welfare had been the associations' guiding principle since their inception, and protecting this principle was the Grupo's moral responsibility (interview, February 23, 2011).

By the late 1990s the Grupo's ambition to balance diverging community and state interests had become untenable, reflecting a sociological phenomenon observed by Alejandro Portes: when community affiliation demands loyalty, external allegiances have little chance of survival (1998, 15–18). Had it kept the demands of the Chinese community at arm's length, the Grupo could have maintained a functional relationship with the state. However, leveraging "the strength of weak ties" (Granovetter 1973) was a remote possibility for the Grupo as its community loyalties were too strong. Consequently, despite the government's calls for tighter regulation of local trade, the accounting procedures of Barrio Chino's associations, restaurants, and other economic actors remained obscure.

For four years Eng Menéndez and her team brokered deals between the Cuban state, Barrio Chino retailers, and their suppliers in China, but the rising tide of foreign trade raised the stakes of allegiance and accountability. To monitor the Grupo's activities more vigilantly, in 1998 the municipal government forced it to give up its independent status and become a state institution. Formalization brought executive power as the Grupo became officially responsible for Barrio Chino's general economic development. It also brought a raft of internal changes, the most drastic of which was the replacement of the Grupo's founding members with external career administrators. By 2004 the Grupo was led by an executive council with departments of investment and accounting, together employing some 400 people. One of its leaders was quoted by a German development agency as describing the Grupo as "a state within a state, like the Vatican" (quoted in Par Darmstadt 2004, 133).

The transformation of any informal association into an official institution inevitably involves compromise. As grassroots loyalties and allegiances are formalized, weakened local autonomy should, in theory, be compensated for by expanded economic and legal capacities for community protection and advocacy. Johannes Fedderke, Raphael de Kadt, and John Luiz describe this process as the "rationalization of social capital" through "the gradual replacement of informal associations and networks by formal administrative structures, and the impersonal market mechanism no longer tied to individual identities. . . . In effect trust is rendered abstract rather than concrete" (1999, 719–20). Accordingly, the Grupo's institutionalization should have given Barrio Chino's community leaders the ears of senior politicians committed to achieving broadly beneficial development outcomes.

A convergence of structural and personal weaknesses threw Barrio Chino's development off course. Central Havana's municipal government, now the Grupo's line manager, was already overburdened with responsibilities and lacked sufficient resources to develop regulations tailored to the district's unique socioeconomic needs. Restaurants connected to the associations were subjected to general civil codes designed for Cuban nongovernmental organizations (NGOs), and as such were required to deposit their profits in designated bank accounts and could not then withdraw funds without written permission from the Ministry of Justice. As the number of their foreign and national customers grew, this monolithic management framework generated easy opportunities for illicit personal gain in both the restaurants and the Grupo. The "rationalization of social capital" ultimately failed because it subordinated interpersonal trust and community identity to the authority of anonymous bureaucrats who had no personal stake in local development. Irregularities became so pronounced that after eight years as a state institution, the Grupo was disbanded.

In 2006 the Council of State appointed the Office of the Historian of the City to replace the Grupo and oversee a new approach to Barrio Chino's economic and civic governance. The Office was charged with ensuring the transparency of bookkeeping and rescuing—as the Council of State put it—cultural traditions to attract foreign tourists and finance local development projects. I discuss the Office's successes and failures in this endeavor below, but first it will be useful to examine Barrio Chino's entrenched informal sector, which constitutes the most serious challenge facing any external institution aiming to build trust in the district.

INFORMAL CONNECTIONS IN BARRIO CHINO

Throughout Cuba's colonial, republican, and revolutionary years, Barrio Chino's informal sector survived the attempts of successive governments to regulate it. For over a century the tight-knit mutual aid and trade networks of the Chinese associations guarded the interests of their members from public hostility and discriminatory legislation. In the early twenty-first century, a legacy of what Alejandro Portes and Julia Sensenbrenner call "solidarity born out of common adversity" (1993, 1328) continues to underpin Barrio Chino's capacity to resist the law.

The spate of formal agreements between Cuba and China in the early 2000s was accompanied by a flow of informal trade in both directions. Cigars, for instance, were becoming popular among China's emerging wealthy class and resident foreign executives, who were paying upward of 250 renminbi ($40) for a Don Diego from the Dominican Republic, a Flor from Honduras, or a Cohiba from Cuba. At this price cigars are beyond the reach of most Chinese people, but in a country of 350 million cigarette smokers (one-third of the world's total), where conspicuous consumption has become increasingly pervasive, demand for cigars has grown. The British tobacco giant Altadis has developed a strategy for meeting Chinese demand: a less expensive line of synthetic cigars, flavored with vanilla and cognac. Unconvinced, aspiring aficionados opt instead to buy genuine Cuban *puros* on the streets of Beijing's cosmopolitan San Li Tun district or under the table in trendy cigar bars for the standard price of 100 renminbi ($17). Owing to a combination of high import duties and a shortage of official retail licenses, contraband is alleged in one Chinese report to represent approximately 90 percent of cigar sales in Beijing, Shanghai, Shenzhen, Guangzhou, and Zhuhai (Hua 2005, 37).

The early 2000s also saw an expanding flow of Chinese goods into Cuba. A combination of low commercial returns and insufficient wages in Barrio Chino's registered kiosks and marketplaces quickly drove retail of Chinese consumer goods—many of which were imported by the Grupo—underground. By 2006 it was possible to obtain not just lip balm, soy sauce, and shoes on the so-called *mercado chino* (Barrio Chino's black market), but also DVD players, rice cookers, pressure cookers, and other Chinese appliances.

The appearance of Chinese electronic goods on the mercado chino reflected the progression of Sino-Cuban economic relations. Hu Jintao's 2004 visit to Havana secured the initial supply of these items for approved state stores and authorized individuals, but long-standing networks of *socios* and middlemen ensured spillover into the informal sector (see chapter 1). "Temporarily" assuming presidential powers in 2006, Raúl Castro declared an assault on corruption, and by the time Hu visited again in 2008 the supply chain was secure enough to permit direct sale of electronics, supplied mainly by China, to the Cuban public. As discussed below, in 2006 the Council of State charged the Office of the Historian with taming Barrio Chino's informal sector, a development that the Chinese Cuban writer Manuel Chiong Lee perceived as an attempt to stem a problem that had been growing since the 1960s:

> My relatives owned three restaurants and five grocery stores. This was before 1959, so the businesses were privately owned and the accounting was meticulous. In the early revolution many of the Chinese businesses were nationalized and the neighborhood fell into stasis. The only way for people to make a profit since then has been to work *bajo el tapete* [literally, below the cover] with the societies [Chinese associations] and producers. . . . The corruption has always had its limits. It's petty

fiddling, and nobody has a yacht or anything like that. But it's been growing. It didn't used to be as rampant. So the government has now decided that it is time to put an end to this. The Office of the Historian is the tool for achieving it. (interview, February 24, 2006)

Fortunate enough to work in Barrio Chino during this administrative transition, I found by late 2005 that many of the relatives, friends, and acquaintances visiting my host family's apartment were conducting more than social calls. Unassuming debates about dinner recipes and the narrative twists of blockbuster Hollywood movies segued into calculated negotiations about price markdowns, bartering arrangements, and discreet delivery. I recorded the business practices of my neighbor, Felipe, in my research diary:

BELOW THE BAR IN BARRIO CHINO

Since a local bar frequented by tourists charges $4 for a bottle of beer, and roughly the same for a rum *mojito*, Felipe has developed a business venture with its staff. Shortly after the delivery truck makes its weekly round, one of the waiters calls and tells him the serial numbers on the containers of beer and rum. Felipe then drops by some of the liquor stores supplied by the same truck, buying twenty bottles of beer (at $1 each) and five bottles of rum (at $4 dollars each), making sure they have the same serial numbers as his accomplice's. Late at night he pays a surreptitious visit to the bar and sells the beer to his associate at $2 per bottle and rum at $10. The waiters serve their foreign clientele as usual, but frequent lapses of memory prevent them from recording sales in the account book. If the manager becomes suspicious, her only recourse is to verify the serial numbers to make sure the products came from the official supply truck, which they did.

Felipe said his days of conducting business bajo el tapete are drawing to a close, as he no longer has energy or time for such things. I asked him about the two bottles of rum he was trying to push on a Spanish tourist earlier this week, the fee he charged me for arranging interviews in Barrio Chino, and his informal bicycle rental business. I couldn't argue with his answer: "That Spanish tourist has been coming here for years, and I know him like a friend. I didn't charge him much because it was more of a gift than anything, just like I'm not charging you much for the interviews because you're a friend, and notice also that I only rent my bicycles to friends."

—Havana, October 25, 2005

Felipe's expansive circle of "friends" provided a ready network of informal commercial partners. Although I never discerned the full extent of its radius, I learned over time that his circle overlapped with other webs of unregistered "friendship" and trust. I visited Felipe every year between 2005 and 2015, and I observed the increasing sophistication of his operations. By 2013 he seemed to have even more time and energy than when I first met him, and he described himself as a "product placement specialist." He was working with a young Chinese Cuban entrepreneur, Daisy, who told me about one of their income-generating schemes, or *mecánicas*: "My brother works in a *taller* [workshop or office] that handles Chinese rice cookers and kitchen appliances. They get sent to him for repair when they don't work properly or get damaged. . . . He has an arrangement with his supervisor to keep the ones that can't be repaired quickly, and then to repair them privately and resell them. I have good relationships with some of the shops here [in Barrio Chino] so I help him. They put my products on the shelf and keep a commission" (interview, May 16, 2013).

Opportunities to work under the table are growing in step with the flow of foreign and national visitors to Barrio Chino's restaurants. Restaurants are the district's primary source of income and employment: the ten I surveyed between 2011 and 2014 earned between $2,000 and $5,000 net income per day. Restaurants in the famed Cuchillo Lane are the legacy of the Grupo, which in the mid-1990s acquired authorization for descendants of Chinese immigrants to operate them with fewer restrictions than those imposed on other Cuban family restaurants (*paladares*). For instance, the independent owners of restaurants in Cuchillo Lane have always been permitted to seat an unlimited number of customers and to purchase equipment and ingredients from dedicated wholesale warehouses. However, as discussed below, the Office of the Historian taxes them heavily and maintains meticulous oversight over their activities. In contrast, restaurants owned by the Chinese associations are classified for tax as NGOs and are afforded corresponding rights to internal financial management. However, they are required to comply with the central policy guidelines of the Ministry of Justice, under which they must deposit profits in a designated bank account, as mentioned above.

The different codes governing Barrio Chino's two varieties of restaurants have produced contrasting results, with important implications for the informal sector. Those subjected to the decentralized regulations, taxes, and bookkeeping requirements of the Office of the Historian have a better record of forthright and transparent accounting, but they are considerably less profitable, and consequently cannot offer steady employment. Paradoxically, those subjected to the elaborate top-down codes of the Ministry of Justice are flourishing because inadequate enforcement of central directives has enabled their owners to undertake private and undisclosed investments in staff, equipment, and maintenance. The disparity highlights how excessive oversight and unrealistic tax margins can stifle economic viability, while at the other extreme, the absence of locally sensitive oversight can give rise to fraud and tax evasion.

The Cuban informal sector—replete with exploits like those of Felipe, Daisy, and the Chinese restaurants—is primarily a domestic concern, but Barrio Chino's circles of illicit trade have begun to extend overseas. The number of visiting Chinese officials and businesspeople is growing, and many of them have formed cooperative relationships with their Cuban counterparts and community leaders. Just as foreign investors seeking opportunities and contracts in mainland China have historically relied on informal connections with Communist Party officials (often brokered through intermediaries in Hong Kong and Taiwan), the evidence emerging from Cuba, Mexico, and other Latin American countries suggests that Chinese commercial initiatives in the region are also preceded by the pursuit of trust and goodwill from influential public- and private-sector authorities and prominent figures in overseas Chinese communities.

Unofficial pathways to trade and investment extend from China into both Cuba and Mexico, but the Cuban urban planning specialist Rosa Oliveras cites Mexico City's rampant black market as the pitfall that Havana must avoid at all cost (interview, February 24, 2011). Mexico's comparatively deregulated economic environment, she says, is ill equipped to contain the unrelenting flow of Chinese contraband into informal street markets like Tepito. Furthermore, three decades of state retrenchment in Mexico have left local governments with insufficient resources to engage citizens in strategies for breaking out of the informal sector. Among the consequences is a growing rift between lawful conduct and local practice, which Mexican authorities have tried—unsuccessfully—to close with so-called iron fist (*mano dura*) approaches to policing (discussed in chapter 4). In contrast, the Havana government's Grupo para el Desarrollo Integral de la Capital (Group for the Integrated Development for the Capital) argues that assertive regulatory intervention is the best way to "bridge the widening gap between state structures and community life" (2001, 1).

Cuba's political and business environment is clearly more restrictive than Mexico's, and in this regard it is less susceptible to large-scale organized crime. However, the experimental and sometimes haphazard introduction of market reforms has opened loopholes for unregistered foreign finance and supply. A Barrio Chino administrator estimated that between 2006 and 2011, twenty neighborhood homes were converted into small businesses or restaurants with Chinese financing. These ventures resulted either from Chinese family ties to the property holder or undisclosed partnerships with local residents. This practice not only skirts foreign investment laws and property rental levies, but it also saves the business 96 percent on electricity, water, and gas, since utilities are charged to citizens in Cuban pesos (*moneda nacional*) rather than "convertible" pesos (*convertibles*) (interview, February 27, 2011).

For Chinese diplomats and entrepreneurs interested in exploring opportunities in Cuba, Barrio Chino is an inevitable port of call. There they usually seek out a man with unparalleled public and private influence: the renowned Chinese Cuban master of wushu martial arts, Roberto Vargas Lee (see figure 3.4). After his return from a year of study in Shanghai, Vargas Lee worked with the Grupo to establish the Cuban School of Wushu in 1995. With over 1,700 students in the city of Havana ranging from four to ninety years of age and a weekly martial arts television show, Vargas Lee has come to command broad popular respect. The school, he says, teaches more than martial arts:

> We are the only country in the world in which an overseas Chinese community fought in a national war of independence. Chinese blood has been spilled in Cuba because our patriotic Chinese brothers saw the need to defend Cuba's independence. . . . The School of Wushu is a symbol of friendship and a bridge between Cuba and China, and the work we do is closely united with the programs of the Chinese embassy. Chinese visitors, diplomats, and students consider the school to be a bedrock of mutual cooperation. . . . China is not seeking to dominate Latin America but rather to establish stable commerce and

FIGURE 3.4 Balancing the forces: Roberto Vargas Lee. Photo by the author.

gain respect from the ground up. Its support for our transportation, education, and medicine sectors is a symbol of Chinese goodwill that we teach our students about, and I hope it becomes known throughout the region. (interview, December 20, 2008)

Among the school's daily functions is popular education about Cuba's deepening relationship with China. While official media inform the masses about Chinese history, culture, and political solidarity with the Castro government, public knowledge about bilateral economic initiatives and actual development projects is limited. Hungry for information on Sino-Cuban affairs, the school's students and their families provide an enthusiastic audience for visiting Chinese officials, who share their thoughts on world development, commercial relations with Cuba, and the growing sophistication of Chinese products. As a beginning student of tai chi and the editor of a book for which Vargas Lee was coauthoring a chapter (Montes de Oca Choy and Vargas Lee 2008), I was permitted to enroll in the school's daily training sessions in 2005 and 2006. Below is an excerpt from my research diary:

FIGHTING FOR THE REVOLUTION

It is peaceful when I arrive at 7:20 AM. There are around a hundred students between fifteen and eighty years old chatting quietly, their shiny tai chi suits standing out in the dim light. Before starting class we stand in rows in the school's courtyard as the Cuban flag is raised. Next to the flag is a bust of José Martí (figure 3.5) with a phrase inscribed on the wall above it. We all shout the phrase together while striking our left palm with our right fist: "Wushu: salud y vida; una arma de la revolucion!" (Wushu: health and life; an arm of the revolution!). . . .

Around 9:00 AM Roberto Vargas Lee arrives with three Chinese officials and his elite students, who are carrying a Chinese flag, swords, curved axes, and other impressive looking weapons. The instructors tell us to form a circle around Master Lee in the center of the courtyard, where he addresses us in a clear and decisive tone. He will soon be leaving for Hanoi in Vietnam and Hainan in China with the school's best students, he says, to represent Cuban wushu: "China has always been a brother to us, and now it is also a friend. We are going to show the world that China lives in Cuba."

He describes China's advances in clean energy and the positive consequences for

FIGURE 3.5 Bust of José Martí in the courtyard of the Cuban School of Wushu below the words "Wushu: health and life; an arm of the revolution." Photo by the author.

Cuba's transportation industry and then speaks in Mandarin with one of the visitors, who steps forward to address us. Through his translator, the official thanks Master Lee and the Chinese embassy and then tells us about the expansion of trade between China and Cuba and says that he hopes Cuban students will find Chinese computers to be helpful in their studies. By this time, onlookers have gathered at the school's circular front gate, pushing for a glimpse through the metal bars. I don't know if they are more interested in listening to the official or watching the wushu demonstration that usually follows these kinds of speeches. . . . At the end of class, at 12:00 PM, the twenty or so people in the novice group have to stand at the front and recite the phrase. Many of us can't remember it and have to turn to read it off the wall, causing two of my fellow beginners to laugh. Our instructor looks upset and shouts at us that wushu is no joke, and that Martí deserves better. "Do it again," she orders, "and this time with the fist [wushu salute] and some conviction!"

—Havana, November 16, 2005

As a champion of Chinese culture in Cuba, the school fills multiple functions. Opening a personal channel of communication between Chinese officials recommended to Vargas Lee by their embassy and hundreds of Cuban students—and potentially thousands of their family members—it is a source of information about Chinese perspectives on the world and the implications for Cuba and Barrio Chino. There is no pretense of detailed reporting on the environmental impact of Sino-Cuban industrial ventures or on the labor standards, hiring practices, or remuneration policies of Chinese firms operating in Cuba. Even so, spontaneous presentations directly from Chinese VIPs on the goals and achievements of bilateral projects provide a valued supplement to official news coverage (figure 3.6). They also provide the Chinese government with an unmediated platform for explaining these initiatives and promoting forthcoming Chinese products. The crowds that regularly gather around the school's gate, whether to glean insights from visiting dignitaries (figure 3.7) or to steal a glimpse of the acrobatic performances staged for them, reveal considerable curiosity about China's growing impact (figure 3.8).

The school's lessons are conveyed through a powerful blend of political and cultural symbols: beneath the Cuban flag and the gaze of Martí, students young and old practice an ancient Chinese art, learn how to count in Mandarin, and become proud of their connection to an emerging superpower. Their pride adds newfound confidence to a long-standing dia-

FIGURE 3.6 Celebrating at the Cuban School of Wushu, May 10, 2013. From left to right: Jorge Chao Chiu (secretary general of the Casino Chung Wah), Xu Kezhu (the Chinese consul), Juan Eng (president of the Casino), Zhang Tuo (the Chinese ambassador), General Gustavo Chui, and General Armando Choy. Photo by the author.

sporic process observed elsewhere by Rhacel Parreñas and Lok Siu: "To be part of a diaspora is to reference one's relationship and belonging to some larger historical cultural-political formation—a people, a culture, a civilization—that transgresses national borders. It is a way of reformulating one's minoritized position by asserting one's full belonging elsewhere" (2007, 13).

Far from a handicap, being "minoritized" appears to be an asset for Cuba's wushu students. Their physical appearance generally shows little evidence of Asian heritage, but their enthusiastic embrace of Chinese martial arts asserts a statement of belonging to a distant homeland whose growing power is globally recognized. However great their enthusiasm, though, the students must accept an implicit hierarchy of devotion: as *una arma* (an instrument, tool, or arm) of the revolution, the school—and, by extension, the Chinese culture it represents—is subordinate to the larger political organism, the Cuban state. It is within this hegemonic structure that students and their families learn from Chinese visitors

FIGURE 3.7 General Moisés Sío Wong delivers a speech at the Cuban School of Wushu, November 2005. Photo by the author.

FIGURE 3.8 A window into the future? The entrance of the Cuban School of Wushu, January 2012. Photo by the author.

about the products, services, and new possibilities that are changing their lives: affordable refrigerators and rice cookers, energy-saving light bulbs, inexpensive medicines stocking previously bare pharmacy shelves, Panda television sets screening weekly Chinese movies, low-emission buses and trains that run on time, and the encompassing message that Cuba's future is secure. As China's impact reaches further each day into the lives of ordinary Cubans, it is logical that the school should diffuse a vision of order that accommodates this impact within the hegemony of Cuban state nationalism.

Another indispensable contact for business-minded Chinese visitors is Vargas Lee's father-in-law, Tao Jin Rong, an entrepreneur from Shanghai who moved to Barrio Chino to invest in the restaurant sector. He and a small group of colleagues assist prospective investors by arranging visas, coordinating meetings with interested counterparts, and helping them navigate Cuba's complex and changeable business environment. His acclaimed Tien Tan (Temple of Heaven) restaurant has gained a reputation among Chinese businesspeople as an auspicious venue for meeting accommodating Cuban officials. Among its patrons are Ramiro Valdés, Cuba's vice president and minister of information, who has overseen a joint venture with the Chinese firm Haier to produce consumer electronics in Cuba (see chapter 1). Former Foreign Minister Felipe Pérez Roque and Vice President Ricardo Cabrisas, both advocates of closer engagement with China, have also conducted meetings with Chinese officials in the restaurant's private dining room. Omar Pereira Hernández, the former director of tourism at the Cuban embassy in Beijing, notes that he would frequently refer outbound Chinese officials to the restaurant, since "in Cuba money alone cannot rule; it has to be backed up by political approval and social connections" (interview, June 14, 2010). The time invested by Chinese officials in cultivating relationships with Vargas Lee, his father-in-law, and Cuban diplomats indicates their familiarity with this code of practice.

Coordinating the potentially chaotic multiplicity of demands from the Cuban and Chinese governments and Barrio Chino's residents, Vargas Lee treads with precision. The task of balancing all of these interests is complicated further by internal differences between two subgroups of the Cuban state (the Ministry of Justice and the Office of the Historian) and two subgroups of the Barrio Chino community (the Chinese associations and local entrepreneurs, discussed below). In Nan Lin's (2001, 67) terms, Vargas Lee is a bridging individual, adroitly navigating the distinct but overlapping demands of these interest groups.

The encounters Vargas Lee orchestrates at the Cuban School of Wushu and the Tien Tan restaurant are infused with opportunities for Barrio Chino's stakeholders. The school gives Chinese government officials and executives a platform for explaining the benefits of Sino-Cuban cooperation and Chinese products directly to hundreds of Vargas Lee's students and their families. In the more intimate environment of Tien Tan's VIP room, the Chinese acquire insider knowledge on trade and investment from the elite of Cuba's China enthusiasts and inevitably express the merits of economic liberalization. The Chinese government has compensated Vargas Lee for his work: the school's gold-painted minivan is hard to miss as it zips around Havana displaying a message stenciled conspicuously on its side: "donation of the embassy of the People's Republic of China."

For their part, the Chinese associations and the independent restaurant operators of Chuchillo Lane are hopeful that with Vargas Lee's support, reforms in Barrio Chino under the Office of the Historian will bring new opportunities for commercial expansion. The lack of such opportunities to date has led to reliance on informal connections, illustrated in the infamous case of a Barrio Chino association elder observed by Cuban agents at the Fair of Canton in Guangzhou with a U.S. investor purchasing supplies, equipment, and decorations for the elder's restaurant. Clearly articulated legal codes that permit foreign financing and commercial expansion are foremost on the wish list of Barrio Chino's Chinese associations, a growing pool of self-employed small business owners, and the Chinese embassy. Vargas Lee advocates this goal from a solid foundation: he has a personal stake in the restaurant sector and is a former member of the executive board of the Chinese community's foremost body, the Casino Chung Wah.

To mitigate any top-down doubts about his revolutionary loyalty, Vargas Lee often begins his public speeches with a positioning statement: "I speak to you in the name of the state." There is nothing hollow in this claim, as the state has benefited considerably from his work. His centrally conferred functions extend beyond building diplomatic ties and demonstrating the Cuban government's regard for traditional Chinese culture. He also advances a century and a half of official attempts to regulate Barrio Chino's informal sector. As the depth and reach of Cuban linkages with China intensify, he ensures that emerging connections are disclosed and integrated into an official framework of bilateral cooperation. Respected by elders and embedded in local networks, he has the capacity to convey community priorities upward and official requests downward, which has proven particularly useful to the Office of the Historian since 2006.

The next section examines the Office of the Historian's efforts to achieve in Barrio Chino what no other state institution has been able to: clamp down on the black market while stimulating economic growth. Implicit in the Office's agenda is an attempt to rationalize social capital in a more consensual way than has previously been the case, by integrating community networks intact into official programs for promoting tourism and neighborhood revival. To their own detriment, external administrators have long overlooked the benefits that sensitivity to Barrio Chino's history, culture, and people could bring to their projects. Local opinions of the Office's civic stewardship reveal that it has improved on past practice, but that it still has much learn before it can harness Barrio Chino's most powerful but elusive resource: the trust of residents.

FORMALIZING THE INFORMAL: THE OFFICE OF THE HISTORIAN IN BARRIO CHINO

Cuban and foreign observers agree that strategies for containing the island's black market are desperately needed. The Havana-based Grupo para el Desarrollo Integral de la Capital has been arguing for over a decade that the most pressing task facing the nation is to "formalize the informal" (2001, 1). Tighter regulations may help, but, as Archibald Ritter writes, top-down controls can be counterproductive: "Paradoxically, in attempting to control everything in the past, the government has ended up controlling very little. The effectiveness of stricter state controls actually leads to weaker genuine control due to their promotion of illegalities, corruption and the ubiquitous violation of unrealistic regulations" (2011, 20). As discussed in chapter 1, decentralized authority and functional supply chains will help overcome this problem, but to achieve the "absolute observance of legality" stipulated in *Lineamiento* 12 (República de Cuba 2011, 11), greater bottom-up respect for the state and the rule of law will also be necessary.

As Cuba moves beyond the political stability of the Castro presidencies, the state must find new ways to marshal popular support for its leadership and regulatory systems. Social allegiances embedded in neighborhood identity, protective solidarity within ethnic communities, loyalty galvanized by religious kinship, and other forms of group membership therefore have considerable influence in contemporary Cuba. As a hub of unregistered trade, headquarters to the nation's Chinese associations, and a source of emerging ties to China, Barrio Chino is a case in point. Transpacific ties are augmenting the capacity of community leaders to contest top-down directives and pursue alternative development agendas. Adopting the position that the support of residents holds the key to administrative success in Barrio Chino, in January 2006 the Office of the Historian of the City became the latest institution to propose a new regulatory framework for the district.

The Office assumed managerial control of Barrio Chino at a time when the long-standing grievances of municipal administrators over inadequate decentralization were at last catching the ear of national lawmakers. In 2000, as noted in chapter 1, Decree Law 91 had divided Havana into 93 (subsequently 105) Popular Councils, but the councils' ability to implement economic development projects that might draw citizens out of the informal sector was undermined by inadequate financial devolution. Cuban officials acknowledge that the transfer of executive power to Raúl Castro in 2006, while motivated by Fidel Castro's failing health, generated broad optimism that there might finally be progress toward decentralization (both administrative and economic). The prospect of growing the formal economy through local reinvestment and business development was on the horizon. New commercial powers and territorial jurisdictions subsequently conferred on the Office of the Historian afforded cautious hope, though it was not until the 2011 *Lineamientos* that decentralization was officially recognized as a catalyst for cooperation between state-owned enterprises, local governments, and small businesses.

There is no Cuban institution more experienced in simultaneously reining in informal practices and expanding registered commerce than the Office of the Historian. Its principal objective is to design and implement commercially viable urban development programs that draw on local cultural heritage. Founded in 1938, the Office was directed by the Cuban intellectual Emilio Roig de Leuchsenring until his death in 1964, when it came under the directorship of the new historian of the City, Eusebio Leal Spengler. In 1981 the Office assumed administrative jurisdiction of Old Havana, the municipality adjacent to Central Havana (where Barrio Chino is located). The Office has developed stable cooperative synergies with actors ranging from Old Havana's seven local governments (Popular Councils) to religious communities and unregistered artistic ensembles (Hearn 2008a; Scarpaci, Segre, and Coyula 2002).[5]

The Office's economic plan—managed since 1994 by its commercial enterprise Habaguanex—centers on establishing hotels, shopping centers, and bars oriented to foreign tourism and reinvesting revenues in municipal development projects. While residents have benefited indirectly from this plan, most cannot afford to patronize the chic lounges and hotel lobby restaurants springing up around them. Leal's strategy has nevertheless created jobs, and those willing to commercialize their cultural heritage have found ready demand for their talent on cabaret stages. Folkloric performances of Afro-Cuban religious traditions and other cultural exotica have done especially well (Hearn 2004). The political upshot is the incorporation of a broad range of local actors, some of whom might otherwise seek to develop independent unregistered operations, into officially regulated projects.

Leal's plan for reinvesting profits from tourism in municipal development was propelled by the austerity of the early years of the Special Period, which left the Office without a central subsidy, and by the 1993 collapse of a revered eighteenth-century heritage site, the Colegio del Santo Ángel (Hill 2007, 59). The incident paved the way for Decree Law 143 of 1993, which designated Old Havana as a Priority Zone for Conservation and made the Office a national exemplar of decentralized municipal economic management (replicated in the late 1990s in the smaller historic centers of Santiago de Cuba, Camagüey, and Trinidad). Henceforth the Office answered not to the provincial government of Havana but directly to the Council of State, in this way acquiring legal authority to establish relations with foreign investors and to tax economic actors in its territory. This authority was expanded in 1995 through Accord 2951, which recognized Old Havana as a Zone of High Significance for Tourism and eased restrictions there on foreign investment, gastronomy services, and trade in U.S. dollars. In 2003, Accord 4942 extended the boundary of the Priority Zone for Conservation from Old Havana to Barrio Chino, though negotiations with the Grupo and local Chinese leaders delayed the Office's administrative takeover until January 1, 2006. The Office's powers were augmented across both districts in June 2011 by Decree Law 283, signed by Raúl Castro, which enhanced its capacity to levy taxes, authorize private businesses, approve new guesthouses, and procure buildings and facilities.

Leal expressed interest in Barrio Chino as early as 1992. In his keynote address at a conference titled "Tourism and Its Importance for Understanding the History and the Culture of the People," he stated: "Barrio Chino: Is there anything more beautiful and interesting in Havana? And yet I'm convinced that Barrio Chino will die in the coming years if a fundamental task is not accomplished. What is the task? To keep the Chinese community alive . . . it is not a matter changing or adorning the Barrio; it's a matter of making it live, and life always comes from the inside out" (quoted in A. Wong and Baez 1993, 7–8). Leal's advocacy of bottom-up development reflects the Office's long-standing attempt to legitimize commercial initiatives by linking them to widely recognized historical processes, or what Sherry Ortner (1991) calls "cultural schemas." Just as Afro-Cuban religious heritage in Old Havana has provided the Office's cabaret clubs with ready material for what it calls "folklore tourism," Chinese settlement in Barrio Chino in the late nineteenth and early twentieth centuries provides a widely recognized theme for the district's commercial "revival." In both contexts the Office has leveraged vague but enthusiastic local and foreign understandings of Cuban history as a basis for specific development projects.

How genuinely history informs the Office's work is debatable. As Clifford Geertz observed four decades ago, invocations of the past to justify the present always involve creative manipulation, or the transformation of a "model of tradition" into a "model for tradition" (1973, 93). Such a transformation is evident in the Office's approach to Barrio Chino, where Mandarin has become the officially endorsed Chinese language and a statue of Confucius the latest photo opportunity. Mandarin, taught at the Confucius Institute (soon to be relocated from the University of Havana to Barrio Chino), was unknown to Cuba's Cantonese-speaking Chinese immigrants. They would have been similarly unfamiliar with Confucius, whose statue is now the centerpiece of a park in the heart of Barrio Chino. Unveiling the statue to inaugurate Confucius Park in December 2012 with the Chinese ambassador and the president of the World Confucian Academy, Leal expressed his vision of multicultural harmony: "Chinese people joined Cubans to form a family; they did not exclude the Cuban family of which they are today a part" (quoted in People's Republic of China Ministry of Foreign Affairs 2012). Invoking the past to shape the present, Leal's mastery of cultural schemas appears to be aimed at encouraging Chinese Cubans to follow the historical disposition of their forebears to cooperate.

Over the decades Confucius Park has itself been reinvented, in step with the changing currents of Cuban politics (figures 3.9–3.12). Eng Herrera recalls that its visitors were previously less concerned with the wisdom of Confucius: "Until 2012 that place was known as Shanghai Park because, before the Revolution, it sat next to the Shanghai Theater, the most notorious adult venue in Barrio Chino. That's where people would go to meet *fleteras* [literally, flirting women] after watching pornographic films and shows. One thing's for sure: its conversion into Confucius Park couldn't be further from its roots" (interview, May 17, 2013).

Shanghai Park's makeover reflects Kathleen López's observation that, "rather than being restored to an approximation of what it once was, Havana's Chinatown is being 'remade' into something new, both out of demographic and economic necessity" (2009, 197). As López implies, the Office's mission is both to promote Cuban heritage and to govern, a dual responsibility that has yielded a pragmatic approach to history: authenticity derives in large measure from local endorsement. This position is logical for an institution whose success depends on the support it builds among citizens. Whether in Old Havana or Barrio Chino, ensuring local benefits is a priority for Leal, who argues that tourism is contiguous with Cuban history because it represents

> a recuperation of the capacities the city has historically enjoyed. We endeavor to look at the past as a point of departure, but with our eyes on the future, which is the only way to conserve one's patrimony while confronting the dynamic challenge of sustainability. . . . The point is to

FIGURES 3.9–3.12 The changing face of Shanghai Park. Top left, a community recreational space (2006); top right, vacant and closed to public (2011); bottom left, a handicrafts and souvenir market (2012); bottom right, rebranded as Confucius Park (2013). Photos by the author.

use tourism as a mechanism for development. I calculate that for every one Cuban employed in tourism, ten people live from their income. That said, we reject the idea of turning our historical center into a theme park and novelty show; instead, we work to improve schools, living conditions, participation, and jobs. (interview, April 29, 2002)

Quick to note the historical precedent of tourism as a Cuban "capacity," Leal nevertheless appears determined to break with past practice, particularly the essentialization of cultural heritage for foreign audiences. The spillover benefits he envisions confirm John Kirk's observation that "tourism remains a premier influence in showing Cubans a different approach to development" (2007, 416).

FIGURE 3.13 A sign erected by the Office of the Historian in Barrio Chino, which reads: "The hand executes what the heart demands." Photo by the author.

The need for a different approach to development is nowhere more pressing than Barrio Chino. A historical reputation smeared by shameless foreign thrill seekers and overregulation of the district's once thriving businesses substantiate the need for innovative governance. Excepting the efforts of the Grupo, local concerns rarely figured into Barrio Chino's management prior to 2006, a deficiency the Office has tried to correct by creating opportunities for residents to participate actively in their neighborhood's revival (figure 3.13).[6] As Kathleen López puts it, "second-, third-, and fourth-generation descendants of Chinese, by taking advantage of special economic opportunities and learning about and participating in Chinese traditions, are claiming an ethnic and cultural heritage and redefining themselves. In the process, they are ultimately forging new spaces along the margins, where the expression of identity and the satisfaction of intellectual curiosity may develop" (2009, 197).

Aware of Barrio Chino's historical subjection to external pressures, Leal acknowledges that solutions must come from within. Prior to officially taking over the district, he commissioned a series of studies from prominent Chinese Cubans to assess local perspectives on tourism. Held in the archives of Barrio Chino's House of Chinese Arts and Traditions, these studies shed light on how residents imagine their neighborhood fitting into Cuba's broader strategy for tourism development. One report states:

> We feel we must diversify and amplify as much as possible the options for tourism and break the scheme of beach and hotel tourism. We want to encourage tourists to come and spend time getting to know the people and places that, unfortunately, are often left out of their programs. . . . In our opinion we are not exploiting all the possible ways to satisfy the desires of tourists in order to promote our industry's objectives and increase the inflow of currency that our country needs. . . . *In Cuba, in our city, in our municipality we have a Barrio Chino; let's convert it into one more of our country's products for tourism.* (quoted in Wong and Baez 1993, 8, 9, and 12; emphasis in original)

To achieve this objective, another report recommends attracting tourists from the adjacent municipality of Old Havana by employing actors to walk around its plazas wearing traditional Chinese clothes, imitating the fruit and vegetable street vendors of the late nineteenth and early twentieth centuries. Similarly, small groups of actors portraying religious figures such as the Afro-Cuban Changó, the Catholic Saint Barbara, and the Chinese San Fan Kon (or Kuang Kong), would draw attention to the contribution of Chinese spirituality, alongside African and European influences, to the formation of Cuba's multicultural heritage (Chong López 2006, 6).

A third report recommends establishing a museum of Chinese Cuban culture and a Chinese-style hotel where visitors can enjoy massages and tea. To capture the market potential of the emerging Chinese middle class, the report advises: "We must make Chinese visitors feel at home. Consequently, Asian visitors will recommend the hotel to their families and friends as the best place for a comfortable stay in Cuba, since upon arrival at the hotel, the negative reactions provoked by the encounter with unfamiliar customs will be alleviated." The report concludes that key factors in Barrio Chino's capacity to develop such facilities will be upgrading the infrastructure and improving relations with foreign tour operators, since "the success of such an initiative inevitably depends on how well it is organized" (quoted in Alay Jó, Alay Jó, and Alay Jó 2002, 30).

Perhaps following the report's advice, in 2007 Cuba established a Chinese tourism office and signed an Operational Plan for Chinese Group Tourists Visiting Cuba with the Chinese government, permitting Chinese tour operators to bring package tours to Barrio Chino. That year the number of Chinese tourists in Cuba exceeded 10,000 for the first time, leading Raúl Castro to declare during Hu Jintao's 2008 visit that tourism and training in hospitality would become focal points of cooperation between their two countries. By 2013 there were more than 22,000 Chinese tourists annually, substantiating this goal and affirming the Office of the Historian's efforts to refashion Barrio Chino as an attractive destination.

The Office set about "rescuing traditions," as it had previously described its work in Old Havana, by renovating Barrio Chino's historically prominent streets, refurbishing the Cuban School of Wushu, creating Chinese-themed shops and markets operating in convertible pesos, erecting street signs written in Chinese, and arranging guided tours of the Chinese association buildings. One resulting highlight is the altar of San Fan Kon, the patron saint of the Chinese Cuban community, which is one of only three in the world (the others are in Singapore and Malaysia). Until the Office of the Historian renovated the altar in 2011, it was a focal point of private reflection and celebrations of community weddings, birthdays, and funerals. Members and guests of the Lung Kong Association could visit the altar to participate in the tradition of *kau cim* (求籤) divination, in which a vessel containing a hundred short sticks is shaken by hand until one of them falls to the ground, corresponding with a short metaphoric text read from a book of prophecies. The altar is now open to tourists, who for a "donation" can also receive the wisdom of kau cim (figure 3.14).

Barrio Chino's revival has brought opportunities for generating revenue from the display of Chinese heritage, a phenomenon not unique to Cuba. Sylvia Van Ziegert writes: "It is precisely the commodification of Chinese culture which helps it to circulate throughout diasporic spaces. . . . Traditional Chinese forms and ideas are repackaged and deployed in order to bridge time and space, and create new Chinese cosmopolitanisms. This new transnational Chinese imaginary seeks to use hip,

Sociedad Lung Kong

龙岗公所

¡Visítenos y pruebe su suerte!

FIGURE 3.14 Tourist brochure for the altar of San Fan Kon. The caption reads: "Visit us and try your luck!"

glitzy appeal to attract new audiences, including many non-Chinese and second generation Chinese" (2006, 10–11).

The Office's efforts to repackage history are generally undertaken with local consent, but its selection of some projects instead of others has produced competitive tensions. Graciela Lau Quan, president of the Lung Kong Association, noted that the restoration of the altar (and the accompanying renovation of the restaurant downstairs from it) provoked jealously from associations less likely to attract tourism (interview, February 25, 2011). The deterioration of community goodwill has become evident in the annual Chinese New Year dinner, which for years brought the associations together in a show of grassroots unity. This changed in 2006, when the Office became the dinner's official sponsor and began hosting it in the Office's new Columnas shopping center. Since then, the associations prefer to celebrate New Year independently, though their presidents typically make a brief appearance at the Office's party.

To convince Barrio Chino's community leaders of the broad benefits flowing from its intervention, the Office established a restaurant called La Muralla de China (the Great Wall of China). Combining traditional Chinese decor with stricter accounting standards and market research, the restaurant was to provide a model for the conduct of local business. La Muralla quickly attracted Cuban and foreign clients, who were hungry for the low-cost pizza and spaghetti that appeared on its menu alongside fried rice, spring rolls, and other ostensibly Chinese food also available from its competitors. Chinese Cuban elders were furious that the limits of tradition had been pushed so far and mobilized some forty association members and independent restaurant owners to protest the erosion of cultural heritage in the heart of Barrio Chino. According to one protestor, "How could the Office of the Historian have any idea about our culture? It is run by white people who live in El Vedado and Miramar [comparatively wealthy districts of Havana], and it has its own plan. Since it came to our neighborhood there's nobody we can negotiate with" (interview, March 11, 2006). While unwelcome commercial competition surely galvanized local opposition, La Muralla's outsider status provided a powerful theme for unifying dissent. At a time when the Office was seeking to build community support and distinguish itself from the state's previous attempts to assimilate Barrio Chino into the revolution, the incident exposed the contrast between the Office's economic rationalism and the Grupo's bottom-up approach.

The Office's popularity deteriorated further when it subjected Barrio Chino's private (*cuenta propia*) restaurants to a meticulous bookkeeping scheme aimed at bringing their informal supply chains into the official economy. Owners objected to the financial impact of the plan: in addition to an existing tax levied by the Organización Nacional de Asuntos Tributarios (National Organization of Tributary Affairs), they would now have to pay the Office a "donation" (in fact, a tax) to fund neighborhood development projects. The restaurants belonging to the associations were also asked to donate to the fund and follow new sourcing restrictions that sought to formalize their supply chains through officially nominated wholesale providers (Cheng 2007a, 40). As they had under the Grupo, the associations argued that the new regulations would force them to curtail or abandon the independent charitable services they provided, including complimentary meals for the most needy local residents. An administrator of the Chi Tack Tong Association lamented that "the Office of the Historian said it would invest our money in local development, but what it meant was advertising for tourism. Look at the buildings and the new streets: all very beautiful and restored, but what about our culture, and looking after the elderly Chinese people?" (interview, February 28, 2011).

Detailed regulatory codes were also introduced to community organizations that maintained foreign linkages, such as the Residencia China, which provides housing, medical care, and other services to many of Barrio Chino's remaining first-generation Chinese residents. According to Kristina Nib, then director of the Residencia, "we've always received donations from foreigners. Usually these have been private individuals, and many of them have been Chinese. The gifts went through the Grupo because we always had a high level of understanding with them. But now, if I need to get a new sofa for the Residencia I will have to first go through a long approval process, and then every penny needs to be accounted for" (interview, January 16, 2006).

The Office's attempt to incorporate local collaborative ties and trust—what Nib called "understanding"—into a scheme of transparent and regulated transactions was criticized openly by the Casino Chung Wah. On December 30, 2005—two days before the Office's takeover, and shortly before his death—Casino President Li San began a public speech in the iconic Cuchillo Lane by invoking a sense of imperiled community: "Our unity is under threat, and we must be stronger now more than ever before." Whether or not this comment was intended to incite noncompliance, the expansion of the informal sector over the next five years turned the Office's objectives on their head. A neighborhood leader, who asked to remain anonymous, described the situation in early 2011: "We are governed by a series of bureaucrats whose eyes have become rounder [physiologically more Caucasian] over the years. Most of them live in El

Vedado, and they know little about our culture. From 5:01 PM until 8.59 AM they are not concerned with Barrio Chino. The new system has problems. Do you know that the leaders of the associations take a cut of about 25 percent before submitting their profits to the Ministry of Justice bank account? That way they can live more comfortably and invest more freely in their restaurants" (interview, February 27, 2011).

Riding the momentum of success in Old Havana, the Office apparently presumed it could transfer commercial regulations from one context to another with little adjustment for local conditions. As a senior Office administrator put it, "Chinese immigrants and their descendants have always been integrated into Cuba. Remember, one of our most famous national icons is the *mulata cubana* [the racially mixed Cuban woman]. Because of Cuba's long history of racial integration we have been able to work in Barrio Chino with no problems. It's just like working here in Old Havana" (interview, February 28, 2011). This optimism has proven counterproductive, as it underestimates the efficacy of trust accrued in Barrio Chino over generations and perpetuated by ongoing perceptions of external interference. As I discussed in the introduction, scholars have shown that social capital is generally not fungible across distinct contexts, and it stands to reason that the same holds true for attempts to rationalize it. Herein lies a core challenge to the Office's plan: trust is a resource possessed by a community of insiders, and it cannot be incorporated into externally administered development projects without that community's consent.

Governments around the world have long attempted to scale up grassroots loyalties into a public good by converting "bonding social capital" into a "bridging" form (Putnam 2000, 22–23), and transforming "particularized trust" into a "generalized" form (Armony 2004, 21; also see Uslaner 1999, 124–25; Yamagishi and Yamagishi 1994). From decentralized health care in India to affordable housing in Brazil, government programs have sought to diminish the prominence of disenfranchised social enclaves rooted in ethnicity, religion, and class that may otherwise turn to informal trade and undermine state authority. In designing such projects, governments often fail to recognize that the more consolidated and inward-oriented trust is, the harder it is to rationalize (Fedderke, de Kadt, and Luiz 1999, 724–26). External pressure to acquiesce tends to reinforce collective internal opposition and over time has been shown to propel resistance horizontally outward to incorporate an ever-growing number of insiders bonded in antagonistic solidarity (Portes and Sensenbrenner 1993, 1343–44). The wider the radius of oppositional trust, the harder it becomes to focus official development interventions.

The Office of the Historian has experienced precisely these problems in Barrio Chino. Meticulous taxation and supply controls were introduced together with practical examples of how businesses should operate, such as La Muralla. These measures were intended to regulate an economy that had long relied on informal networks of tight-knit cooperation and to rescue an imagined tradition of multicultural integration and legally compliant entrepreneurship. In the process, though, they revived perceptions of external interference and unwelcome state micromanagement of local business. The Office's installation of Confucius Park, restoration of the altar of San Fan Kon, and broader gentrification agenda evoked concerns that the historical revival was producing few direct benefits beyond tourism. Community leaders argued that the Office's projects, financed largely by new taxes on restaurants, were undermining their ability to provide welfare services for Barrio Chino's aging pioneers.

Behind the scenes of the Office's eye-catching projects, the Chinese associations have pursued alternative development strategies, including exploring cooperation with a growing flow of enthusiastic Chinese visitors. As the radius of trust that defines Barrio Chino's community of insiders expands overseas, the district's political weight and the capacity of its leaders to negotiate with the state have increased. This changing dynamic is reflected in the Office's evolving approach to governance, which—as the chapter's final section shows—has recently become more flexible and responsive to local priorities.

SYNERGY: TRADITIONAL MEDICINE TO AWAKEN THE BLOOD

Experience has taught the Office of the Historian the pitfalls of coercion and the merits of consensus. Since 2006, one of its more successful tactics has been to work with locally respected intermediaries, such as Vargas Lee. His school has been refurbished by the Office; his students are funded jointly by the Chinese and Cuban governments to compete internationally; his father-in-law's restaurant is one of the most successful in

Barrio Chino; and locals stand in awe of his eloquence, physical prowess, and martial arts television show. After Li San's public call for unity on the eve of the Office's takeover, Vargas Lee addressed the audience with characteristic diplomacy:

> After more than 150 years of friendship with China, Li San is correct that more than ever we need one united Barrio Chino of Havana, under the guidance of our elders in the Casino Chung Wah. . . . The changes that we are going to see in Barrio Chino are going to be very beneficial for us, and we're seeing the results already. There are many things that we want to see, but we know we can't have everything; we entrust these decisions to the wise vision of the city authorities, and we have to have full confidence in them.

Reflecting Leal's proven strategy of recruiting community leaders who command respect and authority in relation to cultural history and neighborhood affairs, Vargas Lee's advocacy distinguishes the Office's activities from earlier external attempts to manage Barrio Chino's development. The Office's approach has opened channels of direct communication with the executive board of the Casino Chung Wah, independent restaurant owners, and other local leaders. As noted, it has also enabled the Office to frame face-to-face contact between visiting Chinese officials and Barrio Chino's residents in a patriotic light.

As China goes global, the outward flow of its diplomats, students, and investors is beginning to overcome the Cuban government's containment strategies. Commercial connections are thickening, as demonstrated above by the association elder caught red-handed at the Fair of Canton. Barrio Chino's emerging small businesspeople will evidently go to great lengths to acquire the products they need, but the need for such lengths is diminishing in step with the arrival of prospective Chinese partners on their doorsteps. Emerging nonstate ties to China have provoked the Office to explore new, more sensitive approaches to neighborhood development. This, it has found, is the best way to learn about and address community needs before entrepreneurial visitors beat them to it.

One of the Office's key projects in Barrio Chino in 2013 and 2014 was the restoration of the Chinese pharmacy, first established as the San Man Woo medical center in the early twentieth century and now the only one of five Chinese pharmacies that continues to operate in Cuba (Alfonso Rodríguez 2009, 40). The project's genesis was a letter to the Office from the Casino Chung Wah decrying the scarcity of medicinal herbs and teas to treat the ailments of Barrio Chino's aging Chinese residents. Eager to pinpoint local needs and identify how they might be resolved, Mayelín Alfonso Rodríguez of the Office's investment bureau took on the project and quickly identified mutual interests. Demand for specialty natural medicines at the Office's recently refurbished Sarrá Pharmacy in Old Havana had been steadily generating revenue for local street lighting and sewer works. If restored in partnership with community leaders, she reasoned, the Chinese pharmacy could finance similar infrastructure upgrades in Barrio Chino while satisfying a local health need (interview, May 14, 2013).

By mid-2013 construction on the new and improved pharmacy was underway, including a museum wing to exhibit the San Man Woo medical center's appearance in the early twentieth century (figure 3.15). Alfonso Rodríguez envisioned the sale of traditional medicines at minimal cost to association members registered with the Casino (as had long been the case), but also an expanded inventory of specialist relaxation and meditation items for sale primarily to foreign tourists at international prices. The project's main problem, she said, was that the Cuban government's medical procurement branch, Empresa Medicuba, was taking too long to secure competitively priced Chinese medicines, herbs, and teas. The delay had provoked some locals to acquire these items independently through friends and associates visiting from China and, in one instance, to sell them to the public at a local restaurant. Arguing that this illicit supply chain could spiral out of control, the investment bureau's director, María Isabel Martínez, convinced the Office of the Historian's head office to prioritize the pharmacy project and authorize her to independently explore low-cost bulk contracts in China. Alfonso Rodríguez and Martínez asked if I could assist by introducing the Office to a Chinese supplier. I did so, and in early 2014 Beijing's Tong Ren Tang wholesale pharmacy was pursuing a supply contract.

Another of the Office's ongoing projects is the *Kwong Wah Po*, a newspaper founded in 1928 and printed (then and now) in Spanish and Cantonese for local readers.[7] Chinese characters are painstakingly arranged by hand for an antique printing press by Guillermo Chiu, the only remaining person with the requisite technical expertise (figures 3.16 and

FIGURE 3.15 Watch this space: The Chinese pharmacy under construction in 2013. Photo by the author.

3.17). Concerned about the newspaper's precarious future, the Casino requested that the Office rescue it as an emblem of cultural patrimony. A series of meetings between the Casino, association leaders, and Alfonso Rodríguez led to an agreement to convert the newspaper into a glossy magazine with news and editorials in Spanish and Mandarin to attract the interest of descendants of Chinese immigrants to Cuba, language students, and Chinese speakers around the world. Produced digitally by word processors, scanners, printers, and five professional staff members, the magazine is expected to generate revenue for upgrading neighborhood infrastructure both through direct sales and by attracting tourists to a museum featuring the working antique press (and presumably a photo opportunity with Guillermo Chiu).

Like the pharmacy, the newspaper reflects the Office's attempt to address local needs while advancing a political agenda. The revamped *Kwong Wah Po* is a way not only of generating revenue, but also of balancing China's growing media presence in Cuba. A journalist from the Cuban newspaper *Juventud Rebelde* noted that Chinese soft power in Cuba has grown through news, current affairs, and artistic media (inter-

FIGURES 3.16 AND 3.17 Guillermo Chiu and the Chinese printing blocks he arranges by hand to produce the *Kwong Wah Po* newspaper, January 2012. Photo by the author.

view, May 11, 2013). *China Today*, *Xinhua*, and other publications are distributed each month by the Chinese embassy in Cuba on the understanding that they be made publicly available in hotel lobbies and at trade fairs, conferences, and cultural centers like Barrio Chino's House of Chinese Arts and Traditions. The new *Kwong Wah Po* will ensure that an official Cuban perspective accompanies these Chinese publications.

The pharmacy and newspaper serve the Cuban state's interests, but the proposals for both were developed through community meetings coordinated by the Casino Chung Wah and then submitted to the Office of the Historian. They were rare instances of local consensus in a context of growing competition for the Office's attention. A prominent Chinese Cuban general, Gustavo Chui, believes that the deliberations that initiated the two projects may set Barrio Chino on a new course of bottom-up development:

> There is no shortage of interest from partners in China in investing in Barrio Chino; the holdup is on our side. The way I see it, this process has to follow a bottom-up formula. The first thing is for the community to agree on solid development proposals; the next is for these to be presented to the Office of the Historian or directly to the National Assembly; and from there, legal changes can happen. With the commercial benefits it brings to Barrio Chino, this process should be enough to awaken the blood [*despertar la sangre*] of the community, and this has finally started to happen with the pharmacy and the newspaper. Remember the case of La Muralla restaurant? When it began selling pizza and spaghetti, the community came together in opposition. No law mandated them to do that; on the contrary, it was direct collective action that brought about change. This is the same kind of activism that is needed for broader change in Barrio Chino today.
>
> Thirteen of Cuba's eighteen Chinese associations are in Barrio Chino [including the Casino Chung Wah], so China's influence in Cuba is entering there first. Young people are important for this process, and the Chinese ambassador and his staff have accepted that they must work with the descendants [of Chinese immigrants]. It's possible we may see new Chinese immigration, and this could help strengthen the embassy's relationships with the Chinese associations. But they won't come unless there are advantages for them in doing so, and unless they

are made aware of these advantages. This will be one of the functions of the newspaper. (interview, May 16, 2013)

Chui believes that bottom-up proposals in Barrio Chino are a starting point for engaging the state and gaining visibility in China. This, he thinks, should generate commercial benefits that will in turn stimulate and "awaken the blood of the community" to propose further neighborhood development projects. Lau Quan of the Lung Kong Association is hopeful that this process will attract Chinese investment:

> The Lung Kong has around two million members and 143 associations around the world, with its headquarters in China. We [in the Cuban branch] receive a lot of Chinese businesspeople, who are ready to invest here because they think the competition will be less than in Canada or other places. But we can't receive foreign investment by law. If that changes, you'll see a real transformation here. The Lung Kong Association could have a general grocery store, for example, and expand the restaurant. There's a ready market for this, and that's what we've been telling the Ministry of Justice. There are thousands of Chinese students living in Cuba, and many have already approached us looking for the daily things they need and the food they are accustomed to. (interview, February 25, 2011)

Association leaders are keenly watching for signals of legal change, particularly as the Raúl Castro administration rolls out reforms to put state and nonstate enterprises on more equal footing. Especially relevant are statements like that of Marino Murillo, vice president of the Council of Ministers, to the National Assembly in July 2013: "The plan for the coming year has to be different. . . . The plan is designed so that a businessman from whatever sector does not have to ask permission to make minor investments to ensure production does not stop" (quoted in Frank 2013). For Barrio Chino's associations, the question is whether such statements will lead to authorization from the Office of the Historian and the Ministry of Justice to receive investments, expand their businesses, and sell imported Chinese consumer goods. The ministry's director of associations, Miriam Garcia Mariño, says that lifting the restrictions would mean breaking with a long-standing policy: "The main thing is that community groups respect the Law of Association, which

Cuba inherited from Spain in 1888. The point of that law is to keep some overall structure in place so that NGOs and other associations stay focused on their original tasks. Without it they would just turn to commerce, as some of the Chinese associations have begun to do through their restaurants. Law 1320 put the associations under our jurisdiction in 1978, and since then they've focused, as they should, on the welfare of the Chinese community. That's their purpose, and it's best that they stay committed to it" (interview, January 9, 2012).

The ministry's intentions may be sound, but its restrictions have caused frustrations as Sino-Cuban ties deepen. The Min Chih Tang's public relations officer reports that its branch in the city of Cienfuegos was in need of a truck to manage a small agricultural project. The Chinese embassy heard of the project and donated a truck, but the Min Chih Tang was forbidden by the Law of Association from accepting it because of the project's commercial nature. The Min Chih Tang crossed the Ministry of Justice again in 2012 when it tried to organize a business forum with fifteen trade representatives from China to mark its 125th anniversary. Invited to speak at the event, I recorded some impressions in my research diary:

NONE OF YOUR BUSINESS

There was supposed to be a Chinese business delegation, but at the last minute the Ministry [of Justice] ruled that the event must be strictly "academic" and focus on cultural themes rather than business networking. This hasn't stopped some determined Chinese entrepreneurs from coming to explore opportunities for setting up supermarkets, electronics outlets, and tourism services. . . . The political attaché from the Chinese embassy, Yu Bo, shares his thoughts with me: "Our young people, including some who have come to this event, are not that interested in traditions and culture. They're focused on making money for themselves. That's not easy to do here because of the restrictions, but they're determined." Flora Fong, the renowned Cuban artist, is also reflecting on the determination of the Chinese visitors. She tells me a fable: "A woman decided that the best way to get from her house to the market was across a mountain rather than around it. People laughed at her, saying it would take a lifetime to build a path across that mountain, but she vowed to do it. By the time she completed the path everyone had forgotten her promise, and they asked how she could travel so quickly to the market. Rather than tell them it was none of their business, she shared her secret openly so that the entire village could benefit." Luis Chang, no stranger to determination judging by the thirty-foot sculpture of the Great Wall he has single-handedly installed on the wall of the Min Chih Tang common room, chimes in: "These folks [the Chinese visitors] are going to find their own mountain here in Cuba, but I doubt they'll be shown the path."

—Havana, January 10, 2012

The Min Chih Tang event demonstrated the disposition of independent Chinese businesspeople to trade and invest in Cuba, but also the difficulty of doing so legally. The reform process headlined by the *Lineamientos* may inspire local optimism, but many people remain skeptical that any resulting legal changes will endure. At the Casino Chung Wah's 120th anniversary celebration in 2013, a member of its executive board described his community's hopes and fears: "We believe that if the laws change, they could just as quickly change back. They have before. Any new law will have to be in place for some time before people are confident enough to invest their time and money. A lot of people lost their entire livelihoods when the unthinkable happened in the 1960s. Cuba's friendship with China is strong at the moment, but things have turned bad before, and what would happen if at some point they turn bad again?" (interview, May 9, 2013).

Reinforced by memories of the Great Revolutionary Offensive, fears of loss continue to dampen the confidence of Barrio Chino's community leaders. Until these fears are overcome, neighborhood proposals for initiatives like the pharmacy and newspaper will remain scarce. In turn, new sources of income, registered partnerships with Chinese business-people, and a sense of creative "awakened blood" will also remain subdued. Trust in the state's ability to fashion a stable and productive legal environmental is therefore a key determinant of Barrio Chino's future.

The Office of the Historian's accountability codes aim to inspire confidence in its ability to govern, but Barrio Chino's ambivalent responses have transmitted an important message in return: bottom-up endorsement is critical to the success of government development policies. A proven pathway to local support is the advocacy of community leaders like Vargas Lee, but as China's influence grows, even this is not enough to ensure trust in the state. Faced with the prospect of deepening illicit business connections, the Office has become more publicly engaged, for instance by responding to neighborhood proposals for the restoration of the Chinese pharmacy and newspaper. This has motivated Barrio Chino's associations to put competitive differences aside in pursuit of collective benefits. The extent to which the pharmacy and newspaper will secure these benefits is yet to be seen, but as I conclude below, these projects and the turbulent local history that gave rise to them crystallize Cuba's broader development challenge: to formulate consensual policy frameworks that accommodate and encourage trust rather than destroy it.

CONCLUSION: SPHERES OF TRUST IN BARRIO CHINO

Barrio Chino's future cannot be divorced from its tumultuous past. The inhumanity of the coolie trade, the xenophobia of colonial administrators, the commercial injunctions of the anti-Chinese movement, the demeaning fantasies of foreign tourists, the nationalization campaign of the early revolution, and the disinterest of a government at diplomatic odds with Beijing produced more than a century and a half of neglect and acrimony. These unrelenting pressures are matched only by the endurance, protection, and promise of the Casino Chung Wah and its affiliated Chinese associations. Historical legacies persist in Barrio Chino, not least through the entrenched informal sector, but contemporary pressures and opportunities are reshaping the civic landscape. These include growing foreign tourism, the Office of the Historian's tax and accountability codes, the Ministry of Justice's administrative red tape, and the increasing presence on the ground of Chinese diplomats and businesspeople. The contemporary regulatory environment seeks to contain the black market while ensuring attention to community welfare, but it also places a toll on the efficiency and viability of daily affairs, from running a soup kitchen to holding a conference.

The Office of the Historian is not alone in the quest for local compliance with the law; around the world administrators and tax bureaus face an uphill battle in convincing citizens that adherence to commercial regulations is worth their while (O'Donnell 2006; Portes and Sassen 1987). Barrio Chino's restaurant operators have yet to accept this proposition, especially in light of the high taxes they pay. They prefer to work quietly at the margins of the formal economy, securing supplies from alternative sources and sustaining a network of unregistered ethnic entrepreneurship that now extends across the Pacific. These independent relationships constitute a potentially valuable resource for the broader Cuban economy if they can be brought out of the shadows, but to achieve this the Office must develop more dynamic and conciliatory state-society synergies. Its task, in deceptively simple terms, is to simultaneously build horizontal and vertical trust.

Barrio Chino's community leaders have clearly identified the threats and opportunities they face. At the dawn of the Office's takeover, Carmen Eng, the director of the House of Chinese Arts and Traditions, was apprehensive about the introduction of new accountability codes but was confident that "with a solid organizational structure, getting things done will be easier. No more doing deals by word of mouth. Instead we'll do things in a more disciplined manner" (interview, March 12, 2006). Nib, director of the Residencia, criticized the growing bureaucracy involved in handling foreign donations and acquiring new furniture, but she also perceived advantages in a more official governance framework: "An advantage is that the Office of the Historian has contacts with foreign NGOs and sources of funds. Now there's an official mechanism for linking up with donors" (interview, January 16, 2006). She also predicted that Barrio Chino's circles of trust and ethnic allegiance would remain intact: "One thing I'm absolutely sure of is that our community will keep working in its own way below the surface, as it always has." This intriguing prediction has proven accurate, striking to the core of the Office's challenge: it must incorporate the broad range of horizontal linkages underpinning Barrio Chino's informal sector, and its nascent connections to China, into its administrative plan.

For all the Office's historical expertise, it has learned the hard way that cultural sensitivity is a prerequisite for grassroots endorsement. The Muralla pizza and spaghetti affair revealed a clash between the Office's commercial goals and community perceptions of tradition, making the Office's outsider status an easy target for detractors. Unveiling a statue of Confucius may have convinced onlookers of Leal's personal respect for traditional Chinese values, but residents are less easily convinced by the Office's broader plan to rescue traditions. Statues, altars, and monuments serve largely to attract revenue from tourism, and the spoils must be shared with Barrio Chino's associations and businesses if they are to endorse the new governance model. As the Office seeks local approval to convert neighborhood heirlooms and artifacts into tourist attractions, it must forge consensus on both the immediate present and the distant past.

Eric Hobsbawm and Terence Ranger (1992) have argued that the "invention of tradition" is standard practice in the building of nations. Barrio Chino's evolution shows that a comparable process is under way at the local level: the commercial recycling of cultural schemas is inherent in the building of trust. The Office is well suited to this task, as its attempts to rescue traditions are appraised largely according to the material benefits they bring. The opening of the San Fan Kon altar to tourists, for instance, was wholeheartedly endorsed by the Lung Kong Association, which retained control of the altar's administrative and financial management. Similarly, the pharmacy and newspaper initiatives indicate an emerging consensus on the interplay of traditional community practice and contemporary economic aspiration.

The cultural convergence underpinning those two initiatives is manifestly political: these are among the first projects in Barrio Chino to be conceived deliberatively, proposed representatively, and received enthusiastically by a governing institution. This process improves on past practice by more genuinely articulating horizontal community linkages with vertical state-society synergies, in effect drawing its stakeholders into a multidimensional sphere of trust. This does not imply rationalization as envisioned by Fedderke, de Kadt, and Luiz (1999), in which social capital is divorced from culture and individual identities. Rather, it treats grassroots allegiances and neighborhood trust as public resources to be harnessed through locally formulated projects. This process should, at its best, encourage the use of informal networks of ethnic entrepreneurship like those of Barrio Chino's associations—as well as previously closed circles of unregistered friends like those of Felipe and Daisy—in the service of a larger national community.

The newspaper and pharmacy projects hold promise, but they are works in progress. Although they were initiated from the bottom up to serve local needs, the benefits they generate may disproportionately flow to the state. Both cases demonstrate improved state-society communication, but they also warrant attention to Bill Cooke and Uma Kothari's (2001) point that participation in official programs does not guarantee positive outcomes or fair treatment. Unless these projects are brought to fruition in ways that carry broadly shared benefits, Barrio Chino's residents will continue to doubt that their concerns matter to official administrators.

Critical to the upward mobility of neighborhood concerns is the support of intermediaries capable of advocating on their behalf to policy makers. Facilitating communication between community groups and government institutions, "amphibians" like Vargas Lee are integral to the conduct of state-society interactions in Cuba (Crahan and Armony 2007, 2). As a former member of the Casino Chung Wah's executive board, major player in Barrio Chino's restaurant sector, host to visiting Chinese officials, and charismatic martial artist, he is embedded in community networks. Among the messages he has conveyed upward is the need for greater leeway in the conduct of local business, including authorization for the associations and restaurants to expand the scope of their services and openly receive investment. With the Office's support, Vargas Lee's martial arts school has become a focal point of Sino-Cuban cultural exchange and a prominent neighborhood landmark. He cannot transform the Office into an insider, but in return for its assistance he has endorsed its stewardship of Barrio Chino's development, enabling it to consult more genuinely with residents.

Vargas Lee's amphibious capacity is also evident in the exposure he affords to visiting Chinese officials. The Cuban School of Wushu is probably the only non-mass-mediated venue in Cuba where foreign VIPs are authorized to deliver impromptu speeches on bilateral relations directly to hundreds of citizens. For all their openness, though, these occasions seek to contain face-to-face ties between citizens of the two nations within an environment trusted by the state to function as "an arm of the revolution." In the absence of such a forum, Chinese visitors would logically turn to the associations, whose independent people-to-people activities would consequently gain momentum. The Office of the Historian's restoration of the Cuban School of Wushu and support for Vargas Lee's international tours indicate the value it places on his service.

Regulating nascent foreign linkages has long been a priority for the Cuban state. Since 1959 it has monitored and largely monopolized international connections as a matter of national sovereignty (Hearn 2005). The Office of the Historian's efforts to establish regulatory codes for mediating partnerships between Barrio Chino's residents and Chinese visitors reflect this preoccupation. Paradoxically, the imposition of tighter rules may ultimately give rise to more open people-to-people ties between Cuba and China. Just as the broader liberalization of Cuba's retail, services, and other sectors depends on the prior establishment of regulated supply chains (see chapter 1), a freer flow of independent actors between the two nations requires that the economic environment in Barrio Chino first be more effectively regulated.

Cuba's Chinese associations are well placed to diversify bilateral relations from the ground up, and more heterogeneous ties would benefit both nations. Association members have knowledge and connections that could attract investment and capital goods from China and open new channels of exports to China. However, as the experience of the Grupo showed, the lack of opportunities to legally conduct business in Barrio Chino has previously driven commercial cooperation underground. How effectively the district's emerging international connections are harnessed for national benefit will depend both on local responses to the Office of the Historian's regulatory designs and on the operational leeway afforded the associations by Ministry of Justice. This complex bottom-up and top-down compromise raises again the encompassing challenge of incorporating local networks and their emerging global connections into official development programs. Barrio Chino's lesson for Cuba—and other nations in transition—is that successful reform requires vertical lines of state-society engagement that support, rather than erode, existing horizontal circles of trust.

Across Cuba the government is taking stock of the benefits brought by small business development and foreign investment. As home to Cuba's first private vegetable markets, stores, and wholesale warehouses since 1959, Barrio Chino provides insights into the pitfalls of state-society alienation and the steps necessary to achieve functional synergies. Considered by many to portend future directions of national reform, Barrio Chino raises pressing questions about the containment of unregistered domestic and international partnerships, grassroots support for the expansion of tourism and economic development, and the introduction of a comprehensive blueprint for managing cooperation with China. It also calls attention to the importance of neighborhood solidarity and trust—whether rooted in ethnicity, historical resistance to oppression, or optimism about new forms of engagement with the state—in shaping Cuba's development agenda.

Mutual aid and internal support structures are prevalent in overseas Chinese communities, but the inward-looking guanxi and other informal connections that have long underpinned these structures present unprecedented policy dilemmas. If the world's emboldened Chinese communities are to willingly permit their social capital to be harnessed by official development agendas, then—as the case of Barrio Chino shows—locally formulated strategies and proposals are prerequisite. This is the case not only in state-led contexts such as Cuba, but also in market-oriented economies like Mexico. As in Cuba, intermediaries embedded in the Chinese communities of Mexico City, Tijuana, and Mexicali are bridging top-down and bottom-up concerns. What they have in common with their Cuban counterparts is the quest for a new balance of horizontal and vertical forces that accommodates the internal social capital they have accrued over a century and a half, and the transpacific trust they are only now beginning to leverage.

While Cuba's aging Chinese immigrants and their descendants gradually reposition themselves in the political economy of the Cuban revolution, their counterparts in Mexico are faced with more urgent problems. Criticized in the mass media for deepening Mexico's trade deficit with China, targeted by thieves and kidnappers, and unprotected by the police, Chinese people have few friends in Mexico and even fewer in high places. Image-conscious private- and public-sector officials are reluctant to openly support trade fairs organized by Mexico's Chinese associations, since these events are widely viewed as conduits for the import of manufactured goods that compete with Mexican products (see chapter 2).

When Mexican officials have seen past the disincentives and engaged local Chinese communities, positive results have quickly followed. The government of the state of Baja California has led the way, harnessing the social connections of Chinese associations in Mexicali and Tijuana to attract investors from China and negotiate access to the Chinese market for Mexican products. However, once these partnerships are off the ground, a lack of regulatory follow-through has left the way open for abuse. Smuggling of Chinese contraband into Mexico is part of the problem, but more serious is the illegal recruitment of employees from China to work in the restaurants and maquiladoras of northern Mexico. Mexico's Chinese associations have sometimes brokered these exploitative connections, departing in every respect from their historical tradition of humanitarian protection, mutual aid, and trust.

This chapter begins by discussing the turbulent lives of the pioneer Chinese settlers in Mexico. Arriving during the revolution of the early twentieth century, thousands of Chinese cotton, copper, and railroad workers found themselves on the wrong side of history. Unlike their counterparts in Cuba, Chinese immigrants in Mexico were excluded from the revolutionary struggle, whose main purpose was to advance the rights and interests of Mexico's disenfranchised indigenous population. As the number of Chinese settlers grew and their businesses prospered, public hostility toward them increased. By the mid-1920s, the Valley of Mexicali was home to nearly ten thousand Chinese, outnumbering the Mexican population and giving rise to a strong backlash against them. Turning inward for economic and social defense intensified their segregation and fueled anti-Chinese campaigns in the 1920s and 1930s and ultimately the expulsion of some ten thousand Chinese people from across Mexico. As Grace Peña Delgado has observed, Mexico's revolutionary vision was rooted in a carefully guarded blend (*mestizaje*) of Spanish and indigenous influences: "*Mestizaje* guided the efforts of post-revolutionary architects to assimilate native populations into mainstream Mexican society, to exclude blacks from the national image, and to expel most Chinese from the country. . . . Chinese Mexicans are nearly absent from the Mexican national narrative" (2012, 5). Despite the efforts of President Lázaro Cárdenas (1934–40) in the 1930s to set Mexico on a more inclusive and progressive course, in the second half of the twentieth century Chinese immigrants and their descendants continued to face prejudice and suspicion, stirred up not least by Mexico's fervent anticommunist movement. From its beginnings, the Chinese diaspora in Mexico was viewed as a foreign intrusion, with no place in the revolutionary vision of national identity.

Echoes from the early twentieth century still resound in the predicament of Mexico's Chinese diaspora. Accusations of unfair commercial practices channeled through obscure Asian networks appear frequently in the mass media, as they did a hundred years ago. But allegations that the Chinese community and its trade fairs are deepening the bilateral deficit are only the tip of the iceberg. Even more confrontational are reactions to Chinese involvement in Mexico's massive informal sector. The chapter's second section looks at a bitter debate that has broken out in Mexico City's historic center, where small business owners complain that the influx of Chinese contraband toys, shoes, DVDs, and other products is forcing them to close their shops. As Chinese suppliers gain a foothold in the notorious Tepito black market district on the perimeter of the historic center, critics have even accused Mexico City's former mayor, Marcelo Ebrard, of colluding with Chinese businesses to "invade our capital city" (*Uno más Uno* 2007). Proposals for containing the black market and its Chinese connections range from the expulsion of street vendors to the provision of more weapons to police, but strategies for managing the social dimensions of the informal sector are yet to emerge. The latter would involve engagement with Chinese communities and their social networks, a course of vertical synergy that Mexican leaders have been reluctant to explore. To do so would not only expose them to public criticism but also require them to demonstrate their trustworthiness to Mexico's Chinese associations.

As is the case in Cuba, Chinese networks in Mexico have long coalesced around ethnic associations. The chapter's third section examines the work of the Chinese associations of Mexicali and Tijuana, two of the country's most active. The state government of Baja California has been more active than its federal- and state-level counterparts in forging cooperative synergies with Chinese associations. Its endorsement of Chinese street fairs, marketplaces, and business networking have promoted public awareness of Chinese cultural heritage, facilitated trade and investment with Chinese partners, and helped to improve Sino-Mexican diplomatic relations. The Chinese government has also offered financial and logistical support to Baja California's Chinese associations, on the condition that they agree to publicly adopt the One-China policy, break ties with Taiwanese institutions, conduct official business in Mandarin, and assist Chinese firms to expand into Mexico. Association leaders describe these commitments as a matter of building trust between investors, suppliers, customers, and ultimately between Mexico and China, but they have yet to convince local Mexicans that they stand to benefit.

The fourth section explores the human fallout from the Chinese associations' hot pursuit of business ties with China. The associations' advocacy of corporate interests has sometimes clashed with the very humanitarian commitments they were founded to honor. As well as promoting bilateral trade in commercial goods, the associations also help northern Mexico's factories and restaurants recruit Chinese employees. As the associations increasingly focus on business consulting, matching employers with workers, and arranging visas, they have turned a blind eye to the plight of exploited laborers. The victims of this process live on the margins of a marginalized community, unable to turn to the associations for help and cut off from nearly all avenues of support. One of the few avenues open to them is a Baptist church in Mexicali, whose congregation of past and present Chinese contract workers has traveled there from around the region in search of protection. Introduced by their minister, these individuals speak of the pressures they face to keep quiet about their situation. To break their silence or associate with anybody beyond their immediate community invites retribution against themselves and their families. This extreme form of enforceable trust has underpinned a tightly guarded system of migration and employment, underscoring the need for regulatory follow-through once deals are struck between Mexican businesses and Chinese suppliers.

China's relations with Mexico have great potential, including the potential for abuse. To reduce commercial and humanitarian exploitation will require forms of cooperation between the Chinese associations and the Mexican government that extend beyond business facilitation. Jointly conducted visa monitoring, workplace audits, and commercial inspections are possible first steps. As President Enrique Peña Nieto endeavors to set Mexican relations with China on a more amicable and productive course, the Chinese associations and their wider communities have much to gain from proactive engagement with state and society. As well as establishing themselves as credible brokers of Sino-Mexican trade and investment, they might also begin to turn back the tide of public distrust that has surrounded them for over a century.

REVOLUTION: EQUALITY FOR WHOM?

A bold statement adorns the iconic central library of the National Autonomous University of Mexico (UNAM): "por mi raza hablará el espíritu" (my spirit will speak through my race; figure 4.1). Inspired by the indigenous pride of the Mexican Revolution, Secretary of Education José Vasconcelos penned the motto in 1921 while also serving as UNAM's presi-

FIGURE 4.1 The coat of arms of UNAM. Photo by the author.

dent. The statement openly challenged a European legacy of racial and cultural stratification by vindicating the *raza bronce* (bronze race) as a source of dignity rather than shame.

Vasconcelos would have known that thousands of Chinese migrant workers had by then settled in the arid lands adjacent to the United States to pick cotton and mine copper. Many arrived after abandoning the search for gold in California and finding themselves denied permission to work or bring family members to join them in the United States (Portes and Sensenbrenner 1993, 1328). Laws passed in California between 1850 and 1870 prohibited Chinese employment in chartered corporations, required Chinese people to live outside of incorporated towns, and even banned the carrying of poles laden with goods on public sidewalks. Many of these laws were overturned because they violated federal jurisdiction, but as Adam McKeown (2008, 129) notes, this drove California's senators in Washington to advocate more centralized restrictions. The federal 1882 Chinese Exclusion Act made Chinese people "the first group specifically designated by race to be barred from entering the country" (Hu-DeHart 2007, 41) and made Mexico a more practical destination for Chinese immigrants.

The Treaty of Friendship and Navigation between Mexico and China, signed in 1899 and ratified in 1900, facilitated direct migration from China, as had Peru's and Brazil's treaties with China in 1874 and 1881, respectively. The introduction of Chinese contract laborers indirectly supported Mexico's revolutionary cause: populating the northern states diminished the chance of a second U.S. annexation. Arriving in Mexico both directly and via the United States, Chinese immigrants established themselves as the fourth largest minority group in the country, representing 11 percent of the population.

Commercial and migratory ties between Mexico and China had commenced in the mid-sixteenth century. The Manila Galleons, known in Mexico as the *Nao de China,* would set sail once (later twice) per year from the Philippines, then a node of contact between the Chinese and Spanish empires. Landing in Acapulco, the *Nao* unloaded Asian silk, porcelain, medicines, and high-quality furniture for distribution throughout the Spanish American colonies and on the return voyage carried silver from across the Americas. This pattern of trade between China, the Philippines, and the Americas persisted for some 250 years. The first Chinese migrant workers arrived in Mexico in 1864, contracted by U.S. employers first to build railroads between the cities of El Paso, Chihuahua, and Juárez and then to expand the rail network in the 1880s to the cities of Sonora, Tampico, and Tamaulipas. By the mid-1890s, 1,800 workers had been contracted from Macao and Hong Kong to work in Mexican agriculture, but nearly half died from disease and extreme working conditions (Auyón Gerardo 2003, 32).

The ratification of the Treaty of Friendship and Navigation in 1900 was expected to boost trade and migration between Mexico and China, but Mexico's ambassador to the United States, Manuel de Azpiroz, argued that the treaty would signal to the world that his country was "demonstrating sympathy for that barbaric nation . . . that has no idea about modern international law" (quoted in Valdés Lakowsky 1981, 255–56). Azpiroz's opinions of China were widely shared, and by the time Vasconcelos became president of UNAM, negative perceptions of Chinese immigrants, reinforced by the revolution's racial pride, were beginning to fuel violence against them (Young 2014). In the chaos that followed the 1910 fall of José Porfirio Díaz's government, the immigrants' hopes for protection and representation from China collapsed, as did the Qing dynasty in 1911. On May 15, 1911, the revolutionary troops of Antonio Madero, led by Francisco "Pancho" Villa, took the city of Torreón, where Chinese immigrants had set up convenience stores, banks, and small agricultural operations. With the assistance of local residents, the troops rounded up and killed some three hundred Chinese people and destroyed their businesses. A commission led by the prominent Chinese diplomat Woo Chung-yen traveled to Mexico to investigate these events and, with the assistance of an Anglo-American law firm, secured the signing of the 1912 Protocol of Indemnity on Chinese Interests (R. Romero 2010, 154). The protocol settled on a compensation of three million one hundred pesos, but the 1913 military coup that installed President Victoriano Huerta ensured that this was never paid (Connelly and Cornejo Bustamante 1992, 43).

From its inception, the Mexican Revolution was closely tied to the politics of race. As early as 1908 Emiliano Zapata, a speaker of Nahuatl, was advocating the land rights of rural indigenous and mestizo people in his home state of Morelos (Horcasitas 1968). In a tense environment saturated by racial politics, economic grievances were directed at ethnic "others." The Chinese community was a convenient target and became an example of a well-established sociological premise: the consolidation of solidarity among insiders entails the simultaneous rejection of outsiders. Galvanized by popular pride in the raza bronce, the revolution found no convenient place for linguistically and visibly distinct foreigners (Sato 2006).

Deeply embedded in Chinese Mexican historical lore is the arrival of the first group of Chinese people in the Valley of Mexicali in 1908. Abandoning the copper mines of Sonora in search of opportunities in the town of Mexicali, 160 Chinese sailed across the Gulf of California to San Felipe and were advised to walk the remaining 121 miles across the state of Baja California to their destination. After three days in temperatures of 125 degrees Fahrenheit, they became disoriented in the desert without a compass and began to die of thirst and exhaustion; only a handful reached Mexicali. The desert where they perished came to be known as the Sierra de los Chinos or El Chinero by locals, who report that those willing to visit this place of tragedy and sorrow have found coins and other objects abandoned by the Chinese pioneers. The former director of the Chinese Association of Mexicali, Eduardo Auyón Gerardo, told me that "when clouds gather over El Chinero, you can still hear their voices screaming for water" (interview, October 7, 2008).

The horrors of El Chinero were prelude to a turbulent period of settlement for the Chinese of Baja California. The size of the community grew through the activities of the Mau Li and Chung Hwa corporations, which by 1921 were operating across Mexico and had contracted between 40,000 and 50,000 Chinese laborers to work in mining, construction, and agriculture (mainly cutting sugarcane and picking cotton). Assisted by the sympathetic immigration policies of Baja California's Governor Esteban Cantú (1915–20), Chinese traders came to dominate niche economies in cities across the state, while making deep commercial inroads into the neighboring state of Sonora and onward into the state of Sinaloa. They manufactured tobacco and other agricultural products, furniture, leather goods, and clothing, all of which were distributed through a network of convenience stores stretching from the town of Culiacán in Sinaloa through Mexicali to San Francisco, laying the foundation of Mexico's commercial infrastructure (Chou 2002, 17).

As noted above, by the mid-1920s Chinese settlers in the Valley of Mexicali outnumbered the local Mexican population (Velázquez Morales 2001, 59; Werne 1980, 16). The tendency of Chinese companies in Mexicali and across Mexico to trade primarily with each other and to employ staff members from within their ethnic community provoked popular resentment and legal action. As in Cuba and Panama, anti-Chinese campaigns in the 1920s and 1930s convinced the federal government to implement laws requiring Chinese businesses to guarantee that 80 percent of their workforces were national citizens.

Public hostility gave rise to protective measures among Chinese mutual aid associations, which since the early 1920s had underpinned the development of the Chinatowns of Mexicali and Mexico City. Many people outside the community perceived the alternative framework of trade, distribution, and finance provided by the Chinese associations (seventeen of which were registered in Mexicali in 1920) as giving Chinese immigrants an unfair advantage. Media articles and pamphlets of the time described the solidarity and mutual aid of the Chinese community as a reflection of its inherent "meanness" and "selfishness" (Monteón González and Trueba Lara 1988, 41; also see J. Romero 1911; Velázquez Morales 1989). *La Frontera* and other northern Mexican newspapers were prominent forums for spreading anti-Chinese sentiment, publishing statements such as: "[The Chinese community] is rejected not for the mere fact that it is Chinese, nor for racial hatred, nor for its color, and much less for its ambition to imitate our Northern neighbors. . . . It is rejected because it is the incarnation of a rotten tree trunk: selfishness. . . . And the selfish Chinese community par excellence sows a bad seed wherever it implants itself" (quoted in Velázquez Morales 2001, 270).

The reputation of Mexico's Chinese communities suffered further as conflicts erupted between supporters of the conservative Manchu Chee Kung Tong faction and the National China League (later the Chinese Nationalist Party), which followed Sun Yat-sen. The two groups undertook violent actions against each other, including the assassination of leaders, which gave the Mexican government a pretext for the expulsion of Chinese people from the country. In the words of President Álvaro Obregón (1920–24), "our office firmly believes in the need to impose order and prevent our country from becoming a theater for the intrigues and assassinations driven by the passions of foreign gangs" (quoted in González Oropeza 1997, 49–50).

Obregón chose his interior minister, Plutarco Elías Calles, to succeed him as president (1924–28), paving the way for the anti-Chinese campaign to expand. Together with his son, the governor of Sonora, Calles endorsed the prohibition of Chinese-Mexican intermarriage and the forced closure of Chinese businesses. In 1924 the Pro-Race Committee (Comité Pro Raza) of Baja California proposed the expulsion of all Chinese people from Mexico, while the Anti-Chinese Committee (Comité Antichino) of Sinaloa backed a law requiring Chinese people to live in districts segregated from the rest of Mexican society. The municipal president of Nogales, Walterio Pesqueira, alleged that "the isolation of the Chinese race is a matter of public interest, considering that they have monopolized all of the local sources of wealth," while his counterpart in the municipality of Huépac proposed abrogating the Treaty of Friendship and Navigation "to ensure the health of la raza" (quoted in González Oropeza 1997, 53, 54).

The first Grand Convention of Anti-Chinese Committees of the Republic of Mexico was held in Nogales in 1925, augmenting the movement's visibility and giving rise to a series of subgroups. These included the Anti-Chinese Youth Subcommittee of Mazatlán, anti-Chinese associations in Durango and San Luis Potosí, and the National Anti-Chinese Workers' League, which declared that Mexicans "find themselves at risk of losing their noble Latin heritage" (quoted in González Oropeza 1997, 55). With the slogan of Mexico for Mexicans, the various groups shared four goals: the prohibition of Chinese immigration, expulsion of illegal Chinese immigrants, prohibition of Chinese-Mexican intermarriage, and establishment of special residential districts for Chinese people. The movement drew inspiration from a concurrent surge of xenophobia in the United States, among whose victims were Mexicans. Manuel González Oropeza notes that "on February 12, 1926, Francisco Martínez wrote to President Calles to suggest the expulsion of all Chinese, whom he categorized as a 'stench,' just as officials in the United States had announced in Brawley, California, in relation to Mexicans; Martínez suggested taking advantage of this idea" (1997, 51).

In the late 1920s the Grand National Pro-Race League (Gran Liga Nacional Pro-Raza) had come to champion the anti-Chinese cause at the national level. The historian Catalina Velázquez Morales has collected the organization's numerous press releases and pamphlets, including one titled "La bestia amarilla" (The yellow beast) that offers the following advice: "Fathers—do not allow your daughters to the get close to the Chinese. Mothers who are proud of your bronze complexion, who carry in your veins the blood of Cuauhtémoc; matrons who have inherited the language of Cortés! Do not mix the blood of jackals with the blood of Incas. How deep is the misery and abundant the filth that Hong Kong has thrown at our shores! For Mexico and our race—if you are a patriot of good stock, be sure this notice circulates profusely throughout the Republic" (Gran Liga Nacional Pro-Raza 1927).

The pamphlet describes the Mexican race as hybrid, yet a resource whose purity should be protected and preserved. Citizens of "good stock" are enjoined to take pride in both their indigenous Latin American ancestry (via Cuauhtémoc) and their Spanish heritage (via Cortés). In the spirit of the Mexican Revolution, indigenous and European ethnicity are placed on equal footing, and both are elevated above the "filth" of Chinese impurity.

Nationalist movements are fertile ground for the reification of race and moralization of place, as China's own revolutionary history attests. Two decades before "La bestia amarilla" was circulated in Mexico, Sun Yat-sen's supporters were imploring Chinese settlers in southeast Asia to limit their foreign commitments, return home, and join the insurgency against the Qing dynasty. A patriotic appeal to racial loyalty permeates the *Geming Ge* (革命歌; Song of the revolution), which nationalist sympathizers promoted among overseas Chinese communities:

> It is hard to be happy all one's life,
> You need but little conscience to feel shame.
> What then is the most shameful matter?
> To forget one's ancestors deserves the greatest hate!
> If not that, then to register as a foreign national,
> Forgetting that you come from Chinese stock. (quoted in Wang G.
>   2000, 69)

The *Geming Ge* offers overseas Chinese settlers a stark choice: return home to fight for the national cause and be exalted, or remain abroad and be hated. Like "La bestia amarilla," it invokes racial stock as a moral compass for orienting its audience to the preferred decision. Both works limit the possible choices to two extreme alternatives that carry momentous consequences and afford no middle ground. If the Chinese revolutionaries tried to force this moral hyperbole on men living in southeast Asia, in Mexico it was local women, writes Peña Delgado, who were forced to choose between the extremes of becoming national "gatekeepers" or "traitors": "In reinforcing women's primary role in the revolutionary project, state-makers simultaneously cast women at two extremes of the moral-political tandem: as traitors of the Mexican state by way of marriage to Chinese men, and as gatekeepers of the revolutionary state by way of marriage to Mexican men. To choose one over the other circumscribed women's relationship to Mexico's revolution" (2012, 10).

Adding further tension to this vitriolic blend of race, nationality, and gender, in the early 1930s the Great Depression forced the mass return of unemployed Mexican men from the United States. Angered and hardened by the expulsion of its citizens, the Mexican government deported around ten thousand Chinese nationals and their descendants, citing violence between rival Chinese gangs and illegal lending and exclusionary hiring practices as the reason (Carr 1973; Rojas Peña 2009). This hardline policy reflected the continuing influence of Calles, who by then had declared himself Mexico's *jefe máximo* (maximum political chief) and had quietly supervised the short presidencies of Emilio Portes Gil (1928–30), Pascual Ortiz Rubio (1930–32), and Abelardo L. Rodríguez (1932–34). Many Chinese immigrants were sent with their Mexican wives and children to Macao and Hong Kong, leaving behind only five thousand Chinese people in Mexico, according to the census of 1940 (Pardiñas 1982, 478–79).

Mexico's rejection of China and its people would have continued into the late 1930s had it not been for the diplomatic skill of Cárdenas. Calles had trusted Cárdenas—they had served together in the military—and expected to manipulate him as he had the previous three presidents (Buchenau 2006). However, Cárdenas gradually removed Calles's allies from office and eventually had Calles arrested and deported to the United States in 1936, where he became acquainted with several known fascists and forged a friendship with Vasconcelos, the designer of UNAM's coat of arms and motto.

Cárdenas sought to reverse many aspects of Mexico's economic and social trajectory, including the treatment of Chinese migrants. In 1937 and 1938, as war broke out between China and Japan, he repatriated four hundred previously expelled Mexican women and a large (but undocumented) number of Mexican Chinese children (Schiavone Camacho 2009, 560; Schuler 1998, 57 and 94). Despite these advances, the Cárdenas administration maintained a restrictive view of Mexican nationhood, which, as Julia Schiavone Camacho writes, denied Chinese men the right to return with their families: "Families that had not split up had to decide whether to do so, since Chinese men remained barred from returning to Mexico. The choice brought immense heartache to families who had wanted to stay unified but saw no other option than to be divided for the well-being of the women and children in a climate of war and uncertainty in China" (2012, 122). Mexico's former economic consul to China, Juan José Ling, was personally affected by these developments:

My grandfather moved from Taishan in Guangdong Province to Tampico during Mexico's oil boom in the early twentieth century. He met my grandmother there, but they were forced to go to China when things turned nasty for Chinese people in the early 1930s. My grandmother finally returned to Tampico with her seven children, but not my grandfather, on one of the ships sent by Lázaro Cárdenas at the end of the 1930s. One of the children was my mother. In my community people were basically ashamed to be Chinese, and I think many still are. Have you noticed that in many photographs and in public, even recently, Chinese people like to wear sunglasses? That's to blend in better, because apart from our eyes we don't look that different to Mexicans. In my whole family I am the only one who has married a woman of Chinese descent, and the only one with an interest in Chinese culture. The rest all wanted to be more Mexican. (interview, June 8, 2010)

Like thousands of Chinese Mexicans, Ling's family endured forced migration, division, and ethnic discrimination. Their predicament was not helped by a steady flow of postwar movies, television, and radio productions (many imported from the United States) that negatively portrayed Chinese people and their government. Witnessing this renewed hostility, Ling recalls that for at least three decades after Mao Zedong established the People's Republic of China (PRC) in 1949, Chinese Mexicans were perceived to be associated with communism. As the historian Wang Gungwu writes, "after 1949, especially in the anticommunist nation-states, every Chinese was suspected of being a communist, or at least a sympathizer, whose loyalty could never be trusted" (2000, 82). Nothing was further from the truth for most Mexicans of Chinese ancestry, particularly those who cited their rejection of communism as ground for their being repatriated from China. Championing their cause in the 1950s, the political activist Ramón Lay Mazo argued that thousands of people who had been expelled from Mexico were stranded in China, hoping for the Mexican government to save them from communism (Schiavone Camacho 2012, 145–46).

Although *China Popular*—a Spanish-language magazine that supported the Chinese government—was available in Mexico in the 1950s, its voice was drowned out by a wave of anticommunist literature. Citing

China as the epitome of political depravity, articles such as "If Communism Comes to Mexico" (1961, 9) were widely distributed in rural and urban Mexico by the U.S. Christian Anti-Communism Crusade to show "what would happen to the Mexican people in the event of a Communist takeover." Mexico's first ambassador to the PRC, Eugenio Anguiano Roch, believed that the persistence of these fears into the 1970s was inflammatory and damaging to bilateral relations, and after his return to Mexico he attempted to dispel them (interview, June 9, 2010). Between 1973 and 1980 he tirelessly lobbied the Ministry of Education, urging it to permit Chinese students to study Spanish at the Colegio de México. The ministry finally granted two hundred visas on the condition that the Chinese students live in a designated dormitory with minimal public contact, and in this way be impeded from spreading communism.

Mexican fiction also portrayed China and Mexicans of Chinese descent in a negative light, focusing on the criminal activities of gangsters and opium dealers. Rafael Bernal's (1969) novel *El Complot Mongól* (The Mongolian conspiracy) describes the corruption of the Mexican political system, which is surpassed only by the inadequacies and moral shortcomings of the protagonist, a Chinese Mexican police detective named Filiberto García. Meanwhile, history textbooks made no mention of Mexico's Chinese diaspora and—according to Yolanda Trápaga Delfín, a China specialist at UNAM—generally still do not (interview, June 16, 2010). Both the Mexican and Cuban Revolutions were underpinned by class struggle, but as Gerardo Rénique (2000 and 2003) has shown, narrow nationalistic notions of racial identity have continued to shape Mexico's development. This has complicated the lives of Chinese people in Mexico, as have political differences between the two countries—from Mexican anticommunism in the mid- to late twentieth century to recent tensions over the so-called disloyal competition of China's state-backed manufacturers (see chapter 2).

Like their Cuban counterparts, leaders of Mexico's Chinese community are attempting to leverage China's growth to advance their interests. But unlike the situation in Cuba, Chinese people and their descendants in Mexico face public opposition to the expansion of their transpacific commercial ties. Journalists have fervently described the damage inflicted on Mexican industries as Chinese imports—both legal and contraband—flood into the country and deepen the bilateral deficit. Fear of public criticism has discouraged state and private-sector engagement with the Chinese diaspora, impeding the development of consensual efforts to regulate its deepening business partnerships with China. The next section argues that this vertical disjuncture has fueled the expansion of informal Sino-Mexican trade, evident in Mexico City's notorious Tepito district.

CHINA GOES GLOBAL: PRODUCTS, PEOPLE, AND PERCEPTIONS

China's unparalleled economic growth, recorded by the World Bank (2015a) as averaging 9.3 percent between 1980 and 2014, is sustained by a massive flow of exports to the world. Overseas Chinese communities have played an important role in familiarizing mainland suppliers with foreign markets. To consolidate a sense of belonging, loyalty, and Chinese cultural identity among emigrants, in 1978 the State Council of China provided new funding for the Overseas Chinese Affairs Office (OCAO). The office had been established more than sixty years earlier, shortly after Sun Yat-sen's nationalist forces overthrew the last Qing emperor and founded the Republic of China in 1911. Initially OCAO focused on extending diplomatic protection to Chinese expatriates, but it increasingly dedicated resources to promoting their cultural affinity and national allegiance.

Wang notes that prior to the Republican period, successive imperial regimes professed that overseas travel could erode subjects' moral commitment to their homeland and discouraged anything more than temporary "sojourning": "Throughout the centuries since the Song dynasty (since the tenth century), the Chinese who went overseas in the ports across the South China Sea were not supposed to have left China permanently. If they were good sons who were filial and loved their homes, they would always have planned to return. Thus when they were away from China, they would not have stopped being Chinese. This normative approach clearly represented a view from the top, an elitist view describing an ideal type. There was ample evidence throughout those centuries that it was often not practicable, and often not true" (Wang G. 2000, 44–45).

Struggling to publicly justify the growth of enduring overseas Chinese communities, imperial lawmakers had categorized émigrés as *huaqiao* (华侨), a term borrowed from classical poetry to describe dutiful foreign service while temporarily sojourning. The creation of OCAO under the Republican government went much further, signaling for the first time that Chinese leaders not only approved the practice of overseas work and settlement but also "confirmed it as a patriotic obligation" (Wang G. 2000, 70). This break with the past nevertheless sustained a quintessentially imperial ethos: Chinese people, wherever they may live, should remain trusted subjects of their motherland.

Today, OCAO assists overseas Chinese communities to create opportunities for trade with China, to overcome linguistic and cultural misunderstandings, and ostensibly to build "harmony with the governments and communities that host them" (Minor 2010). OCAO's Mexican activities (discussed below) range from trade facilitation to advocacy of the One-China Policy, but the prospect of harmonious public- and private-sector relationships remains distant. A remark made in 2008 by China's then consul general in Tijuana, Gao Shoujian, remains true today: the convergence of economic competition with persisting social and diplomatic tensions constitutes a formidable challenge to any Chinese effort to build trust with the Mexican government, let alone with Mexican customers (interview, November 5, 2008).

Mexico's trade deficit with China is the largest in Latin America, surpassing $60 billion in 2014 (United Nations Commodity Trade Statistics Database 2015). For more than a decade, a pervasive effect of the economic imbalance has been a homogenizing tendency in the Mexican public sphere to equate Chinese businesses, products, and people with the global ambitions of the Chinese state (Haro Navejas 2007, 457). This tendency is strengthened by the frequent appearance in the mass media of domestic and foreign articles critical of human rights abuses in Chinese state-operated factories, the substandard quality of the products they manufacture, and the unfair competition they represent for Mexican businesses (González Alvarado 2008; *La Prensa* 2005). As illustrated by the assault on the Chinese travel agency described at the beginning of this book, Chinese resident in Mexico are viewed by many as the foot soldiers of China's commercial invasion.

According to Mexico's most recent census (conducted in 2010), the country is home to 6,655 Chinese-born individuals, the twelfth largest foreign group. The Chinese embassy counts 20,000 Mexicans of Chinese origin, and community leaders report that Mexicali and Tijuana alone are home to some 60,000 Chinese people (including Mexican-born descendants of Chinese immigrants). Even in light of these informal reports, this is a small populace compared to the 738,103 expatriates from the United States, the largest foreign group (Instituto Nacional de Estadísticas y Geografía 2010).

Unofficial reports estimate the number of U.S. citizens residing in Mexico to exceed one million, many of them unregistered. These figures are not surprising considering that in 2014 U.S.-Mexico trade amounted to $537 billion (more than seven times the value of China-Mexico trade) (United Nations Commodity Trade Statistics Database 2015). Commercial ties, though, are only part of the explanation. The other part concerns the aging U.S. population: in 2005 some 250,000 U.S. senior citizens were living in gated villages on Mexico's Pacific coast, where Spanish is barely spoken and "you can't really tell you're in Mexico" ("Retiring Americans: Go South, Old Man" 2005). These communities are growing, promoted by a Mexican government plan to attract some five million U.S. retirees by 2025 (Oppenheimer 2010). This objective reveals a sharp divergence of public attitudes toward U.S. and Chinese migrants, though the reasons for this extend beyond historical familiarity and trade integration and other economic considerations. As a student at the Autonomous University of Baja California explained, "Even though we hate the gringos, we wish we could be like them. It bothers us that they look down on us, so we pass this feeling on, especially to Chinese people" (interview, October 31, 2008).

It does not require a detailed investigation to reveal that multiple ethnic origins, historical backgrounds, political affiliations, and economic aspirations have produced considerable diversity in Mexico's Chinese diaspora. Communities descended from Chinese migrant laborers of the nineteenth and twentieth centuries, for instance, did not automatically embrace the 1949 establishment of the PRC and have generally maintained only distant relations with its diplomatic missions. For thousands of Chinese Mexican entrepreneurs, diplomatic indifference has stemmed less from political considerations than a reluctance to expose their blend of local, global, formal, and informal business activities to the scrutiny and regulatory designs of Chinese and Mexican authorities. For their part, the governments of both countries have shown little interest in Mexico's Chinese community or even in each other, instead focusing what little cooperation they have on the upper echelons of transnational business. Their failure to find bilateral solutions to Mexico's chronic trade deficit with China has not as yet provoked serious efforts from Mexico's federal government to harness the entrepreneurial capacities of resident Chinese communities.

Identifying missed opportunities for engagement, Chinese entrepreneurs and their descendants in Mexico City—as in Havana—have begun to develop commercial initiatives with partners in China. Conscious of these thickening international ties, the Chinese embassy has pressured resident Chinese communities to register their activities officially, advance opportunities for Chinese firms through local political and business connections, and explicitly articulate support for the PRC's One-China Policy. In response, the Confederation of Chinese Associations of Mexico (CACHIMEX) has sought open endorsement from the Mexican and Chinese governments for its commercial expos and trade fairs. However, as noted in chapter 2, official support from either government has been hindered by the political sensitivity of Mexico's trade deficit with China and popular perceptions that such activities are dedicated to importing Chinese products—legally and otherwise—into Mexico.

Chinese communities in Mexico—like those in Cuba—have faced pressure to integrate into their surrounding economic and legal environments, but unlike in Cuba, in Mexico the pressure has been intensified by commercial competition on the ground. Cuban industries do not compete with China, especially in the commercial sector—which prior to the revival of Sino-Cuban relations in the 1990s relied on consumer goods imported from the Soviet Union. The Cuban state's dependence on allies for manufactured goods, combined with the U.S. embargo's detrimental impact on economic diversification, has produced a vacuum that Chinese products fill without opposition. No such vacuum exists in Mexico, where industrialization in the 1970s and subsequent market reforms underpinned the growth of manufacturing to meet U.S. demand for consumer goods. Since the 1980s Mexico's liberal democratic governments have remained committed to free trade in spite of the recent wrangling over customs tariffs on Chinese exports and allegations of disloyal competition.

Extending to the activities of Chinese importers resident in Mexico, anti-Chinese allegations emanate mainly from small and medium-sized

Mexican enterprises unable to compete with the flood of inexpensive Chinese consumer goods. These sectors perceive a chronic lack of fairness and transparency in the apparent ethnic exclusivity of Chinese trade fairs, the labor conditions and low wages in Chinese factories, the piracy of traditional Mexican handicrafts, and the seemingly ungovernable expansion of illegally imported Chinese textiles, shoes, toys, office equipment, and steel products.

Criticism of Chinese people in Mexico has drawn on long-standing beliefs about Chinese cultural and economic practices. This legacy did not go unnoticed by the historian Jorge Gómez Izquierdo, when the Chinese Mexican drug trafficker Zhenli Ye Gon was arrested in 2007: "Prejudice comes to us from a past era, in which the Chinese community in Mexico was the object of resentment, jealousy, and violent assault carried out by nationalistic groups backed by a range of state institutions. In the mass-mediated lynching of [Zhenli] Ye Gong, a series of Mexican social perceptions of China and its people have reappeared. Prejudice and ignorance, as always, go hand in hand when mobilization draws on the formation of phobias. . . . The racist hostility toward 'the Chinaman' is not new in our country" (2007, 5–6).

Media reports have perpetuated essentialist portrayals of Chinese culture, suggesting that Chinese people in Mexico are "reserved, because their culture forces them to be . . . they are determined to generate their own sources of employment" (G. López 2009). Some articles, Internet sites, and radio broadcasts are overtly malicious, criticizing the disloyal, opportunistic, and dishonest nature of Chinese business activities, which have allowed "China to invade us with its products through disloyal competition" ("¿Y la soberanía?" 2007; also see El Economista 2008; A. Simón 2007). Chinese immigrants and their descendants are publicly associated with Mexico's diminishing productivity and competitiveness as local producers are squeezed out of the market (Páramo 2008). They are also publicly accused of importing counterfeit goods, including traditional Mexican handicrafts such as blankets and pottery for the domestic and tourist markets.[1]

Just as the xenophobic pamphlets of the 1930s urged Mexicans to ostracize the "yellow beasts" whose "selfish" and "mean" mutual aid activities gave them an unfair economic advantage, contemporary Mexican websites—as discussed in chapter 2—carry inflammatory titles such as

"Pinche Chinos" (Damn Chinese), "Fourteen Reasons Not to Buy Chinese Products This Christmas," and "Buying Fraud from China." As Chinese Mexican businesses and associations become more active in establishing commercial partnerships with mainland Chinese exporters, the historical parallels are deepening. A Tijuana taxi driver shed light on local perceptions of China's impact:

> It's sad because we were proud of our industrial advancement, but now we've been undercut. I know this is the free market and globalization, and I accept that there will be winners and losers, but people like me are the losers. I was a manager in a factory making microchips, well paid, and in charge of a team of thirty-five workers. Now look at me: driving a taxi. Not only have Chinese workers taken our jobs, but the products we used to make are now being sold to us, and the Chinese people here in Tijuana are helping to make it happen. To answer your question, yes, I do blame them. Chinese people have come here, set up their import businesses, and we've suffered the consequences. (interview, December 20, 2011)

An emerging focal point of face-to-face tension between Mexican critics and Chinese vendors is Tepito, a notorious outlet for unregistered merchandise on the eastern perimeter of Mexico City's historic center. As early as the 1870s Tepito was known as the "Thieves Market," where "stolen merchandise could be sold three months after the theft, without fear of prosecution" (Piccato 2001, 37). By the mid-1970s the Tepito district had evolved into a labyrinth of tents and stalls (known as *tianguis*) dedicated to the sale and bartering of clothing, food, live animals, and practically anything else (figure 4.2). By 2006 it had grown to more than seventy-five city blocks, accommodating some 150,000 vendors (Mondragón 2006). It has since expanded to a hundred blocks and 175,000 retailers, who—according to a representative of 500 vendors—perceive little need for external law enforcement: "The police leave us alone because we have our own security systems and our own rules for organizing the district" (interview, June 21, 2010). Research by John Cross (1998) and Carlos Alba Vega (2012) confirms this point, noting sophisticated modes of representation and advocacy developed by Mexican street vendors to protect their commercial interests. Another Tepito organizer put it this way: "our basic needs are more important than official legal regula-

FIGURE 4.2 The informal market of Tepito, which is expanding into Mexico City's historic center, May 2012. Photo by the author.

tions; street vending is a safety valve" (quoted in Mondragón). Former Economic Consul Ling agrees: "Mexicans should realize that their informal sector, which constitutes something like 40 percent of business in the country, is something they need. The official figure of 5 percent unemployment is a blatant lie. There is an abundance of people we call *nini*: *ni trabajan ni estudian* [neither work nor study]. They need informality to survive. The real problem is the lack of government support for education, training, Mexican companies—which should be actively finding new markets, including in China—and creating jobs. Without Tepito, Mexico would be in trouble. There'd probably be another revolution!" (interview, June 8, 2010).

Tepito's steady expansion since the 1870s demonstrates its ongoing appeal for thousands of Mexicans in search of inexpensive consumer goods, but not everybody perceives its value as a safety valve for averting "another revolution." Residents of the adjacent historic center, for instance, contend that tourism to their neighborhood and the commercial viability of their businesses are being negatively affected. Unable to compete with low-priced contraband, owners of the historic center's 17,670 registered enterprises are increasingly converting their shops into warehouses for the 40,000 unregistered merchants who have spilled over from Tepito (M. López 2006a). At the forefront of the campaign against the expansion of Tepito is the Unión del Centro Histórico, which has lobbied the city government to place restrictions on where vendors can set up their stalls. The Unión points out that some 80 percent of merchandise sold in the historic center is contraband from China, and that the street vendors who sell these products do not pay taxes to help pay for the physical maintenance and legal governance of the district.

The Unión alleges that government officials have taken bribes to allow some 17,000 Chinese and Korean immigrants to illegally take up residence in Tepito and establish 2,500 registered businesses to import contraband from China (Bazán 2005). According to the Unión's president, Victor Cisneros Taja, "the historic center has been kidnapped and is a lawless territory" that could follow Tepito's lead in becoming a safe haven for drug-related activities (quoted in S. González 2006; also see M. López 2007). Local authorities, he lamented in a 2010 interview, are not willing to intervene:

> We've raised the problem with the city government, but the officials have a convenient excuse: contraband is a federal problem, so not their responsibility. This is actually not the case, because it's written into law that if something is going on in the streets under your jurisdiction, then it's your responsibility. Because of Tepito over 80 percent of what is sold in the historic center is contraband, nearly all of it from China. You can see the Chinese vendors in their stalls in Tepito. They used to do this in the [historic] center, but in October 2007 we started to get them out. They mostly sell women's goods because those items sell fast—handbags, watches, shoes, and clothes that are copies of brand names. We're talking about organized crime. There are showrooms in China where Mexicans go to look at products. The Chinese even pay for the twenty-hour charter flight to go over and look at their merchandise, and you can simply pay for the products at Western Union here in Mexico City. We recently denounced Western Union for this in the press, and they came out a few days later with a public statement saying that it's not their responsibility. Apparently it's nobody's responsibility. (interview, June 18, 2010)

To interrupt the flow of Chinese contraband, Cisneros Taja sent a list to the city government of 250 businesses that illegally rent their shops to unregistered traders (Solis Peña 2006). Constant lobbying by the Unión and thirty-two prominent business leaders to strengthen the Law of Merchant Establishments (Ley de Establecimientos Mercantiles) finally led the city government, on October 12, 2007, to order vendors to remove their stalls from the thirty-four restored blocks of Mexico City's historic center (Osorio 2007). To diminish resistance from the informal sector, Cisneros secured a commitment from registered businesses that they would also remove merchandise from public spaces outside their shops and stores. Street vendors, he argued, should be relocated to delineated open-air plazas so that the historic center could once again become orderly, "like it was in the era of the conquest" (quoted in Osorio and Díaz 2007).

Unimpressed with this vision of history, representatives of the informal sector confronted Cisneros in a public forum, arguing: "We street vendors are the pride of Mexico. . . . We do not want more commercial plazas; street stalls are better because people can buy from us as they walk by" (quoted in Páramo 2007). To build public support for their case, informal traders—the majority of whom are Mexican—turned on the mayor of Mexico City, Marcelo Ebrard, and accused him of conspiring with Chinese businesspeople in his plan to redevelop the historic center:

> They [government officials] want to expel the people into the street, and give their territory over to companies that will build large commercial centers, but not for the informal vendors or even for registered businesses, but rather for the Chinese. Marcelo Ebrard, the interviewees say, is destroying the local informal sector; he is going to take it away by force on October 12, from one day to the next, leaving nearly 10,000 street vendors with no way to feed their families. The local government is complicit, but everyone loses out. The only people benefiting from the expropriation, with the protection of the city government, are the Chinese businessmen who will find ways to sell contraband and their merchandise freely. . . . [Ebrard] is helping Asian networks to invade our capital city. (*Uno más Uno* 2007)

It is well known that Mexico City's government is eager to accept Chinese investment in tourism, communications, and information technology (Courtade 2013), but the historic center's street vendors are concerned about the influx of Chinese products and people that might accompany this investment. Alleging collusion between the city government and Chinese businesspeople, the vendors have publicly distanced themselves from Chinese merchandise, which is widely associated with the massive growth of the informal sector and its deleterious economic impact (M. López 2006b). Cheap Chinese-made blank DVDs (1.9 pesos, or 15 U.S. cents, each) and high-speed copying devices are believed to be responsible for the annual production of some sixty million musical CDs in Tepito, which are subsequently distributed around the country and throughout Latin America (Aguiar 2012, 37; Padgett 2005; Sierra 2004).

Ling argues that allegations like these use China as a scapegoat: "Actually China produces much more than cheap goods, and the Mexican Chinese community isn't that involved in piracy. Ninety percent of piracy is operated by Mexicans, including those who import goods from China and then change labels to 'made in USA' or 'made in Mexico.' To escape the attention they blame the Chinese community" (interview, June 8, 2010). Ling's contention is supported by evidence that Chinese contraband is smuggled and distributed in partnership with Mexicans, including unscrupulous officials on the country's southern border with Guatemala and northern border with the United States (M. González 2005; Ochoa León 2008). As one report has it: "Whether it be with shoes, clothes, 'brand name' perfumes, or 10 percent of the value of fake jewelry, the Chinese traffickers pay the officials to smuggle their merchandise during the night through the Suchiate River [on Mexico's border with Guatemala]. . . . Most of the Chinese mafia operating in Tepito are actually owners of distribution centers" (J. García 2008).

Cisneros Taja of the Unión del Centro Histórico does not deny Mexican collusion, but he argues that it results from the irresistible overtures of Chinese traffickers and providers. The latter, he says, pay Mexican "big sellers" to visit factories in Guangdong and Zhejiang Provinces, buy cheap consumer goods in bulk, and sell them in Tepito and other organized street markets (interview, June 18, 2010). They have become especially attracted to the city of Yiwu in Zhejiang, which allegedly operates "as a sort of 'Wall Street' for the counterfeiting industry" (Fingleton 2008, 41). This arrangement gives Chinese wholesalers a presence in Mexican street markets to which their access would otherwise be limited (Ellis 2012, 71).

The informal networks that enable the movement of undeclared products from factories in Guangdong and Zhejiang across Mexican borders and into street markets are expansive, robust, and evolving. By 2014 Cisneros saw evidence that Tepito's illicit supply network was changing, and for his own safety he stopped campaigning against it:

> Since we met in 2010, middlemen have become less prominent because Chinese traders now have a foothold and *dan cara* [show their face] directly in Tepito. Some of the old guard don't like it, but the Chinese distributors have bought their way into retail and even have their own building for coordinating supplies from China. In a place like Mexico, where there is little enforcement of the law, they can do what they like. . . . The Partido Revolucionario Democrático [Party of the Democratic Revolution, PRD] asked if I'd like to represent it, but it became dangerous. My denunciation of the city government for not enforcing commercial laws shone a light on a bigger problem. Drugs and arms are being traded, and a lot of money is changing hands between criminals and local politicians. I wasn't trying to expose this, but once you look under the rock you can't help uncovering things. The city government ran a campaign to trash my name, and it affected my family. I'll take on anybody one on one, but we're talking about fighting an enormous monster. You can't win, so it's better not to try. And safer. (interview, May 30, 2014)

Counterfeit merchandise is one strand in Tepito's intricate web of informal goods and services, sustained by connections that have flourished in step with a well-documented lack of regulatory enforcement. The resulting scenario, described by Cisneros Taja as a "culture of impunity," has permitted the expansion of illicit trade in everything from consumer goods to narcotics and arms. It has also further eroded public trust in the state's ability to govern (evident in the Latin American Public Opinion Project and National Electoral Institute surveys noted in chapter 2), particularly since public servants appear to be bound up in the "enormous monster" of organized crime.

Policy recommendations for stemming illicit commerce range from mandatory taxation of bank deposits through the system of Impuesto Empresarial a Tasa Única (Unified Business Tax Rate) to arming customs officials and police officers with more powerful weapons to combat offenders (Ayón et al. 2009; Dussel Peters 2009; Organisation for Economic Co-Operation and Development 2009, 59). These and other proposals reflect the enormity of Mexico's informal sector, but they have placed growing emphasis on negative rather than positive reinforcement: sticks instead of carrots.

Fighting the hard edge of organized crime has entangled Mexican police in de facto warfare along with the armed forces, deployed by President Felipe Calderón in 2012 to combat drug cartels. Critics argue that this strategy and the broader U.S.-financed Plan Mexico, also known as the Mérida Initiative, are counterproductive because they have militarized police and security services that are themselves implicated in violations of the law (Behrens 2009). They also leave few resources for policing the softer dimensions of the informal sector, a point that has not escaped the attention of sensationalist reporters eager to expose Chinese involvement in Mexico's black market:

> Could it be that pursuing one kind of criminal network has obscured the pursuit of another, which is responsible for even more damage by causing unemployment, putting the textile, shoe, electronics, toy, and accessory industries out of business, and furthermore, operating in a totally illegal way in the very center of the Republic? . . . If we compare the damage caused by the traditional criminals of Tepito, however associated with cartels they were, with the damage caused by the Chinese, the differences are enormous, gigantic, because the latter are leaving millions of Mexicans with nothing to eat, nowhere to work, and without opportunities to develop, and nobody stops them. (Arellano 2013)

To pin Mexico's structural problems on Chinese contraband is facile, but the allegation that criminal cartels have drawn police attention away from the broader informal sector merits consideration. There is evidence that the allocation of resources to hard-line mano dura law enforcement has compromised the resilience of civilian police forces and impeded more socially engaged containment strategies (Casey-Maslen 2014, 13).

Among the casualties of socially disengaged policing is vertical trust between state and society, already fragile in Mexico owing to successive electoral scandals, economic mismanagement, and collusion between politicians and criminal networks. A more constructive policy orientation to Mexico's informal sector and China's role in it would set out to understand, engage, and harness the social capital underpinning its cooperative networks. This proposition has recently been tested in the northern state of Baja California, where local government initiatives have tried to accommodate unregistered trade in regulated street markets and an official chamber of commerce. Baja California is a historical settling place of Chinese people in Mexico, and the Chinese associations of the region have long been a hub of regional business connections—registered and otherwise. Identifying and collaborating with the leaders of these associations has opened a channel of community engagement for the state government and revealed the practical benefits of culturally sensitive policy design.

The next section draws on research I conducted in Tijuana and Mexicali between 2008 and 2012 to examine how Mexico's oldest Chinese associations are forging new partnerships both in China and with the Baja California state government. Resulting as much from a gradual process of relationship building as from more immediate economic goals, these partnerships have the added capacity to overcome popular distrust built up over more than a century.

CHINA GOES LOCAL: THE CHINESE ASSOCIATIONS OF MEXICALI AND TIJUANA

The problems endured by Chinese people in Mexico City have also emerged in the northern state of Baja California, where a vicious circle of hostility and protection has long revolved around the region's Chinese associations. Despite these conditions, geographic and legislative distance from federal politics has afforded government officials in Baja California more room than their peers in the capital to reach out to the associations. The presence of Chinese people in the state for over a century has favored this process, since their associations in the cities of Mexicali and Tijuana have provided a longstanding institutional platform for official communication.

MEXICALI

From 1990 until 2006 Eduardo Auyón Gerardo served as president of the Chinese Association of Mexicali, a position he used to initiate communication with outward-looking commercial exporters in China. In 2001 his efforts to connect Chinese exporters with Mexican retail networks were recognized by OCAO, which appointed him as one of its thirty-two worldwide "assessors." Providing a stable nexus for bilateral trade, together with the related advertising, matchmaking, and visas, have made Auyón (as he is known) a key node of contact for entrepreneurs from both sides. Building commercial networks under the auspices of OCAO, he says, has provided a robust and enduring framework for business development:

> The important thing is security. Some Chinese businesses have shipped their products over only to find that the market has turned against them because of exaggerated media reports about product safety and competition with Mexican producers. As an assessor for the Overseas Chinese Affairs Office I am responsible for selecting trustworthy clients who will follow through with their commitments. This has worked very well for us with electronic products and home appliances. Mexicali is on the same latitude as the Sahara Desert, so we are sourcing a new line of powerful air conditioners under our "Kooling Air" and "Dragón Refrigeraciones" brands and selling these through the network. (interview, October 7, 2008)

Auyón was born in Zhongshan, Guangdong, shortly after his Chinese father and Mexican mother were expelled from Chiapas, Mexico, in the 1930s. In Zhongshan they reestablished themselves as small traders, but they lost their business in 1949 when the communist government seized power. Again facing political hostility, they migrated to Macao, where Auyón studied visual arts. He eagerly seized an opportunity to visit his brother in Mexicali in 1960 and soon became one of Baja California's foremost painters of traditional Chinese and Chinese-Mexican themes (figure 4.3). His trademark series of celestial horses drew acclaim, enabling him to work his way into the executive ranks of Baja California's School of Fine Arts. Among Auyón's students were the school's former director and the secretary of education of Baja California, people he later drew on to support cultural exchanges with China, such as a visit by forty members of the China Central Opera and a series of artistic expositions in the 1980s. "These relationships," he says, "gave me a platform for making contacts in China. . . . I have blood from both countries, and

FIGURE 4.3 Eduardo Auyón Gerardo's renowned mural on the outside of a Mexicali nursery school, whose students are mostly Chinese or descendants of Chinese immigrants. Photo by the author.

I've always wanted to be a bridge between them" (interview, November 9, 2008).

Auyón's aspiration to become a "bridge" between Mexico and China is no doubt stimulated by his fragmented family history, but as David Palumbo-Liu writes, among Chinese and other diasporic communities "there is an abiding possibility that the cultural identification with home is more than (merely) sentimental" (2007, 283). For Auyón, the gradual construction of bilateral ties has the added advantage of increasing market opportunities to import Chinese products. This is evident in the delegations of forty to fifty Mexican businesspeople (mostly of Chinese descent) that he brings four times each year to Beijing, Shanghai, and Guangzhou.

The delegations visit important historical and cultural sites in China, but their primary focus is the Fair of Canton. Sponsored by the government of Guangdong and the Chinese Ministry of Commerce, the fair is China's largest trade convention, bringing together thousands of the country's leading exporters. Each year the fair has a theme, such as medicine or interior design, around which Auyón designs his trips. At the fair, the Mexican visitors contract suppliers, collect product catalogues, and organize visits for Chinese business partners to Baja California. "Last year [2007]," explained Auyón, "we arranged for slightly over a hundred Chinese businesspeople we had met at the fair to visit trade expos that we organized in Mexico. The Chinese Association is not a government organization, but we work through the Chinese consulate in Tijuana and the Mexican embassy in Beijing to arrange the visas" (interview, November 9, 2008).

Throughout his career, Auyón has cultivated relationships to facilitate cultural and commercial initiatives between Mexico and China. In 2004 he began arranging meetings for the governor of Baja California, Eugenio Elorduy Walther, with Chinese counterparts such as the governor of Jiangsu Province, Liang Baohua. When President Hu Jintao visited Mexico in 2005 to discuss strategies for reducing the trade imbalance, he recognized Auyón's leadership in facilitating new business linkages. The government of Baja California praised the potential benefits of these connections during National Immigration Week in October 2008. Seven Mexican states participated in the festivities, but the Baja California branch of the National Institute of Migration (Instituto Nacional de Migración, INAMI) dedicated the week specifically to Chinese immigration, holding all related events and ceremonies in the main hall of the Chinese Association of Mexicali (figure 4.4). The city's mayor, Rodolfo Valdez Gutiérrez, described the Chinese community as "a motor of the local economy" (Mejía 2008), while Javier Reynoso Nuño, Baja California's delegate to INAMI, promised to simplify the process of visa acquisition for relatives of local Chinese people (*La Crónica* 2008).

The Baja California government first showed its interest in working with Auyón by sponsoring Chinese festivals, parades, and marketplaces. These initial activities, he says, have matured into broader public-private partnerships:

> The Baja California government wanted to work more closely with China, so we set up the Sister City relationship between Mexicali and Nanjing in 1991. In 2005 when Hu Jintao came to Mexico I met him personally, and the Mexican government started to see our community as a bridge to China. We created the Chamber of Chinese Enterprises of the Northwest [in 2010]. The Chamber takes advantage of the relationships we've built up with the Baja California government and businesses in the area to export Mexican food and other products to

FIGURE 4.4 The headquarters of the Chinese Association of Mexicali. Photo by the author.

China, and to promote Chinese investment in Mexico in the copper mining and the energy sectors. (interview, December 19, 2011)

The Chamber of Chinese Enterprises coordinates the activities of some four thousand businesspeople living in the states of Baja California, Sonora, Coahuila, and Chihuahua. As well as working with the Baja California government, it also benefits from the logistical support of OCAO's Guangdong office, which views such initiatives as an opportunity to advance the Chinese government's worldwide aspiration to become "the central force of the Chinese community" (Barabantseva 2005, 17). Through the Chamber, Auyón aims to "generate a bridge to support commerce between Chinese entrepreneurs and producers in Asia and those in this region of Mexico," particularly in the maquiladora and automotive sectors (Minor 2010).

Embedded in his dislocated personal history, Auyón's attempts to build connections between Mexico and China resonate with OCAO's more overtly instrumental goals. Overlapping personal pursuits and political strategies, writes Khachig Tölölyan, are a common feature of diasporic communities, which have often been complicit in the projects of the nation-state (1991 and 1996). Indeed, as Palumbo-Liu observes, the concept of diaspora entails not only "longing for home, but political strategizing for a nation-state.... Historically the notion of diasporic identity (a shared disseminated/dispersed identity) was in large part a compensation for the loss of a state. Diaspora was precisely the condition of statelessness read as homelessness. It mourned deeply that loss, yet retained the possibility of its recovery or re-creation" (2007, 283).

Whether or not OCAO aspires to expand the global reach of the Chinese nation-state, Auyón believes his work serves Mexico by helping to place its products in the Chinese market and attracting Chinese investors to copper mining projects and renewable energy initiatives in Mexicali's emerging Silicon Border complex. His nephew, Alfonso Auyón, a businessman who works in the U.S. border town of Calexico, shares his uncle's vision of win-win cooperation: "We've been looking at how we can export products to China, like tequila, abalone, beets, and shark fins for soup and medicine. We're also working with Chinese investors in Mexican copper mining in Chihuahua and the central states. On the other side of the coin, we're always looking for opportunities to help Chinese exporters enter the Mexican market, and where possible the U.S. market. It's important that the benefits flow both ways.... We're Mexican as well as Chinese, and the last thing we want is to be attacked for being against Mexico somehow" (interview, December 21, 2011). Mutually beneficial outcomes are sorely needed for both Mexico and its Chinese communities, whose difficulties stem largely from public perceptions that they have monopolized economic opportunities rather than extending them beyond their tight-knit business networks. Support from Baja California politicians, their Chinese counterparts, and OCAO may prove decisive in this regard, as institutionalized cooperation would enable the diversification and formalization of previously narrow trade ties and reduce perceptions of unfairness and illegality. Conscious of the power of perceptions, Auyón has undertaken a media campaign to publicly demonstrate the mutual benefits of Sino-Mexican cooperation brokered by Mexicali's Chinese community. Luis Ongay Flores, director of the Institute of Cultural Research at the Mexicali Museum, has observed this firsthand:

Some time ago Auyón donated part of his collection of Chinese-Mexican artifacts to the museum, and every so often he visits with Chinese government officials, Mexican politicians, and an entourage of photographers. I don't really know what they want, besides to snap some photos together. I guess they do their business and then have a symbolic moment for the press. The museum is a symbol of Mexicali's multicultural heritage and of human ties between China and Mexico in general, so it makes for a good visual backdrop. When those photos appear in the press in China and in Mexico, they demonstrate respect for local history and culture. (interview, December 21, 2011)

The photographs imply that Mexico's Chinese community is ensuring the continuity of a historical human connection, and in the process doing its part to advance Mexican national interests. This message is not trivial, especially in light of the negative reactions to the Chinese diaspora that China's growing impact has provoked. Hostility has taken an especially visible form in Tijuana, where the city's Chinese association has been overwhelmed by the growing frequency of attacks on its members' businesses.

TIJUANA

The Chinese Association of Tijuana, 135 miles west of Mexicali, has also positioned itself as an intermediary of bilateral trade. Its secretary general, Willy Liu Ke Wei, was a key lobbyist in a local effort to persuade the airline Aeroméxico to operate a direct flight between Shanghai and Tijuana. The effort paid off, and in May 2008 the new route was launched with the ambition of attracting 30,000 Chinese tourists per year, inspiring Liu to set up a travel agency catering to Chinese entrepreneurs exploring opportunities in Mexico. The agency set out to generate new Chinese trade and investment at a time when the global financial crisis had reportedly caused the earnings of Baja California's Chinese businesses to decline by 30 percent (G. López 2009).

To stimulate business partnerships Liu initially focused on building Chinese and Mexicans' understanding of each others' cultural traditions, since in his view "commerce and culture are like sisters, and if you go down the path of culture, you arrive at the path of business" (interview, October 21, 2008). The path forged by Liu's agency was paved with both culture and commerce, bringing Chinese entrepreneurs to Tijuana three times a year to meet Mexican business partners at conventions and banquets coinciding with the Chinese New Year, the PRC's Independence Day, and the Qingming Festival (which commemorates ancestors). By 2012 these events had expanded through a partnership with the Autonomous University of Baja California that enabled a series of trade exhibitions inspired by CACHIMEX's annual Expo China (see chapter 2).

Between 2005 and 2014 Liu's events were accompanied by public parades and Chinese-themed street markets, coordinated by his association at the invitation of the Tijuana city government. The Chinese consulate contributed resources to support these occasions, for as Liu says, "the PRC needs our help in creating a good public image" (interview, October 21, 2008). Consul General Gao confirmed this point, noting that the expansive networks developed by the Chinese Association of Tijuana function as a catalyst for advancing China's political as well as economic interests (interview, November 5, 2008). For instance, with OCAO's support, Liu's association has been instrumental in convincing other Chinese associations to break their ties with Taiwan. To this end, in 2001 OCAO established the Chinese Peaceful Pro-Unification Alliance of Baja California, which the state's three Chinese associations (in the cities of Tijuana, Mexicali, and Ensenada) immediately joined, adopting Mandarin as their operating language as a condition of membership.

For the Chinese Association of Tijuana, 2001 marked the first time since its 1918 founding that it did not conduct its annual meeting in Cantonese, the first language of 98 percent of its members. The adjustment, along with vigilance against anti-PRC and pro-Taiwan activities, appears to be the price of institutional recognition. This recognition, says Liu, has enabled the association to attract additional support from the Baja California government and begin to develop officially endorsed business activities, like its counterpart in Mexicali. Operating in Mandarin is fundamental to this process, and therefore translators fluent in Cantonese, Mandarin, and Spanish are in demand. One such person is Li Zhuohong, who is contracted by the association as an intermediary for Chinese and Mexican lawyers:

> When I was fifteen I came to Mexico to join my father, who had been here for three years. I'm from Guangdong, so I speak Cantonese, like most Chinese people here. The problem is that to do business with

China these days, you have to speak Mandarin. I learned Mandarin in school in China, and then I improved here in the Chinese Association of Tijuana. Then the association hired me to teach Mandarin to the children of newly arrived Chinese. From there I've become a sort of translator and interpreter. . . . I was hired by Geely [a Chinese carmaker] to help it negotiate the establishment of a factory in Guanajuato. If there are legal documents that Chinese firms need, then I point them in the right direction. I also get a lot of calls from the Chinese consulate, which sends Chinese businesspeople to our association because we have good relations with practically all industries in the Tijuana area. Some of these are restaurants, some are maquiladoras, and some are retail outlets. (interview, November 11, 2008)

In 1998 the Chinese Association of Tijuana published a set of guidelines for its members, titled "Laws of the Chinese Community of Tijuana." Circulated in Mandarin and Spanish, the document spells out the organization's four primary responsibilities: (1) assist the government of the PRC in any way possible; (2) strengthen the unity of the Chinese community, promote its peaceful development, and secure maximum possible benefits for it; (3) build friendship between Chinese and Mexican people and their countries through economic and cultural exchange; and (4) encourage the Chinese people of Tijuana to compensate other members of the community for losses resulting from calamities with donations and support (Chinese Association of Tijuana 1998).

While the first responsibility leaves the association's political allegiance to the PRC in no doubt, the second and fourth reveal a specific preoccupation with the community's well-being. Considering the adversity faced by Chinese people in Mexico, past and present, this is a logical concern. Indeed, while the efforts of people like Liu, Li, and Auyón to build Mexican trust with mainland Chinese businesses are recognized and praised in China, anti-Chinese "calamities" are commonplace in Baja California (*Xinhua* 2007; Zhan 2002). Liu laments that his community has borne the brunt of this hostility:

In the last five years, things have gotten worse for our community. All of our businesses, 100 percent, have been robbed or assaulted in some way, some of them four or five times in one year! We don't go to the police because we feel they won't resolve anything for us and we'll just waste more time and money dealing with them. Criminals target us because they know the police won't investigate. My agency was robbed three times this year. That's why my door is locked with a buzzer. If you don't have an appointment or we don't know you, we don't let you in. Now Chinese businesses have to hire security guards. . . . We're suffering, and we're running out of hope. Many are scared, and many are leaving. When your businesses are attacked you have to make a choice. You can either turn around to make a fuss or you can go on without looking over your shoulder. We choose to go on and not draw even more attention to ourselves. (interview, October 21, 2008)

In the second half of 2008 alone, the Chinese Association of Tijuana registered over ten attacks on its members' businesses, prompting Consul General Gao to publicly denounce the assaults. The perpetrators, he said, were probably emboldened by expectations of police indifference to Chinese immigrants and their descendants. Liu had previously expressed his dismay to the newspaper *La Frontera* about the fact that the law cannot help his community: "We want protection, but we do not know which institution or individuals to go to because we don't trust the authorities, the police, or others" (quoted in Ramírez 2007). When I followed up with Liu in December 2011, he noted that little had changed: victims of abuse still preferred not to involve the police, instead turning to the association for social and financial support.

Faced with ineffective law enforcement and fears of police discrimination, it is no surprise that community protection should reemerge as a core activity of Mexico's Chinese associations. While adversity has renewed the associations' purpose, their members' reliance on customary internal procedures rather than the police and institutional legal defense has further ingrained their reputation as a community unwilling to integrate. As Alejandro Portes puts it, "sociability cuts both ways" (1998, 18). Liu acknowledged his community's part in perpetuating this reputation: "I am aware that our silence is partly to blame for society's lack of understanding of us. It's one of the things we have to change" (interview, October 21, 2008). More than three years later, Liu conceded that beyond the creation of a group that performed folk music and a festival of Chinese food, the association had made little progress in building external trust: "culturally things are going well, but people are still suspicious; the problem is politics" (interview, December 22, 2011).

Mexico's Chinese associations have long protected and advanced their members' interests, but deepening business ties to China may be compromising this humanitarian tradition. Their networks now include Chinese providers of low-skilled labor for Baja California's industries, not least the maquiladora sector. Oppressive working conditions and inadequate safety standards have brought misery to thousands of Chinese immigrants, whose passage to Mexico has been overseen by the associations. Severe consequences await those who complain or even discuss their predicament outside a tight circle of fellow employees. The next section examines this closed circle of trust and how a lack of regulatory oversight has let it spin out of control.

ENFORCING TRUST: THE DEPTHS OF NEGATIVE SOCIAL CAPITAL

Investors from mainland China and Taiwan have taken a keen interest in northern Mexico's maquiladoras, whose geographic location and rapid turnaround times have made them responsive to the fluctuations of the U.S. market and enabled the region to retain a foothold in the textile, electronics, and automobile industries (Hu-DeHart 2003, 248). The Han Young maquiladora in Tijuana, for instance, manufactures truck chassis, which under the North American Free Trade Agreement are shipped free of duty to the Hyundai assembly plant in San Diego and sold on the U.S. market. The success of this model owes much to the long working hours of maquiladora employees, and, according to the workers' rights activist Antonio Velázquez Loza, "it is not only Mexican workers who are victims of low wages and ill treatment; Chinese laborers who work in these plants suffer even worse abuses" (quoted in Gómez Mena 2006). Employed in China as technicians, most Chinese maquiladora workers live onsite, are prohibited from interacting with Mexicans, and have limited access to medical attention. Like the Chinese immigrants of the early twentieth century, they arrive in Mexico with hopes of earning a respectable living, but according to Veláquez Loza soon find themselves "practically living in slavery."

The Chinese associations assist Mexican and Chinese companies to navigate the legal procedures of sponsoring and contracting Chinese employees. This assistance is not limited to the maquiladora sector; other major importers of labor include northern Mexico's thriving Chinese restaurants and clothing retailers (Spagat 2005). Tijuana and Mexicali are each home to approximately six hundred Chinese restaurants, but approximately one-third of these are reportedly not formally registered. The labor force that supports this wide range of businesses is similarly diverse. It includes migrants seeking to enter the United States, who have traveled for weeks or months from mainland China and Hong Kong by air to Colombia and then by a combination of land and sea voyages to Panama and across Central America (*Protocolo* 2007).

In the border cities of Tijuana and Mexicali, unregistered Chinese migrants work alongside descendants of Chinese immigrants and a growing pool of laborers who enter Mexico on temporary work and study visas and remain indefinitely. Depending on the complexity of their passage, Chinese migrant workers incur costs ranging from $30,000 to $60,000 per person, and according to a senior figure in the Chinese community of Tijuana, these costs must be repaid: "It's very expensive for Chinese workers to come. Officially the cost to arrange a work visa for an employee is 800 pesos [$80], and there was a point when this worked, especially for chefs. But things have tightened up, and now, after paying lawyers to push the case through, it costs about $8,000 per employee just for the paperwork. When they get here they work extremely hard, almost without sleep, so the restaurant and factory owners make their money back in this way. It can take fifteen or twenty years to pay back the debt" (interview, October 2, 2008).

Bound to their sponsors until their debts are paid, Chinese immigrants are in no position to formally advocate for improved working conditions. To do so would leave them destitute, subject to retribution, and in many cases exposed to prosecution under immigration laws. Their fate illuminates the underside of globalization, as observed by Wanni Anderson and Robert Lee: "Many thousands of Asian migrants who belong to the transnational working class, the new hewers of wood and haulers of water in the global economy, are tied to 'homelands' by debt, familial obligation, and statelessness" (2005, 13).

In a context of extreme pressure against independent unionization, Chinese migrant workers in Mexico have few sources of support. Even the Chinese associations have not extended their assistance, in part because their efforts focus on Chinese migrants and their descendants who have already established themselves in Mexico, but also because their business commitments impede them from doing so. According to Juan Arroyo, a Baptist minister who works with Chinese newcomers in Mexicali, the associations' tradition of humanitarian support to marginalized workers has been turned on its head, since their assistance goes instead to the managers of factories and restaurants in the name of building bridges to China: "The leaders of the Chinese associations are too busy arranging business deals for wealthy mainland investors to pay attention to the problems of these people. Most of the new arrivals are victimized. They are targets of discrimination in hospitals, in workplaces, and in public . . . [they are] denied services and refused legal representation. When they have difficulties learning Spanish they are humiliated, and sometimes they are even physically abused" (interview, October 12, 2008).

The Chinese associations have provided unofficial channels of migration into Mexico, and onward to the United States, since the mid-nineteenth century (Taylor 2002). Whether or not they have abandoned their humanitarian tradition, as Arroyo believes, they continue to broker a social contract that commits new arrivals to pay for their passage by working hard and keeping quiet. For the few who refuse to honor these terms in northern Baja California, Arroyo has been a beacon of hope. His congregation, which consists mainly of Chinese contract employees, has grown to include over a hundred migrant workers who have walked away from exploitative factory and restaurant jobs and others who are considering doing so. After a Sunday worship service in a Baptist outreach center in downtown Mexicali, Arroyo invited me to his nearby house for lunch.

THE DEFECTORS

Arroyo takes me from room to room, introducing me to groups of people standing with bowls of fried beef and pork with rice in hand, conversing in Mandarin. In each room he describes me, in Spanish, as an anthropologist from the Autonomous University of Baja California [where I was working at the time] doing a research project on Chinese people in Mexico. I'm here, he explains, because I want to learn more about the outreach activities of the Baptist church, and I am a trustworthy person who won't reveal people's information to the authorities. My Mandarin salutations evoke smiles and soon lead to conversations about where people are from and how they are finding Mexico. I hear stories about unexpected hardship, the impossibility of acquiring legal residence papers, the constant threat of corrupt police officers, and the unrelenting demands of sponsors. A restaurant worker says she was kidnapped last year, and a diabetic factory worker says that his sponsor threatened to harm his family in China if he continued to take sick days. The hub of activity is a grill outside the back door, around which four men and two women busily take requests and sizzle thin strips of beef. Arroyo suggests that we all take a photo together, but polite smiles accompanied by exaggerated waves of the hand force him to abandon this idea. His mobile phone rings, and he says we need to leave. Another victim has asked him to come and help at the hospital.

—Mexicali, November 5, 2008

Some of Arroyo's guests that Sunday were also staying with him, their former accommodation withdrawn by their sponsors when they left their jobs. One young man said the official fee for coming to Mexico and acquiring residence papers is $18,000, but that unofficial payments of thousands of dollars are also necessary to advance the paperwork and upgrade a tourist visa to a work visa. The restaurant owner who had employed him had still not paid these unofficial fees, and after two years he was still working illegally. An older man had been stopped by the police, and when they found he was without his residence documents, they asked him to pay an impossibly large fine on the spot. His sponsor, a prominent member of Mexicali's Chinese association, paid the fine but then required the man to work days and nights without rest in an electronics assembly plant. A woman spoke of the unsafe conditions at the plastics factory where she worked, which had resulted in her young daughter burning her hand. She had to wait eight hours for treatment in the public hospital.

These and other stories revealed frequent abuse by sponsors, neglected labor standards, and public discrimination. Arroyo's church was doing all it could for its desperate congregation, he said, but it did not have the resources to sustain the growing number of new arrivals. Other religious groups, including Baptist congregations in Mexicali, had "cut us off," Arroyo said, because they did not want to be publicly associated with Chinese workers and face the potential vengeance of their employers. During my subsequent visits, Arroyo answered several calls on his mobile phone each hour, providing advice, making appointments, and responding to the latest crises. Driving through Mexicali with me, he pointed out apartments housing ten to twenty Chinese laborers in one or two rooms. "You don't see them," he said during one of our meetings, "and nor does anybody else. They leave for work before light and return after dark." As Liu confirmed, Chinese immigrants are disproportionately targeted by kidnappers emboldened by their victims' illegal status, and by confidence that their sponsors will pay a high price to recover their investments (interview, October 21, 2008; also see Ramírez 2007).

The detail in which Arroyo introduced me to his congregation reflected its delicate predicament and the circle of trust defining its boundaries. The understandable reluctance of its members to be photographed, even at Arroyo's request, suggested the danger of transgressing these limits. To do so could expose them to their sponsors' wrath in the form of longer work hours, withdrawal of access to housing, and even threats to family members in China. These sanctions constitute an extreme form of "enforceable trust," a concept that Portes (1998, 8) borrows from Max Weber ([1922] 1947) to describe informal sanctions applied within a community to ensure compliance with rules of conduct. For Arroyo's congregation, the rules are clear: focus on your work, do not complain, speak to nobody, and in return you will be safe and eventually free. These conditions make it almost impossible for hundreds of Chinese migrant workers in Mexico to build linkages and friendships beyond each other. Prevented from doing so both by the fear of retributions from their sponsors and the insecurity of being Chinese in Mexico, they live on the margins of a marginalized community.

There is no shortage of solidarity among Baja California's Chinese migrant workers, but as Raphael De Kadt (1994) and Johannes Fedderke, Raphael de Kadt, and John Luiz (1999) have shown, the benefits of social capital result more from optimization than from maximization. Optimization in this case would mean extending relationships outward, with Arroyo's help, to potential allies and advocates. Barred from this path by ruthless employers and recruiters, the members of Arroyo's congregation were almost entirely isolated from external connections. Ronald Burt (1992) describes such scenarios as "structural holes," social vacuums that confer especially high value on intermediaries who endeavor to fill them. Arroyo was such an intermediary and embodied this point: he provided a lifeline to pull the Chinese workers out of their hole and sought only spiritual fulfillment in return. As Nan Lin (2001, 39–40) writes, cooperation across community boundaries requires a reciprocal flow of rewards, whether social, economic, or divine.

The problem for Arroyo and, consequently, his congregation was that his own external affinities were weak. Facing rejection from his broader religious network for his association with Chinese immigrants, Arroyo risked being trapped in the social void he had dared to enter. The missing ingredient for him was vertical synergy—with the church, a nongovernmental organization, a business, or a government outreach office—that might lift him and his congregation out of isolation and into contact with potential friends and allies. Without vertical institutional support, they had no way to develop horizontal alliances.

Closer economic cooperation between Mexico and China will not in itself create vertical structures capable of addressing the predicament of Chinese migrant workers and may even do the opposite. The Peña Nieto administration's negotiations with China to establish more direct flights to and from Mexico and to increase the number of Chinese tourists from the current 50,000 (only one-tenth the number of Chinese who visit the United States) could result in further abuse, as could INAMI's promise to facilitate Chinese immigration to Baja California. As the number of Chinese visitors grows, integrating these efforts into a broader governance strategy will become more urgent. Early attempts to do so have been unsuccessful. In 2008 an official at the Mexican embassy in Beijing proposed to hold information sessions to inform visa applicants of potential risks, but these were not authorized for fear of repelling prospective tourists. A 2010 scheme to track the conversion of tourist visas into work visas was also abandoned owing to insufficient consular resources.

The proven disposition of Baja California's government to work with the Chinese associations of Tijuana and Mexicali could provide a more promising platform for confronting abuse. The associations have previously embraced opportunities for vertical collaboration through cultural festivals, street markets, and the Chamber of Chinese Enterprises of the Northwest. These activities provide a foundation for promoting social responsibility within Chinese business networks. Initiatives could include periodic briefing sessions among INAMI, the Chinese consulate in Tijuana, and the associations; joint outreach services for victimized employees; and audits of conditions in local restaurants, factories, and other sectors powered by Chinese contract workers. The Chinese associations would gain much from actively participating in such schemes, not least an opportunity to improve their reputations as responsible and trustworthy intermediaries. As China's economic and demographic ties to Mexico deepen, official support for such vertical partnerships, and the disposition of the Chinese associations to participate in them, will carry growing political and humanitarian weight.

CONCLUSION

Compassion alone rarely stimulates political action, and Mexican officials are unlikely to engage more closely with their nation's Chinese diaspora unless doing so secures tangible benefits. As in Cuba, motivation for new synergies will come not from goodwill, but in response to perceived opportunities and threats. People-to-people ties with China are generating both. New channels of trade, such as those developed by the Chamber of Chinese Enterprises of the Northwest, have caught the eye—and received the endorsement—of the Baja California government. By supporting the organization's commercial partnerships with China, facilitating trade fairs, and inviting Chinese associations to conduct public festivals, administrators are discovering that their electorates stand to gain when business networks and the trust underpinning them are integrated into formal development strategies.

Failure to engage more assertively with its Chinese communities will leave the Mexican state exposed to an expanding informal sector fueled by imported Chinese merchandise. Cisneros's characterization of Tepito as one limb of "an enormous monster" is worrying, especially since the monster's other limbs reach outward to suppliers across the Pacific and inward to unscrupulous customs officials and politicians. To cage the monster and limit the expansion of illicit trade networks, Cisneros advocates more assertive policing and stricter enforcement of the Law of Merchant Establishments. Stronger rule of law would no doubt help contain illicit transpacific networks, but inadequate legal resilience extends beyond specific commercial regulations into the daily conduct of politicians.

Allegations of undue cooperation between so-called Chinese economic invaders and civil servants—including Marcelo Ebrard, Mexico

City's former mayor—are symptomatic of broad public suspicion of government. The profound "distrust and disconnect among citizens, and between the population and the government" acknowledged by the National Electoral Institute in 2014 constitutes fertile ground for narratives of unwelcome Chinese informal trading (Saldierna 2014). The electoral, security, and procurement irregularities described in chapter 2 have generated a vertical disjuncture that must be bridged through comprehensive anticorruption measures alongside tighter regulation of the black market. The two problems are intertwined and mutually reinforcing, and neither can be fully understood—or remedied—independently of the other.

Sustainable trust between state and society requires carrots as well as sticks. As the case of Baja California showed, social engagement strategies have made headway in integrating informal Chinese networks into registered markets. Experiences of state-society collaboration in Mexicali and Tijuana offer lessons for the broader Mexican public and private sectors, which have been slow to reach out to Chinese networks because of public concern about the national trade deficit with China and the supposed role of the resident Chinese community in deepening it. Evident in the press, on Internet sites, and in violent acts against private businesses, popular antagonism toward the Chinese diaspora in Mexico echoes the nationalism of the early twentieth century, predicated on the perceived selfishness of Chinese people. The response from Chinese communities—then and now—has been to avoid direct confrontation with opponents and seek protection within the long-standing mutual aid and economic assistance services of the Chinese associations.

External hostility and internal protectionism constitute a perennial vicious circle surrounding Mexico's Chinese communities, but as the circle revolves over time, the distrust it generates has extended outward. According to analysts at UNAM's China-Mexico Research Center, aggression toward Chinese interests is discouraging Chinese investors and importers from proceeding with their Mexican projects. This is detrimental to Mexico, as Chinese investors and importers possess more power than anybody else to restore some measure of balance to the bilateral trade relationship. The potentially massive demand of Chinese markets for Mexican products, coupled with the apparent inability of the two governments to formulate projects that produce genuine mutual benefits, endows the activities of intermediaries like Eduardo Auyón, Willy Liu, and Li Zhuohong with considerable gravity. The challenge lying before these individuals and the Chinese associations they represent is to expand the scope of their networks horizontally beyond Chinese suppliers to Mexican exporters, and vertically to secure government endorsement at the state and federal levels.

The community support structures of the Chinese diaspora in Mexico have benefited those with a stake in the international expansion of Chinese firms, but for thousands of Chinese migrant workers, conformity to internal codes of loyalty has been less beneficial. Indebtedness and subservience to employers has subjected them to inhumane working conditions and to the threat of kidnappers seeking to cash in on their precarious legal standing and their value to commercial sponsors. The predicament of Chinese laborers in Mexico bears out a truth observed by Peter Evans (1997): social capital is no more inherently beneficial than financial capital.

The concept of enforceable trust among Chinese migrant workers helps illuminate the conditions they endure, but the facts on the ground warrant cautious application of this and other sociological constructs. The control exercised over desperate migrant laborers by powerful sponsors belies the existence of a cohesive Chinese diaspora in Mexico. At most a Weberian ideal type, "the term diaspora holds within it a series of contradictions that the name itself seeks to elide" (Palumbo-Liu 2007, 282). More accurately understood as a hub of diversity than uniformity, the Chinese community in Mexico demonstrates the extent of inequality, fragmentation, and diversification created by twenty-first-century labor migration. With this process comes the need for conceptual tools that are less reliant on bounded notions of community and more sensitive to the globalization of trust in all its forms.

Social and financial capital are interacting in new ways as the reach of mainland Chinese formal and informal institutions extends further overseas. Emerging labor markets and production chains are creating new contexts for the deployment of trust, and trust is enabling the creation of new niches in the global economy. This book's conclusion argues that a looming challenge for the governments and citizens of Mexico, Cuba, and other nations that are pursuing closer relations with China is to more effectively harness the resulting social affinities to create inclusive development opportunities. Implicit in this challenge is the formulation of analytic concepts capable of grasping the social as well as economic implications of China's historic rise.

CONCLUSION
CHINA AND THE FUTURE OF HISTORY

As China's brand of state capitalism goes global, developing countries have become at once alarmed and inspired. For two decades prior to the global financial crisis, Western policy analysts confidently advised governments around the world—those of China, Cuba, and Mexico among them—to scale back their interventions in economic affairs. The apparent Cold War victory of liberal democracy, markets, and civil society as the prime movers of development led Francis Fukuyama (1992) to famously declare that the world had reached "the end of history."

The fact that Cuban history continued defiantly along a state-centric path is noteworthy, but even more so is the Chinese government's mastery of international markets. Over the past decade China has contributed around 25 percent to global economic growth, more than any other country. Set against the backdrop of today's financial volatility in the West, China's rise has institutions from the International Monetary Fund to the U.S. government questioning whether we are witnessing "the return of history" (Kagan 2008).

For all the trepidations of the world's liberal democracies, one thing is certain: history is not repeating itself. Despite its communist underpinnings, the Chinese government now looks outward with a brand of economic pragmatism unknown to Cold War contenders. Furthermore, formal and informal cooperation forged through the Chinese diaspora is advancing a unique blend of materialist and idealist agendas. David Shambaugh has recognized the hybrid approach of Chinese actors and has suggested that their growing global influence is internationalizing a tradition that diverges from Western protocol: "for the Chinese, cooperation derives from trust—whereas Americans tend to build trust through cooperation" (2009). There is nothing essentialist about Shambaugh's claim; efforts to build trust are embedded from the start in Chinese projects throughout Latin America. Across the region, Chinese enterprises have offered the confidence of long-term cooperation, agreeing to purchase energy and agriculture products for more than a decade into the future and taking on considerable risk through potentially irrecoverable trade credits and loans.

Cuba illustrates Shambaugh's point, having accrued an estimated $6 billion debt to China, including $115 million pledged during Xi Jinping's 2014 visit to upgrade the Port of Santiago de Cuba. The fact that China continues to financially and politically support the Cuban government illustrates Beijing's faith that reforms on the island will eventually yield economic results, among them the repayment of loans. Mexico underscores the human dimension of trust as a prime mover: support from the Chinese government's Overseas Chinese Affairs Office (OCAO) has used transpacific ethnic affinities to foment the personal confidence necessary for commercial partnerships between leaders of the Chinese diaspora and exporters in mainland China. Where official attempts at bilateral engagement have failed, informal cooperation has flourished.

Deepening commercial exchanges in the Chinese diaspora, alongside cooperation on development projects with powerful Chinese state enterprises, present new challenges for Latin America. This book has argued that effective responses require more dynamic and inclusive partnerships between people, companies, and their governments. Chinese diasporic communities have begun to leverage a broad set of social and economic resources to stimulate this process from the bottom up. Their dynamism contrasts with the difficulties of large enterprises, both public and private, in responding to the competitive pressures and commercial opportunities generated by China's rise. Whether mandated to source supplies from small providers, as proposed by Cuba's *Lineamientos* (República de Cuba 2011), or forced to share tax and funding benefits with a wider variety of economic actors, as signaled by Mexican lawmakers under President Enrique Peña Nieto, established industrial winners are under pressure to reform.

Although closer dealings with Chinese actors have provoked greater emphasis on local economic dynamism, there is no guarantee that initial responses will consolidate into long-term policies. As China's international influence grows, its preference for state-to-state cooperation may not support the efforts of partner countries to decentralize and diversify their economies. On the contrary, official cooperation agreements orchestrated by foreign ministries suggest an ongoing process of top-down agenda setting. The only significant countercurrent is the proliferation of personal collaborations between overseas Chinese communities and mainland business partners, which is beginning to generate economic results and political responsiveness from the bottom up.

For Cuba, cooperation with China is managed exclusively by the state. As discussed in chapter 1, this top-down approach has served the purpose of coordinating initiatives across the education, electronics, and logistics sectors. It has also enabled the controlled import and distribution of agricultural equipment, automobiles, and electronic goods. Regulated supply chains orchestrated by the Cuban and Chinese governments have diminished the unregistered circulation of these items. As the expansion of Cuba's agricultural cooperatives and deregulation of its automobile market show, lawful supply is a prerequisite for subsequent liberalization.

The incremental growth of private initiative under state hegemony may be one of "China's lessons for Cuba" (Cheng 2007a; Ratliff 2004), but equally salient is the lesson that communist ideology can no longer supersede economic rationalism. Chinese officials have repeatedly conveyed this message to their Cuban counterparts since the fall of the Soviet Union. This was evident in 1995, when Li Peng urged Fidel Castro to start opening the Cuban economy, and in 1996, when China terminated the barter-based trade and payment agreement. The Chinese government has since sent a stream of envoys to advise Cuba on foreign investment and the creation of consumer markets. According to Chinese officials quoted by a U.S. diplomat in Havana, discussions between China and Cuba about carrying out Chinese-style reforms have been tense and at times caused "a real headache" (U.S. Department of State 2010). The changing basis of bilateral relations hit home for Cuba in 2011, when the Chinese firm Yutong insisted that replacement parts for its buses would be sold rather than donated to Cuba. As Omar Pereira Hernández, a former Cuban diplomat, put it, "political trust is still important in our relationship, but now it's a matter of pragmatism, because the Chinese insist that the numbers have to add up" (interview, May 28, 2012).

Numbers that refuse to add up are also a persisting theme of Mexico's relations with China, reinforcing a pattern of governmental interactions fraught with acrimony. As noted in chapter 2, $72 billion of trade with China in 2014 left Mexico with a bilateral deficit of $60 billion (United Nations Commodity Trade Statistics Database 2015). The emerging superpower has progressively encroached on the Mexican handicrafts, textiles, shoes, electronics, and—more recently—automotive sectors. The last is a pillar of the Mexican economy that has also come to face Chinese competition in the U.S. market (Watkins 2013). Powerful lobby groups, such as the Council for Business Coordination and the Mexican Council of Businessmen, have long lobbied their government on behalf of the interests of Mexico's largest companies. These elite organizations have secured state subsidies, tax breaks, and permits for the automotive, telecommunications, and agribusiness sectors. As competition with China intensifies, pressure is mounting on the government to extend these benefits to smaller businesses. This not only would diversify the economy and expand the tax base but would also entice workers out of the rampant informal sector, which is estimated to employ some thirty million people, or 60 percent of Mexico's workforce (Hughes 2013). The need for formal opportunities at the grass roots is becoming more urgent as the flow of contraband Chinese consumer goods into Mexico gains momentum.

Subsidies and other forms of state intervention will not by themselves overcome the much-heralded China threat that Mexico faces, but neither will unsupported initiatives from the private sector and civil society. Solutions will more likely emerge from a framework of engagement between state and society, between independent actors, and between Mexico and China. Chapter 2 identified potential steps toward the creation of such synergies. Tax breaks, rebates, and travel support could be extended to small businesses that present their products in the Fair of Canton and other Chinese trade expositions. Official sponsorship could be offered to China-oriented trade fairs in Mexico, such as the annual Expo China, which attempts to bring together Mexican, Latin American, and Chinese commercial partners. Cases of successful engagement with China, such as Nemak, could be studied with the aim of learning and emulating best practices among a broader range of exporters. Small steps like these, so far impeded by an overemphasis on assistance to large enterprises, would foment trusting relationships among the Mexican state, a broad range of businesses, and their prospective Chinese partners.

The reforms under way in Cuba and Mexico will broaden both countries' international horizons. Cuba is attempting to update its economy through the *Lineamientos* process initiated in 2011, the opening of the automobile and real estate markets, and the revision of the 1995 Foreign Investment Law. The 2014 version of the law protects investors against the nationalization of their assets, exempts them from personal income and labor taxes, and guarantees a profits tax ceiling of 15 percent preceded by an eight-year grace period. The architect of these measures, Marino Murillo, was reappointed as minister of the economy in 2014, affording him the executive authority to supervise implementation. Raúl Castro aspires to attract $2.5 billion of foreign finance, but investors must weigh opportunities in oil exploration, tourism, and the Mariel Special Economic Zone against political risks. For instance, if the U.S. government relaxes its trade embargo, Chinese and U.S. investors will be forced to balance the diplomacy of peaceful coexistence with the pressures of strategic competition. Cuba could become a regional testing ground for Sino-U.S. interactions.

Sino-U.S. encounters in Cuba are becoming more likely as Havana and Washington negotiate steps toward diplomatic and commercial rapprochement. The Chinese political scientist Wang Yiwei (2014) argues that U.S. policy toward Cuba has generated friction across Latin America and that the embargo is akin to "lifting a rock only to drop it upon one's own foot" (搬起石头砸自己的脚). The sentiment is gaining traction in Miami-Dade County, in Florida, where 68 percent of Cuban Americans now favor the restoration of diplomatic relations (Florida International University 2014). More conciliatory public opinion underpinned President Barack Obama's 2014 pledge to advance political détente with Cuba, which has unleashed a flurry of trade and fact-finding missions to Havana by U.S. businesspeople and politicians, including Assistant Secretary of State for Western Hemisphere Affairs Roberta Jacobson and Congresswoman Nancy Pelosi. Opportunities exist for U.S. businesses to supply

Cuba's agriculture cooperatives, emerging small businesses, and underequipped state enterprises, but Chinese competitors have the advantage of trade credits, low-interest loans, and supply contracts deriving from Sino-Cuban presidential accords. Under these conditions, Chinese suppliers are less affected than their U.S. counterparts by Cuba's tight import regulations, dual currency regime, and lack of conventional foreign exchange financing.

Diverging visions of state intervention will continue to generate difficulties among Cuba, China, and the United States. Although Sino-Cuban relations have become more pragmatic, their continuing reliance on the "supreme guidance of the state" (discussed in chapter 1) is at odds with U.S. conventions of transnational business and civic governance (Hearn 2009; Mao et al. 2011). Diverging views of government intervention are intertwined with the impasse over human rights in Cuba. Jacobson said that she broached this sensitive topic in Havana with Josefina Vidal, the Cuban Foreign Ministry's director for U.S. relations, but Vidal emerged from the meeting denying that the issue was even raised ("US, Cuba Move toward Embassies, Disagree on Human Rights" 2015). A key question for future research, as noted below, is whether China's deepening trade and investment relations with Cuba will favor or impede more participatory modes of governance and steps toward financial liberalization. The answer to this question will set the tone for interactions not only between Cuba and China, but for interactions between both countries and the United States.

Like the reforms in Cuba, those in Mexico under Peña Nieto are attracting attention from Chinese investors, who are eager to enter the country's energy, electricity, telecommunications, automobile, and manufacturing sectors. Chinese ambitions in Mexico will also unfold in the context of relations with the United States, whose multinational enterprises are likely to dominate new opportunities. In the oil sector, Exxon Mobil, Chevron, and other U.S. firms will leverage the 2013 U.S.-Mexico Transboundary Hydrocarbons Agreement to outmaneuver Chinese competitors. Similarly, as Mexico's Telecommunication Reform Bill forces América Móvil to reduce its market share to below 50 percent, AT&T has positioned itself to acquire divested mobile and landline assets.

Mexican industries will become further intertwined with the United States if the proposed Trans-Pacific Partnership (TPP) comes to fruition.

The TPP aspires to accelerate investment among its twelve Pacific Rim members, which include the United States and Mexico but not China. A recent study reveals conflicting views of the TPP among senior Mexican advisors, some of whom believe that a better strategy would be to prioritize "triangular" Chinese investments in Mexico that target U.S. markets (Armony, Chávez, and Hearn, under review). Whether or not the TPP is ever implemented, U.S. and Chinese firms (among others) will continue to vie for Mexico's strategic assets. Like their Cuban counterparts, Mexican citizens can therefore expect more intense collective and personal encounters with the conflicting forces of globalization.

While the policy declarations of the Mexican, Cuban, and Chinese governments attempt to define the contours of engagement, interactions between individuals propel relations in unforeseen directions. With or without government approval, independent ties between the Chinese diaspora and partners in mainland China are thickening. This presents a diplomatic challenge for the Cuban state, which since 1959 has left no aspect of foreign interaction to chance, closely supervising external partnerships in line with Lenin's dictum that "trust is good, but control is better." Top-down control of foreign contact has minimized Cuba's exposure to external influences, limited the ability of foreign nongovernmental organizations to foment an independent civil society on the island, and defended against the U.S. government's Cuban Democracy Act, which attempts to reach around the Cuban state to support organizations that could destabilize it (Hearn 2008a, 107–9). Cuban apprehension about foreign intervention, including at the level of people-to-people ties, focuses for good reason on the United States. Meanwhile, Chinese visitors ranging from official delegates to unofficial businesspeople are exempt from visa requirements and, for the time being, free to collaborate with Havana's Chinese associations.

Never before in Barrio Chino's 150-year history has the Chinese Cuban community been able to draw support from an external superpower. With their bargaining power augmented, community leaders have found the Cuban government more responsive than ever to their ideas and proposals. The state's growing disposition to work with the Chinese associations may be strengthened by the commitment of the Office of the Historian of the City to participatory development, but paramount is a top-down desire to maintain control over local affairs. As chapter 3 showed, the revival of Barrio Chino's traditional pharmacy was accorded high priority when the Office became concerned that Chinese visitors might otherwise illegally supply the community with medicines. Similarly, a local proposal to revamp the newspaper *Kwong Wah Po* attracted the Office's interest not only for its capacity to deliver revenue, but also for its ability to balance China's growing media presence with a Cuban perspective.

The introduction of new businesses, restaurants, infrastructure, and tourist attractions into Barrio Chino should be understood in light of the Cuban state's determination to bring emerging entrepreneurs into the fold of its hegemony. Nevertheless, opportunities resulting from this flurry of activity are encouraging the Chinese community to put internal differences aside, collectively formulate proposals, and pursue common goals. A critical question for the future is whether or not the Chinese associations' revived horizontal solidarity will equip them to challenge the state's hegemony and potentially inspire other groups to pursue a similar course. It is noteworthy that the powerful Afro-Cuban religious group Ifá Iranlowo, in the neighboring district of Los Sitios, is keenly aware that registration with the Ministry of Justice has advanced the Chinese associations' goals and is now lobbying for the same status (interview with Victor Betancourt Estrada, leader of Ifá Iranlowo, June 6, 2014; also see Hearn 2008a, 50–52). How deeply and broadly such attempts at local empowerment progress will depend on the degree of state endorsement they attract, and how deftly they leverage this support to consolidate independent circles of cooperation and trust.

Mexico's Chinese diaspora is bound together by more intense pressures than its Cuban counterpart, including a widespread perception that its business activities are exacerbating Mexico's trade deficit with China and fueling the black market. Such perceptions result indirectly from the lack of functional official partnerships between Mexico and China and, as chapter 4 showed, directly from concerns about the unconventional modes of exchange that have emerged in their stead. These exchanges include import and distribution schemes supported by the Chinese government's OCAO, illicit trade and employment practices underpinned by emerging community ties to manufacturers and recruitment agencies in China, and defensive networks of ethnic entrepreneurship and mutual aid consolidated by Mexico's Chinese associations. A sociological lesson from the upheavals that gripped Mexico in the 1930s has apparently not been learned: the stronger the antagonism against Chinese communities, the more they will defend themselves by strengthening internal loyalties, ethnic protectionism, and guanxi. In this environment, the prospect of rationalizing Chinese cooperative networks into formal structures of governance is remote.

The consequences of enclave economies, or what Michael Woolcock calls "integration without linkages" (1998, 172), are on display in Mexico's Tepito district, where thousands of black-market vendors abide by internal rules and procedures that are completely disarticulated from broader legal codes. Opponents of street vending argue that government disinterest has enabled informal traders not only to evade taxes, but also to smuggle Chinese consumer goods and potentially narcotics into Mexico. Proposals for mitigating this "culture of impunity," as noted in chapter 4, aim to contain illicit networks through more aggressive policing and harsher penalties but have so far neglected cooperative solutions. If the goal is to foment stable, law-abiding interpersonal ties to China, then the resident Chinese community is ideally placed to assist, as it has begun to do in Baja California.

The social connections of the Chinese associations of Tijuana and Mexicali bypass government protocols but have nevertheless advanced official efforts to build registered trade and investment relations with Chinese partners. A challenge now facing the Chinese associations and their supporters in the Baja California government is to integrate ethical concerns into their shared economic agenda. To confront the circles of "enforceable trust" that sustain the abuse of twenty-first-century Chinese migrant workers will require broader avenues of state-society engagement, from visa tracking to workplace monitoring. Cooperation on these matters would also build public trust in Mexico's Chinese community, enabling it to work with a wider range of national actors.

Cuba and Mexico show that regardless of the prevailing blend of public- and private-sector carrots and sticks, Chinese communities represent a valuable resource. Whatever their political orientation, governments and citizens stand to reap substantial rewards if the activities of these communities are consensually integrated into broader development strategies. Those who fail to harness the capacities of Chinese networks may find themselves bypassed as the flow of transpacific products, finance, and people intensifies. Conversely, those who build bridges with the Chinese diaspora will unlock exchanges that reach beyond China-towns into other sectors of their own societies and across the Pacific. Whether focused on domestic economic development or international trade and investment, policy makers can draw strength like never before from social engagement at home.

As China reaches out to the worldwide Chinese diaspora, local governments will need to formulate more meticulous strategies for governing Chinatowns. These strategies may be driven by the pursuit of economic growth, efforts to manage and police local-foreign partnerships, or attempts to frame bilateral relations with China in a particular historical light. Whatever their motivations, more assertive efforts to work with Chinese communities will generate opportunities to reconcile the legacies of ethnic marginalization with fresh prospects for future cooperation.

The so-called Asian Century heralded by China's rise involves more than great-power politics. It also involves a reassessment of how politics and society intertwine to shape the trajectory of global change. The growing capacities of Chinese diasporic communities to build cooperation between their countries of residence and mainland China, and to attract support from host country governments, illustrate the interplay of local social dynamics and geopolitical relations. Researchers who wish to grasp the significance of this interplay will need to develop conceptual approaches that blend the broad comparative vista of international relations with ethnographic sensitivity to the lives of individuals.

As the twentieth century drew to a close, Aihwa Ong proposed that the emerging field of diaspora studies would do well to experiment with the "ethnography of transnational practices and linkages" (1999, 5) as a framework for understanding the political economies of overseas Chinese communities. The need for research that blends micro and macro perspectives has increased in step with China's intensifying engagement with Latin America, and as Ariel Armony and Julia Strauss write, this need is set to increase further:

> Future work ought to be designed so as to accommodate the multi-dimensional nature of the China–Latin America interaction and capture the empirical realities of a rapidly changing and complex set of relationships while developing concepts that lend themselves

to a mixture of comparison and generalization. We need to continue to explore China–Latin America from a transnational perspective, understanding how global phenomena are expressed in different ways at the local level, how various actors (governments, corporations, diasporas, non-state organizations and so on) interact with each other, and how international and domestic agendas shape interactions between China and Latin America. (2012, 14–15)

Armony and Strauss concur with Ong that local actors are central to contemporary Chinese transnationalism, and that their endeavors are best understood from the bottom up. To this end, ethnographic study of daily life among overseas Chinese communities enables a sharper appreciation of their diverse identities and aspirations. The facts of life on the ground belie, for instance, the facile tendency of recent public debates whose "keenest interest," writes Wang Gungwu, "has been in the political ramifications of having unassimilated migrants within modern nation-states" (2000, 39). The proposition that Chinese communities remain stubbornly "unassimilated" is an appealing hook for conservative commentators, but in modern nation-states (and their postmodern successors) it is as misleading as the notion of cultural homogeneity. Fantasies of national purity are anachronistic in what Evelyn Hu-DeHart perceives as an increasingly hybrid world: "'China' is enlarged to be wherever Chinese people and their descendants are to be found, and 'America' is not confined to just the United States. Multiplicities of Chineseness interact with multiplicities of Americanness, producing new and unique kinds of *mestizaje* or hybridity" (2005b, 80).

To explore mestizaje on the ground is to discover how old loyalties are maintained, how new alliances are forged, and how resulting compromises transcend any easy association of race and nation. Personal histories of loss, hope, and identity provide a human corrective to the sanitized economic and demographic analyses that characterized early transnational studies and continue to prevail in policy making (Angel-Ajani 2006; Castles 2006).

Personal experiences of transnationalism among Chinese migrants constitute what Donald Nonini and Aihwa Ong call "new Chinese subjectivities found in the global arena" (1997, 4), conditioned at once by local imaginaries, national policies, and international connections (Vertovec 2009; Wilson and Dissanayake 1996). These individual and institutional factors interact in innumerable ways to shape history, but as Fernand Braudel (1982) argued, grand narratives are discernible over the *longue durée*. Historical narratives of socialism and democracy, for instance, are manifest in contemporary Cuban and Mexican interactions among citizens, their governments, and foreign actors. At the dawn of the Asian Century, these grand narratives are entering a transformative phase. China's reemergence as a global power after an often-invoked "century of humiliation" is introducing narratives of personal identity, state-society relations, and international cooperation that support and undermine each other in unforeseen ways. Conceptualizing this interactive process as part of an emerging grand narrative of transnationalism and formulating more comprehensive policies on this basis are among the most important challenges of the twenty-first century.

Recognizing the need for approaches that more effectively bridge personal histories and grand narratives, Armony and Strauss encourage scholars to develop concepts that accommodate local experience and economic globalization in a holistic research design. The "multidimensional" framework they envision underscores Christopher Lee's call for more "inclusive" analyses of Asian diasporas that bridge idealist and materialist perspectives (2007, 32). The building blocks of such a bridge will be unifying themes that have equal relevance to international relations, economic development, and social participation. I have argued that trust is one such theme.

Trust is an inclusive concept that sheds new light on interactions among nations, industries, and people. It is the common denominator underpinning the ethnic affinities that connect mainland China to its global diaspora, the tight circles of bonding social capital that consolidate around emerging business activities, and official attempts to integrate these circles into frameworks of governance and regulation. Trust permeates the horizontal circumstances of diplomatic engagement across borders and network formation across communities, as well as the vertical channels through which local interests intersect with government agendas. Analyzing macro- and micro-level interactions side by side through the lens of trust opens fresh lines of inquiry into the future of China's deepening engagement with Cuba, Mexico, and the world:

- Will deepening formal and informal connections to the mainland enhance the ability of Chinese diasporic communities to secure recognition and support from host country governments, businesses, and publics? Will resulting initiatives provide bottom-up alternatives to the model of top-down state-to-state interactions favored by the Chinese government?
- Will the elite public and private enterprises that currently dominate Cuban, Mexican, and most other countries' relations with China cede space so that smaller actors—including those in the Chinese diaspora—can participate more fully in setting bilateral agendas?
- What kinds of public-private cooperation can overcome exaggerated perceptions that overseas Chinese communities remain locked into allegiance to the Chinese state? To what extent can collaborative endeavors, like those pursued by Baja California's government and the Chinese Association of Mexicali, challenge historically entrenched correlations of race with nation and counteract vicious circles of hostility and self-defense?
- As the capacities of overseas Chinese communities are consolidated, how can concepts like social capital, synergy, linkage, and trust support the development of consensual and responsive regulations? What conceptual innovations will enable policy makers, business leaders, and civil societies to accommodate China's expanding economic and social influence within robust structures of governance?
- What opportunities do China's engagements with Latin America and the world create for researchers to test established theoretical models and sharpen their conceptual tools? Which institutions and forums best enable Chinese and non-Chinese scholars to compare, contrast, and integrate their intellectual traditions in pursuit of original approaches and mutually beneficial policy outcomes?

Implicit in these questions is a core problem of political sociology: how can governments, businesses, and people work together in ways that build trust? The pressures and opportunities created by China's rise have introduced new ideas into this old debate. More dynamic approaches are becoming evident in Cuba and Mexico, where—despite fundamental economic and political differences—there is growing recognition of the value harbored by synergies and linkages that extend beyond traditional partners.

China's engagement with Latin America and the world is stimulating the renovation of existing institutions and the establishment of new ones to question and create knowledge. One of the oldest Chinese institutions in the Americas, Havana's Casino Chung Wah (founded in 1883), now hosts regular research seminars in partnership with the University of Havana's Center for the Study of Chinese Immigration to Cuba. In Mexico, the Latin American and Caribbean Academic Network on China, inaugurated in 2012 at Universidad Nacional Autónoma de México, has brought together over 400 specialists in conferences to foreground regional interpretations of Chinese foreign affairs. In 2015 Renmin University of China launched a Latin America Research Center to promote intellectual synergies related to Chinese development initiatives in the region. In the United States, the Inter-American Dialogue and the Latin American Studies Association have established divisions to advance critical analyses of Sino–Latin American interactions.

Institutional innovations have yielded a decade of quantitative data on Sino–Latin American trade and finance and a growing recognition that these must be more effectively integrated with qualitative analyses. As this book's case studies illustrate, understandings of history, identity, and the state condition the deployment of capital even as they respond to it. A holistic approach that accommodates this interaction of material and cultural factors promises fertile ground for conceptual innovation and policy input. This unprecedented process is redrawing disciplinary as well as institutional boundaries, prompting the world to move away from the end of history and toward a more interdependent politics of diaspora and trust.

2. MEXICO, CHINA, AND THE POLITICS OF TRUST

1. Eradicating prejudices through cultural awareness is also a goal of the Chinese Ministry of Education's Confucius Institutes, five of which are operating in Mexico at the time of writing. The Chinese newspaper *People's Daily* reports that the institutes and related educational programs play a dual diplomatic and educational role: "China hopes to dissolve the misconception of its development as the 'China threat,' by making its traditional value systems known to the world" ("'China Threat' Fear Countered by Culture" 2006).

3. HAVANA'S CHINATOWN AND THE QUEST FOR SYNERGY

1. According to Ernesto, Carlos, and Jorge Alay Jó (2002), the first Chinese arrived in Cuba in approximately 1830, from the Mandarin-speaking Chinese community in the Philippines. Generally able to speak Spanish, these "Chinos de Manila" worked primarily as domestic servants and later as florists and horticulturalists.
2. While Ortiz wrote little on Chinese heritage in Cuba, classic Cuban ethnologists such as José Baltar Rodríguez (1997), Antonio Chuffat Latour (1927), Jesús Guanche (1983), Juan Jiménez Pastrana (1963 and 1983), Juan Pérez de la Riva (2000), and Gonzalo de Quesada (1946) documented the social practices and demographic characteristics of Chinese communities throughout Cuba. Building on this foundation, a new wave of Cuban scholarly interest in Chinese Cuban heritage has emerged. Pedro Cosme Baños (1998) and Ana Valdés Millán (2005), for instance, have published ethnographic studies of Chinese-descended communities in Regla and Guantanamo, respectively. The University of Havana's

Catedra de Estudios sobre la Inmigración China en Cuba (Center for the Study of Chinese Immigration to Cuba), directed by María Teresa Montes de Oca Choy, has produced a multimedia CD-ROM on Havana's Chinese ethnic associations (Montes de Oca Choy 2007). Yrmina Eng Menéndez, former director of the Grupo Promotor de Barrio Chino, wrote a master's thesis on Chinese civic integration in Havana and a chapter on Barrio Chino for the volume I edited on community development in Cuba (Eng Menéndez 2008). A description of Barrio Chino in the early twentieth century by the historian Federico Chang (2007) appears in a volume on Cuban multiculturalism by Raimundo, Gómez Navia, and Graciela Chailloux (2007). The two most comprehensive historical analyses of Sino-Cuban cultural and political interaction are by Mauro García Triana (2003), former Cuban ambassador to China, and the historian Mercedes Crespo Villate (2004).

Recent years have also witnessed a flourishing interest in Chinese Cuban history from scholars outside Cuba. Joseph Dorsey (2004), Evelyn Hu-DeHart (1993, 1999, 2005a, and 2010), Moon-Ho Jung (2006), Kathleen López (2004, 2008, 2009, and 2013), and Lisa Yun (2008) have each made original contributions to the historical record of the coolie trade, describing both the difficulties faced by its victims and the ways they tried to organize and raise their community out of poverty. Earlier publications include Duvon C. Corbitt's ethnographic history, *A Study of the Chinese in Cuba, 1847–1947* (1971), and Beatriz Varela's account of Chinese linguistic influences in Cuban daily life, *Lo Chino en el Habla Cubana* (1980). *The Chinese in Cuba: 1847–Now* (Garcia Triana, Eng Herrera, and Benton 2009) presents the reflections of Mauro García Triana and the Chinese Cuban revolutionary leader Jesús Pedro Eng Herrera in their own words, with annotation by Gregor Benton. Autobiographical accounts of Chinese integration into Cuban revolutionary society are also presented in *Our History Is Still Being Written: The Story of Three Chinese Cuban Generals* (Choy, Chui, and Sío Wong 2006). Emerging at a time of intensifying Chinese engagement with Latin America and the world, this literature provides a historical framework for understanding the significance of Chinese presence in Cuba for both countries.

3. The declaration is now inscribed on a monument in Central Havana, visited by twenty-first-century visitors interested in tracing the tribulations of Chinese immigrants through Cuban history.

4. The Casino Chung Wah keeps meticulous records of the number of Chinese association members in Cuba. Jorge Chao Chiu, who maintains these records, reports that many who left Cuba in the 1960s were not association members and that it is therefore impossible to determine their numbers. The records show a sharp increase in the number of Chinese nationals adopting Cuban citizenship at the time, most likely so they could then enter the United States.

5. The absence of such ties in cases as diverse as Salvador (Brazil), Georgetown (Malaysia), and Madras (South India) has manifested in poor civic participation,

political apathy, and conflicting interpretations of local cultural heritage (Crook 1993; Kahn 1997; Woolcock 1998). Black markets and informal rules often take root in such contexts, posing challenges to institutions seeking to assert economic governance and discourage social fragmentation (Armony 2011; Hilgers 2008).

6. A similar process is evident in Cholon Chinatown in Ho Chi Minh City, where the Vietnamese government has attempted to selectively revive those aspects of Hoa (ethnic Chinese) heritage that attract tourism and portray multicultural harmony. Hoa residents' affinities with traditional and even contemporary Chinese culture, however, are tenuous at best (Yu 2006).

7. For details of the *Kwong Wah Po*'s origins and history, see Garcia Triana, Eng Herrera, and Benton (2009, 32–33, 40).

4. TRUST AND TREACHERY IN MEXICO'S CHINESE DIASPORA

1. Chinese production of Mexican artisanal handicrafts is perceived as piracy in Mexico. It began with the imitation of wooden products from the state of Michoacán and has extended to *rebozos* (traditional Mexican shawls), *tapetes* (decorative rugs), embroidered dresses, *talavera* (traditional pottery from Puebla), baskets, *hojas de lata* (tin plates), and silver and stone jewelry sold in tourist centers and markets around the country. This has outraged Mexican artisans, who claim that their sales have diminished by 70–80 percent. See Cruz García 2003; González Alvarado 2008; Noticieros Televisa 2005.

AgendAsia. 2012. *Agenda estratégica México-China*. Mexico City: AgendAsia.

Agosin, Manuel R., Pablo Rodas Martini, and Neantro Saavedra-Rivano, eds. 2004. *The Emergence of China: A View from Central America*. Washington: Inter-American Development Bank.

Aguiar, José Luis. 2012. "They Come from China: Pirate CDs in Mexico in Transnational Perspective." In *Globalization from Below: The World's Other Economy*, edited by Gordon Mathews, Gustavo Lins Ribeiro, and Carlos Alba Vega, 36–53. London: Routledge.

Alay Jó, Carlos A., and Julio Hun Calzadilla. 2015. *La Danza del león chino en Cuba*. Havana: Ediciones Extramuros.

Alay Jó, Ernesto, Carlos A. Alay Jó, and Jorge A. Alay Jó. 2002. "El Barrio Chino de la Habana: Un producto turístico." Paper presented at the Fifth Festival of Overseas Chinese, Havana, May 31, 2002.

Alba Vega, Carlos. 2012. "Local Politics and Globalization from Below: The Peddler Leaders of Mexico City's Historic Center Streets." In *Globalization from Below: The World's Other Economy*, edited by Gordon Mathews, Gustavo Lins Ribeiro, and Carlos Alba Vega, 203–20. London: Routledge.

Alfonso Rodríguez, Mayelín. 2009. "La presencia China en la conformación de Centro Habana: La farmacia y su rehabilitación." MA thesis, Institute Superior Politécnico José Antonio Echevarría, Havana.

Álvarez Medina, Lourdes. 2007. "La industria automotriz China: Posibilidades de competir con la industria automotriz en México." In *China y México: Implicaciones de una nueva relación*, edited by Enrique Dussel Peters and Yolanda Trápaga Delfín, 191–208. Mexico City: UNAM/CECHIMEX.

Amess, Kevin, Jun Du, and Sourafel Girma. 2011. "Turning to the Govt's Helping Hand." *China Daily European Weekly*, June, 10–16.

Anderson, Wanni W., and Robert G. Lee. 2005. "Asian American Displacements." In *Displacement and Diasporas: Asians in the Americas*, edited by Wanni W. Anderson and Robert G. Lee, 3–22. New Brunswick, NJ: Rutgers University Press.

Angel-Ajani, Asale. 2006. "Displacing Diaspora: Trafficking, African Women, and Transnational Practices." In *Diasporic Africa: A Reader*, edited by Michael Gomez, 290–308. New York: New York University Press.

Arellano, Lilia. 2013. "China en México." EstosDías.com, July 29. Accessed May 25, 2015. www.estosdias.com.mx/blog/archivos/4649.

Armony, Ariel C. 2004. *The Dubious Link: Civic Engagement and Democratization*. Stanford, CA: Stanford University Press.

———. 2011. "The China-Latin America Relationship: Convergences and Divergences." In *China Engages Latin America: Tracing the Trajectory*, edited by Adrian H. Hearn and José Luis León-Manríquez, 23–50. Boulder, CO: Lynne Rienner.

Armony, Ariel C., Nashira P. Chávez, and Adrian H. Hearn. Forthcoming. "Latin American Perspectives on the Pacific Alliance and the Trans-Pacific Partnership." Manuscript unpublished and under review.

Armony, Ariel C., and Julia C. Strauss. 2012. "From Going Out (*zou chuqu*) to Arriving In (*desembarco*): Constructing a New Field of Inquiry in China–Latin America Interactions." In *From the Great Wall to the New World: China and Latin America in the 21st Century*, edited by Julia C. Strauss and Ariel C. Armony, 1–17. Cambridge: Cambridge University Press.

Arrow, Kenneth. 1974. *The Limits of Organization*. New York: W. W. Norton.

Association of Former Intelligence Officers. 2006. "Chinese Signal Intelligence and Cyber Warfare Operations in Cuba." *AFIO Weekly Intelligence Notes*, no. 23-06, June 12. Accessed April 25, 2014. www.afio.com/sections/wins/2006/2006-23.html#ChinaInCuba.

Auyón Gerardo, Eduardo. 2003. *El dragón del desierto*. Mexicali, Mexico: Centro de Investigación de la Cultura China.

Ayón, David R., et al. 2009. *The United States and Mexico: Towards a strategic partnership*. Washington: Woodrow Wilson International Center for Scholars.

Azel, José. 2011. "So Much for Cuban Economic Reform." *Wall Street Journal*, January 10.

Bain, Ben, and Eric Martin. 2014. "Mexico Sets Borrower Standard 20 Years after Tequila Crisis." *Bloomberg*, September 22. Accessed August 4, 2015. www.bloomberg.com/news/articles/2014-09-21/mexico-sets-latin-america-standard-20-years-after-crisis.

Baltar Rodríguez, José. 1997. *Los Chinos de Cuba: Apuntes etnograficos*. Havana: Fundación Fernando Ortiz.

Barabantseva, Elena. 2005. "Trans-Nationalising Chineseness: Overseas Chinese Policies of the PRC's Central Government." *ASIEN* 96: 7–28.

Bate, Peter. 2004. "The Story behind *Oportunidades*." *FOCUS Online Magazine*. Washington: Inter-American Development Bank. Accessed August 4, 2015. www.iadb.org/en/news/webstories/2004-10-01/the-story-behind -10portunidadesi,5552.html.

Bazán, Ligia. 2005. "Inundan coreanos centro histórico." *El Diario*, January 18.

Behrens, Susan Fitzpatrick. 2009. "Plan Mexico and Central American Migration." North American Congress on Latin America, January 12. Accessed June 6, 2015. http://nacla.org/news/plan-mexico-and-central-american-migration.

Bell, Duran. 2000. "Guanxi: A Nesting of Groups." *Current Anthropology* 41 (1): 133–38.

Bernal, Rafael. 1969. *El complot mongol*. Mexico City: Joaquín Mortiz.

Bermúdez Liévano, Andrés. 2012. "La deferencia de haber sido recibida por Xi Jinping refleja la importancia y la madurez de la relación entre México y China: Canciller Mexicana Patricia Espinosa." China Files, April 13. Accessed August 4, 2015. http://china-files.com/es/link/16757/la-deferencia-de-haber-sido-recibida -por-xi-jinping-y-wang-qishan-refleja-la-importancia-la-riqueza-y-la-madurez -de-la-relacion-entre-mexico-y-china%E2%80%9D-canciller-mexicana-patricia -espinosa.

Blázquez-Lidoy, Jorge, Javier Rodríguez, and Javier Santiso, eds. 2006. *Angel or Devil? China's Trade Impact on Latin American Emerging Markets*. Paris: Organisation for Economic Co-operation and Development.

Boltvinik, Julio. 2003. "Welfare, Inequality, and Poverty in Mexico, 1970–2000." In *Confronting Development*, edited by Kevin J. Middlebrook and Eduardo Zepeda, 385–446. Stanford, CA: Stanford University Press.

Branigan, Tania, Julian Borger, and Jo Tuckman. 2009. "Swine Flu: Mexican Citizens Flown Back from China after Being Held in Hotels." *Guardian*. May 5. Accessed July 17, 2015. //www.theguardian.com/world/2009/may/05/swine-flu -china-mexico.

Braudel, Fernand. 1982. *On History*. Chicago: University of Chicago Press.

Buchenau, Jürgen. 2006. "Plutarco Elías Calles and the Maximato in Revolutionary Mexico: A Reinterpretation." *Jahrbuch für geschichte Lateinamerikas* 43: 229–53.

Burawoy, Michael, ed. 2000. *Global Ethnography: Forces, Connections, and Imaginations in a Postmodern World*. Berkeley: University of California Press.

Burt, Ronald. 1992. *Structural Holes: the Social Structure of Competition*. Cambridge, MA: Harvard University Press.

Calderon, Ángel. 2015. "Instability and Uncertainty Follow Killing of Students." University World News, February 20. Accessed February 23, 2015. www .universityworldnews.com/article.php?story=20150218105730190.

Calderón, Felipe. 2008. "Mensaje del Presidente Felipe Calderón sobre el programa para impulsar el crecimiento y el empleo." *La Crónica*, October 9. Accessed April 28, 2014. www.cronica.com.mx/notas/2008/390120.html.

Calva, José Luis. 2012. "Prólogo." In *Nueva estrategia de industrialización*, edited by José Luis Calva, 9–21. Mexico City: Consejo Nacional de Universitarios.

Cámara Nacional de la Industria Textil. 2006. "Noticias de nuestro sector." Accessed August 4, 2015. www.canaintex.org.mx. Subscription required.

Canseco, Mario. 2006. "The Second Campaign of Vicente Fox." *Banderas News*, March 18. Accessed August 4, 2015. www.banderasnews.com/0603/eded -secondcampaign.htm.

Carr, Barry. 1973. "Las peculiaridades del norte Mexicano, 1880–1927: Ensayo de interpretación." *Historia Mexicana* 22 (31): 320–46.

Carrier, James G. 1999. "People Who Can Be Friends: Selves and Social Relationships." In *The Anthropology of Friendship*, edited by Sandra Bell and Simon Coleman, 21–38. New York: Berg.

Casey-Maslen, Stuart. 2014. "The Use of Firearms in Law Enforcement." In *Weapons under International Human Rights Law*, edited by Stuart Casey-Maslen, 3–31. New York: Cambridge University Press.

Castles, Stephen. 2006. *Global Perspectives on Forced Migration. Asian and Pacific Migration Journal* 15 (1): 7–28.

Cattan, Nacha, and Eric Martin. 2013. "Mexico's Peña Nieto Seeks Capital Gains, High Earners Taxes." *Bloomberg*, September 9. Accessed August 4, 2015. www .bloomberg.com/news/articles/2013-09-09/pena-nieto-seeks-taxes-on-capital -gains-highest-income-earners.

Cereijo, Manuel. 2001. "China/Cuba: A New Dangerous Axis." *Guaracabuya*, summer. Accessed April 25, 2014. www.amigospais-guaracabuya.org/oagmc065.php.

———. 2010. "Inside Bejucal Base in Cuba: A Real Threat." *Americano*, August 27.

Céspedes, Benjamín de. 1888. *La prostitución en la ciudad de La Habana*. Havana: Tipografía O'Reilly.

Chang, David W. 1973. "Current Status of Chinese Minorities in Southeast Asia." *Asian Survey* 13 (6): 587–603.

Chang, Federico. 2007. "La inmigración china en Cuba: Asociaciones y tradiciones." In *De dónde son los cubanos*, edited by Raimundo Gómez Navia and Graciela Chailloux, 117–64. Havana: Editorial de Ciencias Sociales.

Chen, Albert H. Y. 1999. "Rational Law, Economic Development and the Case of China." *Social and Legal Studies* 8 (1): 97–120.

Chen Xiaoping, and C. Chao Chen. 2004. "On the Intricacies of the Chinese Guanxi: A Process Model of Guanxi Development." *Asia-Pacific Journal of Management* 21: 305–24.

Cheng Yinghong. 2007a. "Fidel Castro and 'China's Lessons for Cuba': A Chinese Perspective." *China Quarterly* 189: 24–42.

———. 2007b. "Sino-Cuban Relations and Cuba's Future after Fidel Castro." *History Compass* 5 (2): 725–36.

———. 2012. "The 'Socialist Other': Cuba in Chinese Ideological Debates since the 1990s." *China Quarterly* 209: 198–216.

"China and Cuba Co-Develop New Anti-Cancer Vaccine." 2012. *China Daily*. March 29. Accessed August 4, 2015. www.chinadaily.com.cn/m/beijing/zhong guancun/2012-03/29/content_14938029.htm.

"China Confirms Leadership Change." 2012. *BBC News*. November 15. Accessed July 14, 2015. www.bbc.co.uk/news/world-asia-china-20338586.

China National Petroleum Corporation. 2008. "CNPC and CUPET Reach Framework Agreement on Further Cooperation." November 27. Accessed April 25, 2014. www.cnpc.com.cn/en/nr2008/201211/557bf652cd624c64a240a504b beb882b.shtm.

"'China Threat' Fear Countered by Culture." 2006. *People's Daily*, May 29. Accessed April 28, 2014. http://english.peopledaily.com.cn/200605/29 /eng20060529_269387.html.

Chinese Association of Tijuana. 1998. "Laws of the Chinese Community of Tijuana." Booklet for distribution among association members.

Chong López, Alfredo. 2006. "Proyecto: Barrio Chino—Hua Qu." Unpublished report. Havana: Casa de Artes y Tradiciones Chinas.

Chou, Diego. 2002. *Los Chinos en Hispanoamérica*. San José, Costa Rica: Facultad Latinoamericana de Ciencias Sociales.

Choy, Armando, Gustavo Chui, and Moisés Sío Wong. 2006. *Our History Is Still Being Written: The Story of Three Chinese Cuban Generals in the Cuban Revolution*. New York: Pathfinder.

Christian Anti-Communism Crusade. 1961. "If Communism Comes to Mexico." *CACC Newletter*, September 9.

Chuffat Latour, Antonio. 1927. *Apunte histórico de los chinos en Cuba*. Havana: Molina y Cía.

Coleman, James S. 1988. "Social Capital in the Creation of Human Capital." *American Journal of Sociology*, supplement 94: S95–120.

Comisión Económica para América Latina. 2004. *Panorama de la inserción internacional de América Latina y el Caribe, 2002–2003*. Santiago, Chile: Comisión Económica para América Latina.

Connelly, Marisela, and Romer Cornejo Bustamante. 1992. *China América Latina*. Mexico City: El Colegio de México.

Cooke, Bill, and Uma Kothari. 2001. *Participation: The New Tyranny*. New York: Zed.

Corbitt, Duvon C. 1944. "Chinese Immigrants in Cuba." *Far Eastern Survey* 13 (14): 130–32.

———. 1971. *A Study of the Chinese in Cuba, 1847–1947*. Wilmore, KY: Asbury College.

Coronel, Rogelio. 2008. "El rastro chino en la cultura cubana." *Anales del Caribe* 1 (1): 158–77.

Cortés, Cecilia Téllez. 2009. "Admite Calderón: Hay 6 millones más de pobres desde que estalló la crisis." *La Crónica*, October 3.

Cosme Baños, Pedro. 1998. *Los Chinos en regla, 1847–1997: Documentos y comentarios*. Santiago de Cuba: Editorial Oriente.

Council on Hemispheric Affairs. 2011. *Cuban Oil Demands Washington's Attention*. Washington: Council on Hemispheric Affairs.

Courtade, Luis Pérez. 2013. "Mancera entrega las llaves de la ciudad a presidente de China." *Excelsior* (published in Mexico), June 6. Accessed May 2, 2014. http://www.excelsior.com.mx/comunidad/2013/06/06/902676.

Crahan, Margaret E., and Ariel C. Armony. 2007. "Does Civil Society Exist in Cuba?" Florida International University, Cuban Research Institute. Accessed June 6, 2015. https://cri.fiu.edu/research/commissioned-reports/civil-society-crahanoarmony.pdf.

Crespo Villate, Mercedes. 2004. *Legación Cubana en China, 1904–1959: Primeros consulados diplomaticos Cubanos y vivencias historicas con la nacion Asiatica*. Havana: Editorial SI-MAR.

Crook, Larry N. 1993. "Black Consciousness, Samba Reggae, and the Re-Africanization of Bahian Carnival Music in Brazil." *World of Music* 35 (2): 90–108.

Cross, John C. 1998. *Informal Politics: Street Vendors and the State in Mexico City*. Stanford, CA: Stanford University Press.

Cruz García, Hortencia. 2003. "Instrumentos musicales Chinos invaden el mercado nacional." *Xiranhua Comunicaciones*, September, 1–15.

"Cuba Claims Massive Oil Reserves." 2008. *BBC News*, October 17. Accessed April 25, 2014. http://news.bbc.co.uk/2/hi/7675234.stm.

Cubaencuentro. 2009. "Más acuerdos con China. Esta vez en industria básica, transporte e informática." Editorial, November 16. Accessed April 25, 2014. http://cubaencuentro.com/es/cuba/noticias/mas-acuerdos-con-china-esta-vez-en-industria-basica-transporte-e-informatica-223337.

"Cuba Seeks Chinese Investment." 2013. *China Daily*, November 4.

Cuba Standard. 2011. "China, Cuba Agree on Refinery Project, New Loans." Editorial, June 6. Accessed 12 July 2015. www.gasandoil.com/news/south_east_asia/f665a752191284342a49572ae311b70c.

Cypher, James M., and Raúl Delgado Wise. 2010. *Mexico's Economic Dilemma: The Developmental Failure of Neoliberalism*. Lanham, MD: Rowman and Littlefield.

De Kadt, Raphael. 1994. "Modernization and Moral Progress." *Theoria* 83 (4): 43–60.

Délano, Alexandra. 2011. *Mexico and Its Diaspora in the United States: Policies of Emigration since 1848*. New York: Cambridge University Press.

Devlin, Robert. 2008. "China's Economic Rise." In *China's Expansion into the Western Hemisphere: Implications for Latin America and the United States*, edited by Riordan Roett and Guadalupe Paz, 111–47. Washington: Brookings Institution.

Dickson, Bruce, and Chao Chien-Min. 2001. Introduction to *Remaking the Chinese State*, edited by Bruce Dickson and Chao Chien-Min, 1–16. London: Routledge.

Domínguez, Jorge I., et al. 2006. "China's Relations with Latin America: Shared Gains, Asymmetric Hopes." Washington: Inter-American Dialogue.

Dorsey, Joseph C. 2004. "Identity, Rebellion, and Social Justice among Chinese Contract Workers in Nineteenth-Century Cuba." *Latin American Perspectives* 31 (3): 18–47.

Durand, Jorge, Douglas S. Massey, and Rene M. Zenteno. 2001. "Mexican Immigration to the United States: Continuities and Changes." *Latin American Research Review* 36 (1): 107–27.

Dussel Peters, Enrique. 2009. "The Mexican Case." In *China and Latin America: Economic Relations in the Twenty-First Century*, edited by Rhys Jenkins and Enrique Dussel Peters, 279–393. Mexico City: UNAM/CECHIMEX.

———. 2011a. "China's Challenge to Latin American Development." In *China Engages Latin America: Tracing the Trajectory*, edited by Adrian H. Hearn and José Luis León-Manríquez, 91–101. Boulder, CO: Lynne Rienner.

———. 2011b. *México: Hacia una agenda estratégica en el corto, mediano y largo plazo con China. Propuestas resultantes de las labores del Grupo de Trabajo México-China (2009–2010)*. Mexico City: UNAM/CECHIMEX.

———. 2012. "Mexican Firms Investing in China 2000–2011." Washington: Inter-American Development Bank.

Dussel Peters, Enrique, and Samuel Ortiz Velázquez. 2012. *Monitor de la manufactura Mexicana* 8 (9). Mexico City: UNAM/CECHIMEX.

Economic Commission for Latin America and the Caribbean. 2010. Database of the División de Comercio Internacional e Integración. Accessed June 1, 2015. www.cepal.org/comercio/SIGCI.

Economist Intelligence Unit. 2008. *Country Profile: Cuba 2008*. London: Economist Intelligence Unit.

EFE. 2014. "Mexico Gov't Imposes Tariff of up to 30 pct on Footwear Imports." Editorial, August 28.

———. 2015. "Oil Prices to Stay Low for Years, Bank of Mexico Says." Editorial, February 3.

El Economista. 2008. "China produce 90% de las 'banderitas' de México." Editorial, September 15.

El Mural. 2011. "Plantean de nuevo prórroga a apertura." Editorial, December 8.

El Universal (published in Mexico). 2008. "México tendrá catarrito por crisis en EU: Carstens." Editorial, February 7. Accessed July 17, 2015. http://archivo.eluniversal.com.mx/notas/480345.html

Ellis, R. Evan. 2005. *U.S. National Security Implications of Chinese Involvement in Latin America*. Carlisle, PA: Strategic Studies Institute.

———. 2009. *China in Latin America: The Whats and Wherefores.* Boulder, CO: Lynne Rienner.

———. 2012. "Chinese Organized Crime in Latin America." *Prism* 4 (1): 65–77.

Ely, Northcutt. 1961. *Summary of Mining and Petroleum Laws of the World.* Washington: Bureau of Mines.

Eng Menéndez, Yrmina G. 2008. "Revitalización de las tradiciones Chinas en Cuba: El proyecto integral de reanimación del Barrio Chino de La Habana." In *Cultura, tradición, y comunidad: Perspectivas sobre la participación y el desarrollo en Cuba,* edited by Adrian H. Hearn, 200–243. Havana: Imagen Contemporánea.

Epoch Times. 2007. "En México todos le declaran la guerra al 'comercio desleal' chino." Editorial. April 1.

Erikson, Daniel P., and Adam Minson. 2006. "China and Cuba: The New Face of an Old Relationship." *Hemisphere* 17 (22): 12–15.

Evans, Peter. 1997. "Introduction: Development Strategies across the Public-Private Divide." In *State-Society Synergy: Government and Social Capital in Development,* edited by Peter Evans, 1–10. Berkeley: University of California Press.

Fedderke, Johannes, Raphael de Kadt, and John Luiz. 1999. "Economic Growth and Social Capital: A Critical Reflection." *Theory and Society* 28 (5): 709–45.

Feinberg, Richard E. 2011. *Reaching Out: Cuba's New Economy and the International Response.* Washington: Brookings Institution.

Fernández Jilberto, Alex E., and Barbara Hogenboom, eds. 2010a. *Latin America Facing China: South-South Relations beyond the Washington Consensus.* New York: Berghan.

———. 2010b. "Latin America from Washington Consensus to Beijing Consensus?" In *Latin America Facing China: South-South Relations beyond the Washington Consensus,* edited by Alex Fernández Jilberto and Barbara Hogenboom, 181–93. New York: Berghan.

Fernández Soriano, Armando. 1999. "Realidades, retos y posibilidades de los municipios Cubanos en el fin de siglo." In *Gobiernos de izquierda en América Latina,* edited by Beatriz Stolowicz, 165–82. Mexico City: Plaza Valdés.

Fingleton, Eamonn. 2008. *In the Jaws of the Dragon: America's Fate in the Coming Era of Chinese Hegemony.* New York: St. Martin's.

Florida International University. 2014. *FIU Cuba Poll.* Miami: Florida International University Cuban Research Institute.

Fornieles Sánchez, Luz María. 1993. "El Barrio Chino." *Contrapunto* 3 (27): 25–26.

Frank, Marc. 2006. "Trade with China Primes Cuba's Engine for Change." *Financial Times,* March 7.

———. 2012. "Cuba Plans Massive Shift to 'Non-State' Sector." Reuters, April 23.

———. 2013. "Cuba to Embark on Deregulation of State Companies." Reuters, July 8.

Freitag, Markus. 2003. "Beyond Tocqueville: The Origins of Social Capital in Switzerland." *European Sociological Review* 19 (2): 217–32.

French, Howard W. 2007. "Propina crisis de seguridad." *El Mural*, July 15.

Fukuyama, Francis. 1992. *The End of History and the Last Man*. New York: Free Press.

———. 1995. *Trust: The Social Virtues and the Creation of Prosperity*. New York: Free Press.

———. 2000. "Social Capital and Civil Society." Washington: International Monetary Fund.

Fung, Archon, et al. 2004. "The Political Economy of Transparency: What Makes Disclosure Policies Effective?" John F. Kennedy School of Government, Harvard University. Accessed May 24, 2015. http://www.transparencypolicy.net/assets /whatnakesdisclosureeffective.pdf.

Gallagher, Kevin P., and Roberto Porzecanski. 2010. *The Dragon in the Room: China and the Future of Latin American Industrialization*. Stanford, CA: Stanford University Press.

García, Anne-Marie. 2013. "Cuba OKs More Private Businesses, New Regulations." Associated Press, September 26.

García, Judith. 2008. "Burlan chinos estaciones migratorias para llevar fayuca a Tepito." Organización Editorial Mexicana, November 2. Accessed June 6, 2015. www.oem.com.mx/esto/notas/n915852.htm.

García, Myriam. 2007. "Abren la puerta a China." *El Mural*, July 13.

García Triana, Mauro. 2003. *Los Chinos de Cuba y los nexos entre las dos naciones*. Havana: Sociedad Cubana de Estudios e Investigaciones Filosóficas.

García Triana, Mauro, Pedro Eng Herrera, and Gregor Benton. 2009. *The Chinese in Cuba: 1847–Now*. Lanham, MD: Lexington.

García Zamora, Rodolfo. 2009. "Migration under NAFTA: Exporting Goods and People." In *The Future of North American Trade Policy: Lessons from NAFTA*, edited by Kevin P. Gallagher, Enrique Dussel Peters, and Timothy A. Wise, 79–83. Boston: Boston University/Pardee Center.

Geertz, Clifford. 1973. *The Interpretation of Cultures: Selected Essays*. New York: Basic.

Gibson, William E. 2014. "Russia Plunges into Cuban Oil Exploration." *Sun Sentinel*, June 15.

Global Times. 2014. "Premier 'Regrets' Mexico's Scrapping of Rail Deal." Editorial, November 12.

Gómez Izquierdo, Jorge. 2007. "La sinofobia de los Mexicanos: Una historia de prejuicios y estereotipos racistas." Paper presented at the conference "China-Mexico: Oportunidades y tetos de la economía de la República Popular China para México," Faculty of Economics, Universidad Nacional Autónoma de México, September 12.

Gómez Mena, Carolina. 2006. "En condiciones de esclavitud, cientos de trabajadores chinos en Guanajuato." *La Jornada*, February 25. Accessed May 2, 2014. www.jornada.unam.mx/2006/02/25/index.php?section=sociedad&article=045 n1soc.

Gómez Navia, Raimundo, and Graciela Chailloux, eds. 2007. *De dónde son los Cubanos*. Havana: Editorial de Ciencias Sociales.

González, Angel T. 2005. "La milicia china de Castro." *El Mundo*, June 19.

González, María de la Luz. 2005. "El zurcido invisible." *La Jornada*, June 13.

González, Palmira. 2007. "Invierten $142 millones para tecnología en NL." *El Norte*, October 6.

González, Susana. 2006. "Que no regrese el ambulantaje al centro: Comercio establecido." *Reforma*, January 14.

González Alvarado, Rocio. 2008. "Piratería china de artesanías amenaza subsistencia del mercado de la ciudadela." *La Jornada*, July 14.

González Oropeza, Manuel. 1997. "La discriminación en México: El caso de los nacionales Chinos." In *La problemática del racismo en los umbrales del siglo XXI: VI jornadas lascanianas*, 47–56. Mexico City: UNAM.

Graham, Mary. 2001. "Information as Risk Regulation: Lessons from Experience." John F. Kennedy School of Government, Harvard University. Accessed May 24, 2015. http://www.transparencypolicy.net/assets/information.pdf.

Gran Liga Nacional Pro-Raza. 1927. "La bestia amarilla." Pamphlet for public distribution. Collection of Catalina Velázquez Morales, Department of History, the Autonomous University of Baja California.

Granma (published in Cuba). 2008. "Firmados importantes acuerdos." Editorial, November 5.

———. 2014. "Ligero crecimiento turístico en Cuba en 2013." Editorial, January 6.

Granovetter, Mark. 1973. "The Strength of Weak Ties." *American Journal of Sociology* 78 (6): 1360–80.

Greene, Graham. 1981. *Ways of Escape*. New York: Penguin.

Grupo para el Desarrollo Integral de la Capital. 2001. *La maqueta de La Habana*. Havana: Grupo para el Desarrollo Integral de la Capital.

Guanche, Jesús. 1983. *Componentes etnicos de la nación Cubana*. Havana: Editorial Ciencias Sociales.

Guthrie, Douglas. 1998. "The Declining Significance of Guanxi in China's Economic Transition." *China Quarterly* 154: 254–82.

Hall, Derek. 1992. "Tourism Development in Cuba." In *Tourism and the Less Developed Countries*, edited by David Harrison, 102–20. London: Belhaven.

Hall, Simon. 2013. "Asia Faces Competition in Mexico's Energy Sector." *Wall Street Journal*, December 16.

Haro Navejas, Francisco. 2007. "El dominio de las emociones: Percepciones Mexicanas sobre China." In *China y México: Implicaciones de una nueva relación*, edited by Enrique Dussel Peters and Yolanda Trápaga Delfín, 455–70. Mexico City: UNAM/CECHIMEX .

He Shuangrong, ed. 2012. *China–Latin America Relations: Review and Analysis.* Reading, UK: Paths International. Translated from Chinese to English by Liu Maomin.

Hearn, Adrian H. 2004. "Afro-Cuban Religions and Social Welfare: Consequences of Commercial Development in Havana." *Human Organization* 63 (1): 79–88.

———. 2005. "Political Dimensions of International NGO Collaboration with Cuba." In *Cuba Today: Continuity and Change since the "Periodo Especial,"* , edited by Mauricio A. Font with the assistance of Scott Larson and Danielle Xuereb, 209–27. New York: City University of New York Graduate Center.

———. 2008a. *Cuba: Religion, Social Capital, and Development.* Durham, NC: Duke University Press.

———, ed. 2008b. *Cultura, tradición, y comunidad: Perspectivas sobre la participación y el desarrollo en Cuba.* Havana: Imagen Contemporánea.

———. 2009. "Cuba and China: Lessons and Opportunities for the United States." Miami: Florida International University Cuban Research Institute. Accessed February 12, 2015. https://cri.fiu.edu/research/commissioned-reports/cuba -china-hearn.pdf.

———. 2010. "中国在全球一体化下的关键主题" [Transparency and good governance: Key themes in China's global integration]. *Chinese Social Sciences Today.* March 4. Accessed April 24, 2014. http://sspress.cass.cn/news/8127 .htm.

Hearn, Adrian H., and Félix J. Alfonso. 2012. "Antecedentes locales y globales de las reformas cubanas." *Temas* 71: 21–28.

Hearn, Adrian H., and José Luis León-Manríquez, eds. 2011. *China Engages Latin America: Tracing the Trajectory.* Boulder, CO: Lynne Rienner.

Hearn, Adrian H., Alan Smart, and Roberto Hernández Hernández. 2011. "China and Mexico: Trade, Migration, and Guanxi." In *China Engages Latin America: Tracing the Trajectory,* edited by Adrian H. Hearn and José Luis León Manríquez, 139–57. Boulder, CO: Lynne Rienner.

Hernández, Rafael, Yenisel Rodríguez, and Juan Triana. 2011. "Dossier." *Espacio Laical* 1: 24–47. Accessed July 14, 2015. http://espaciolaical.org/contens/25 /2447.pdf.

Hernández Hernández, Roberto. 2012. "Economic Liberalization and Trade Relations between Mexico and China." *Journal of Current Chinese Affairs* 41 (1): 49–96.

Herrera Jerez, Miriam, and Mario Castillo Santana. 2003. *De la memoria a la vida pública: Identidades, espacios, y jerarquías de los Chinos en La Habana republicana (1902–1968).* Havana: Juan Marinello.

Heryanto, Ariel. 1998. "Ethnic Identities and Erasure: Chinese Indonesians in Public Culture." In *Southeast Asian Identities: Culture and the Politics of Rep-*

resentation in Indonesia, Malaysia, Singapore, and Thailand, edited by Joel S. Kahn, 95–114. Singapore: Institute of Southeast Asian Studies.

Hilgers, Tina. 2008. "Recentering Informality on the Research Agenda: Grassroots Action, Political Parties, and Democratic Governance." *Latin American Research Review* 43 (2): 272–81.

Hill, Matthew J. 2007. "Reimagining Old Havana: World Heritage and the Production of Scale in Late Socialist Cuba." In *Deciphering the Global: Its Scales, Spaces, and Subjects*, edited by Saski Sassen, 59–76. New York: Routledge.

Hira, Anil. 2007. *An East Asian Model for Latin American Success*. London: Ashgate.

Hirschman, Albert O. 1984. *Getting Ahead Collectively: Grassroots Experiences in Latin America*. New York: Pergamon.

Hobsbawm, Eric, and Terence Ranger. 1992. *The Invention of Tradition*. Cambridge: Cambridge University Press.

Horcasitas, Fernando. 1968. *De Porfirio Díaz a Zapata: Memoria náhuatl de Milpa Alta*. Mexico City: UNAM.

Hsing, You Tien. 1998. *Making Capitalism in China: The Taiwan Connection*. Oxford: Oxford University Press.

Hsu, Carolyn L. 2005. "Capitalism without Contracts versus Capitalists without Capitalism: Comparing the Influence of Chinese Guanxi and Russian Blat on Marketization." *Communist and Post-Communist Studies* 38 (3): 309–27.

Hua, Shajun. 2005. "Puros en China." *China Hoy* 46 (3): 34–37.

Hu-DeHart, Evelyn. 1993. "Chinese Coolie Labour in Cuba in the Nineteenth Century: Free Labour or Neoslavery?" *Slavery and Abolition* 14 (1): 67–86.

———. 1999. "Race Construction and Race Relations: Chinese and Blacks in Nineteenth-Century Cuba." In *Encounters: People of Asian Descent in the Americas*, edited by Roshni Rustomji-Kerns, 105–12. Lanham, MD: Rowman and Littlefield.

———. 2003. "Globalization and Its Discontents: Exposing the Underside." *Frontiers* 24 (2–3): 244–60.

———. 2005a. "Opium and Social Control: Coolies on the Plantations of Peru and Cuba." *Journal of Chinese Overseas* 1 (2): 169–83.

———. 2005b. "On Coolies and Shopkeepers: The Chinese as Huagong (laborers) and Huashang (merchants) in Latin America/Caribbean." In *Displacement and Diasporas: Asians in the Americas*, edited by Wanni W. Anderson and Robert G. Lee, 78–110. New Brunswick, NJ: Rutgers University Press.

———. 2007. "Latin America in Asia-Pacific Perspective." In *Asian Diasporas: New Formations, New Conceptions*, edited by Rhacel S. Parreñas and Lok C. D. Siu, 29–62. Stanford, CA: Stanford University Press.

———. 2010. "Indispensable Enemy or Convenient Scapegoat? A Critical Examination of Sinophobia in Latin America and the Caribbean, 1870s to 1930s." In

The Chinese in Latin America and the Caribbean, edited by Walton Look Lai and Tan Chee-Beng, 65–102. Leiden, the Netherlands: Brill.

Hughes, Krista. 2013. "Mexico Aims to Bring Shadow Economy into the Light." Reuters, June 26.

Hun Calzadilla, Julio. 2010. "Las sociedades Chinas en Cuba: Escudo y sostén." Monografías.com. Accessed May 1, 2014. http://www.monografias.com /trabajos39/sociedades-chinas-cuba/sociedades-chinas-cuba.shtml.

Hurst, William. 2002. "'Comrade Can You Spare a Dime?' Political Status, Guanxi, and the Transition from State to Market for China's Workers." Paper presented at the annual meeting of the American Political Science Association, August 31.

Hutchinson-Jafar, Linda. 2011. "China's CNPC in Talks for Possible Cuba Oil Block." Reuters, July 13. Accessed April 25, 2014. www.reuters.com/article/2011 /07/13/cuba-china-oil-idUSN1E76C1S620110713.

Iliff, Laurence. 2009. "Remittances to Mexico Fall 36%." *Wall Street Journal*, December 1.

"Importancia de las Pymes." Las Pymes, June 14. Accessed April 28, 2014. http:// laspymes.com.mx/importancia-de-las-pymes.html.

"Indigna en redes, vestuario usado por Angélica Rivera e hija en gira por Londres." 2015. Proceso.com, March 6. Accessed March 9, 2015. www.proceso.com.mx /?p=397721.

Instituto Nacional de Estadísticas y Geografía. 2010. "Censo de población y vivienda 2010." Accessed May 2, 2014. http://www.censo2010.org.mx/.

Jiang Shixue. 2009. *Cuba's Economic Reforms in Chinese Perspective*. Beijing: Chinese Academy of Social Sciences.

———. 2011. "Ten Key Questions." In *China Engages Latin America: Tracing the Trajectory*, edited by Adrian H. Hearn and José Luis León Manríquez, 51–65. Boulder, CO: Lynne Rienner.

Jung, Moon-Ho. 2006. *Coolies and Cane: Race, Labor, and Sugar in the Age of Emancipation*. Baltimore, MD: Johns Hopkins University Press.

Kagan, Robert. 2008. *The Return of History and the End of Dreams*. New York: Knopf.

Kahn, Joel. 1997. "Culturalizing Malaysia." In *Tourism, Ethnicity, and the State in Asian and Pacific Societies*, edited by Michel Picard and Robert E. Wood, 99–127. Honolulu: University of Hawai'i Press.

Keister, Lisa A. 2002. "Guanxi in Business Groups: Social Ties and the Formation of Economic Relations." In *Social Connections in China: Institutions, Culture, and the Changing Nature of Guanxi*, edited by Thomas Gold, Doug Guthrie, and David Wank, 77–96. Cambridge: Cambridge University Press.

Kirk, John M. 2007. "Toward an Understanding of the Tourism Potential in Cuba." *Cornell Hotel and Restaurant Administration Quarterly* 48 (4): 416–18.

Klepak, Hal. 2010. *Raúl Castro, estratega de la defensa revolucionaria de Cuba*. Buenos Aires: Capital Intelectual.

Kuhn, Philip A. 2008. *Chinese among Others: Emigration in Modern Times.* Lanham, MD: Rowman and Littlefield.

Kurlantzick, Joshua. 2007. *Charm Offensive: How China's Soft Power Is Transforming the World.* New Haven, CT: Yale University Press.

———. 2008. "China's Growing Influence in Southeast Asia." In *China's Expansion into the Western Hemisphere: Implications for Latin America and the United States,* edited by Riordan Roett and Guadalupe Paz, 193–212. Washington: Brookings Institution.

Labrador Ruiz, Enrique. 1952. "Chinatown, Havana." *Americas* 4 (8): 6–8, 42–43.

La Crónica (published in Mexico). 2008. "Prometen a Chinos traer a sus familias." Editorial, October 24.

"La economía informal representa 15% del PIB." 2012. Informador.Mx, June 7. Accessed April 28, 2014. www.informador.com.mx/economia/2012/381491/6 /la-economia-informal-representa-15-del-pib.htm.

La Jornada (published in Mexico). 2015. "Militares heridos en los hechos de Tlatlaya también serán indemnizados: CEAV." Editorial, February 22.

Lam, Willy. 2004. "China's Encroachment on America's Backyard." *China Brief* 4 (23): 1–3.

La Prensa (published in Mexico). 2005. "Acusan a China de competencia desleal." Editorial, January 30.

Laverty, Collin. 2011. *Cuba's New Resolve: Economic Reform and Its Implications for U.S. Policy.* Washington: Center for Democracy in the Americas.

Lederman, Daniel, Marcelo Olarreaga, and Guillermo E. Perry, eds. 2008. *China's and India's Challenge to Latin America: Opportunity or Threat?* Washington: World Bank.

Lee, Christopher. 2007. "Diaspora, Transnationalism, and Asian American Studies: Positions and Debates." In *Asian Diasporas: New Formations, New Conceptions,* edited by Rhacel S. Parreñas and Lok C. D. Siu, 23–38. Stanford, CA: Stanford University Press.

León-Manríquez, José Luis. 2011. "China's Relations with Mexico and Chile: Boom for Whom?" In *China Engages Latin America: Tracing the Trajectory,* edited by Adrian H. Hearn and José Luis León-Manríquez, 159–201. Boulder, CO: Lynne Rienner.

Lin Hua. 2012. "Functions of Chinese Communities in the Development of China–Latin America Relations." In *China–Latin America Relations: Review and Analysis,* edited by He Shuangrong, 107–19. Reading, UK: Paths International.

Lin, Nan. 2001. *Social Capital: A Theory of Social Structure and Action.* Cambridge: Cambridge University Press.

Linares Savio, María Teresa. 2000. "Expresiones de la cultura China en Cuba: El teatro, la música." *Catauro* 2 (2): 41–49.

Lo, Ming-Cheng M., and Eileen M. Otis. 2003. "Guanxi Civility: Processes, Potentials, and Contingencies." *Politics and Society* 31 (1): 131–62.

Lombera, Manuel. 2009. "México no supo manejar la crisis: Stiglitz." *El Universal*, November 19.

López, Guadalupe. 2009. "Expanden cultura china." *La Frontera* (published in Mexico), February 12.

López, Johnny. 1942. Vocal performance of "El chinito pichilón" by Ñico Saquito Bimbi, Luis M. Bosch, Hermenegildo Cardenas Bimbi. Recorded on Cuarteto la Playa, Decca [format: 78–10, publish #: 21266–1].

López, Kathleen. 2004. "One Brings Another: The Formation of Early-Twentieth-Century Chinese Migrant Communities in Cuba." In *The Chinese in the Caribbean*, edited by Andrew Wilson, 93–127. Princeton, NJ: Markus Wiener.

———. 2008. "Afro-Asian Alliances: Marriage, Godparentage, and Social Status in Late-Nineteenth-Century Cuba." *Afro-Hispanic Review* 27 (1): 59–72.

———. 2009. "The Revitalization of Havana's Chinatown: Invoking Chinese Cuban History." *Journal of Chinese Overseas* 5 (1): 177–200.

———. 2013. *Chinese Cubans: A Transnational History*. Chapel Hill: University of North Carolina Press.

López, Mario. 2006a. "Cambian giros de comercios a bodegas." *Reforma*, June 5.

———. 2006b. "Reconocen incapacidad en aduanas." *Reforma*, January 16.

———. 2007. "Urgen para tepito plan contra piratería." *Reforma*, January 13.

Lopez, Mark H., Gretchen Livingstone, and Rakesh Kochhar. 2009. "Hispanics and the Economic Downturn: Housing Woes and Remittance Cuts." Pew Hispanic Center Report, January 8. Accessed August 5, 2015. www.pewhispanic .org/2009/01/08/hispanics-and-the-economic-downturn-housing-woes-and -remittance-cuts/.

Lopez-Levy, Arturo. 2011a. *Change in Post-Fidel Cuba: Political Liberalization, Economic Reform and Lessons for U.S. Policy*. Washington: New America Foundation.

———. 2011b. "Reformas económicas y desarrollo en el Este de Asia: ¿Una experiencia para Cuba?" *Espacio Laical* 3: 40–44.

Macaluso, Grace. 2010. "Incentives Sealed Deal with Nemak; City Steps Up to Save Jobs with Tax Breaks." *Windsor Star*, September 29.

Mao, Xianglin, et al. 2011. "China and Cuba: Past, Present, and Future." In *China Engages Latin America: Tracing the Trajectory*, edited by Adrian H. Hearn and José Luis León-Manríquez, 187–201. Boulder, CO: Lynne Rienner.

Mao, Xianglin, Adrian H. Hearn, and Liu Weiguang. 2015. "China and Cuba: 160 Years and Looking Ahead." *Latin American Perspectives* 42 (6).

Marcus, George E. 1995. "Ethnography in/of the World System: The Emergence of Multi-Sited Ethnography." *Annual Review of Anthropology* 24: 95–117.

Marquez, Julio. 1994. "Bad News, Good News: Colosio's Untimely Death Could Mean the Rebirth of Reform." *Reason*, July. Accessed July 16. http://reason.com /archives/1994/07/01/bad-news-good-news.

Martin, Andrew. 2007. "Escándalos favorecen seguridad alimenticia." *El Mural*, June 15.

Mau, Steffen. 2010. *Social Transnationalism: Lifeworlds beyond the Nation-State*. London: Routledge.

Mayoral Jiménez, Isabel. 2011. "México se 'blinda' por contrabando Chino." CNNExpansión, December 6. Accessed April 27, 2014. www.cnnexpansion .com/economia/2011/12/06/mexico-se-blinda-vs-pirateria-de-china.

McKeown, Adam M. 2001. *Chinese Migrant Networks and Cultural Change: Peru, Chicago, and Hawaii, 1900–1938*. Chicago: University of Chicago Press.

———. 2008. *Melancholy Order: Asian Migration and the Globalization of Borders*. New York: Columbia University Press.

Mejía, Javier. 2008. "Festejó asociación China la 'semana de migración.'" *La Voz de la Frontera*, October 24. Accessed May 2, 2014. http://www.oem.com.mx/esto /notas/n904413.htm.

Meo, Paul. 2011. "Change in Cuba?" *ASCE Newsletter*, September 6–10. Accessed August 5, 2015. www.ascecuba.org/c/wp-content/uploads/2014/09/newsletter -2011-09-03.pdf.

Mesa-Lago, Carmelo. 2013. *Cuba under Raul Castro: Assessing the Reforms*. Boulder, CO: Lynne Rienner.

Mesa-Lago, Carmelo, and Pavel Vidal-Alejandro. 2010. "The Impact of the Global Crisis on Cuba's Economy and Social Welfare." *Journal of Latin American Studies* 42: 689–717.

Millán, Ana Valdés. 2005. *Una cultura millenaria en el siglo XX guantanamero*. Guantánamo: Editorial el Mar y la Montaña.

Mingramm, Rafael Valdez. 2012. "2012, Año de oportunidad para renovar votos con China." In *40 años de la relación entre México y China: Acuerdos, desencuentros y futuro*, edited by Enrique Dussel Peters, 97–106. Mexico City: UNAM/CECHIMEX.

Ministry of Foreign Affairs of Cuba. 1960. "Memorandum of the Conversation between Premier Zhou Enlai and Cuban Revolutionary Government Economic Delegation, November 18, 1960." Available from the Wilson Center History and Public Policy Program Digital Archive, PRC FMA 204-00098-02,1-16. Translated by Zhang Qian. Accessed July 9, 2015. http://digitalarchive.wilsoncenter.org /document/115156.

Minor, Milthon. 2010. "Abren en Mexicali cámara de empresarios Chinos del noroeste." *La Frontera*, March 6.

Mondragón, Santos. 2006. "Ambulantes invaden el centro histórico." *Noticieros Televisa*, December 25.

Monteón González, Humberto, and José Luis Trueba Lara. 1988. *Chinos y antichinos en México: Documentos para su estudio*. Guadalajara: Gobierno de Jalisco, Secretaría General, Unidad Editorial.

Montes de Oca Choy, María Teresa. 2007. *Las sociedades Chinas en Cuba: Pasado y presente*. Havana: Imagen Contemporánea, 2007. CD-ROM.

Montes de Oca Choy, María Teresa, and Roberto Vargas Lee. 2008. "Llevando a la práctica la cultura China: La cátedra de estudios Chinos y la Escuela Cubana de Wushu." In *Cultura, tradición, y comunidad: Perspectivas sobre la participación y el desarrollo en Cuba*, edited by Adrian H. Hearn, 162–99. Havana: Imagen Contemporánea.

Morán, Francisco. 2005. "Volutas del deseo: Hacia una lectura del orientalismo en el modernismo Hispanoamericano." *Modern Language Notes* 120: 383–407.

Moreno, Alejandro, and Daniel Calingaert. 2011. *Change Comes to Cuba: Citizens' Views on Reform after the Sixth Party Congress*. Washington: Freedom House.

Morris, Stephen D. 2001. *Corruption and Politics in Contemporary Mexico*. Tuscaloosa: University of Alabama Press.

Morris, Stephen D., and Joseph L. Klesner. 2010. "Corruption and Trust: Theoretical Considerations and Evidence from Mexico." *Comparative Political Studies* 43 (10): 1258–85.

Mujal-León, Eusebio. 2011. "Survival, Adaptation and Uncertainty: The Case of Cuba." *Journal of International Affairs* 65 (1): 149–68.

Murray, Mary. 2004. "China Gives Boost to Cuba's Economy." NBCNews.com, November 23. Accessed April 25, 2014. http://www.msnbc.msn.com/id /6566988/.

Newton, Kenneth. 2001. "Trust, Social Capital, Civil Society, and Democracy." *International Political Science Review* 22 (2): 201–14.

Nonini, Donald M., and Aihwa Ong. 1997. "Chinese Transnationalism as an Alternative Modernity." In *Ungrounded Empires: The Cultural Politics of Modern Chinese Transnationalism*, edited by Aihwa Ong and Donald M. Nonini, 3–33. London: Routledge.

Noticieros Televisa (published in Mexico). 2005. "Productos mexicanos 'made' en China." Editorial, September 13.

Ochoa León, Sara María. 2008. "Corrupción y contrabando en el sector textil en México." Report for the Chamber of Deputies of Mexico. Accessed August 5, 2015. https://www.yumpu.com/es/document/view/10326979/corrupcion-y -contrabando-en-el-sector-textil-en-camara-de-.

O'Donnell, Guillermo. 2006. "On Informal Institutions, Once Again." In *Informal Institutions and Democracy: Lessons from Latin America*, edited by Gretchen Helmke and Steven Levitsky, 285–89. Baltimore, MD: Johns Hopkins University Press.

Oficina Nacional de Estadísticas e Información. 2014. *Anuario estadístico de Cuba 2013*. Havana: Oficina Nacional de Estadísticas e Información.

Ong, Aihwa. 1999. *Flexible Citizenship: The Cultural Logics of Transnationality*. Durham, NC: Duke University Press.

Ong, Aihwa, and Stephen Collier, eds. 2004. *Global Assemblages: Technology, Politics, and Ethics as Anthropological Problems*. London: Blackwell.

Oppenheimer, Andres. 1992. *Castro's Final Hour: An Eyewitness Account of the Disintegration of Castro's Cuba*. New York: Touchstone.

———. 2010. "La gran esperanza de México: Lograr tener 5 millones de Norteamericanos retirados." *Excelsior*, April 30.

Opus Habana (published in Cuba). 2013. "Mensajero de paz y amor." Editorial, March 25. Accessed August 5, 2015. www.opushabana.cu/index.php?option =com_content&view=article&id=3738&Itemid=43.

Organisation for Economic Co-Operation and Development. 2009. *OECD Economic Surveys: Mexico*. Paris: Organisation for Economic Co-operation and Development.

Ortiz, Fernando. 1940. "América es un Ajiaco." *La Nueva Democracia* 21 (11): 20–24.

———. [1940] 1995. *Cuban Counterpoint: Tobacco and Sugar*. Translated by Harriet de Onís, introduction by Bronislaw Malinowski, prologue by Herminio Portell Vilà, new introduction by Fernando Coronil. Durham, NC: Duke University Press.

Ortner, Sherry B. 1991. "Patterns of History: Cultural Schemas in the Founding of Sherpa Religious Institutions." In *Culture through Time: Anthropological Approaches*, edited by E. Ohnuki-Tierney, 57–93. Stanford, CA: Stanford University Press.

Osorio, Ernesto. 2007. "Descarta barrios retirar ambulantes." *Reforma*, August 8.

Osorio, Ernesto, and Mariana Díaz. 2007. "Ofrece el comercio formal liberar banquetas del Centro." *Reforma* August 17.

Oxfeld, Ellen. 1993. *Blood, Sweat, and Mahjong: Family and Enterprise in an Overseas Chinese Community*. Ithaca, NY: Cornell University Press.

Padgett, Humberto. 2005. "Abastece tepito a piratas." *Reforma*, February 15.

Padilla, Art, and Jerome L. McElroy. 2007. "Cuba and Caribbean Tourism after Castro." *Annals of Tourism Research* 34 (3): 649–72.

Padura Fuentes, Leonardo. 1994. *El viaje más largo*. Havana: Ediciones Unión.

Palumbo-Liu, David. 2007. "Asian Diasporas, and Yet . . . ." In *Asian Diasporas: New Formations, New Conceptions*, edited by Rhacel S. Parreñas and Lok C. D. Siu, 279–84. Stanford, CA: Stanford University Press.

Pan, Tao. 2004. "Timeless Theme of International Relations." *Beijing Review* 47 (23), 10 June.

Páramo, Arturo. 2007. "Se alían informales: No rinden la plaza." *Excelsior*, April 28.

———. 2008. "Barrio chino: Muralla productiva." *Excelsior*, August 5.

Parás García, Pablo, Carlos López Olmedo, and Dinorah Vargas. 2011. "Cultura política de la democracia en México, 2010: Consolidación democrática en las Américas en tiempos difíciles." Latin America Public Opinion Project, Vander-

bilt University. Accessed July 18, 2015. http://vanderbilt.edu/lapop/mexico
/2010-culturapolitica.pdf.

Par Darmstadt. 2004. *Factores que contribuyen al éxito de las iniciativas comuni-
tarias a nivel barrial: Casos observados en la Habana, Cuba.* Accessed July 26,
2015. www.academia.edu/9680271/Factores_que_contribuyen_al_%C3%A9xito
_de_las_iniciativas_comunitarias_a_nivel_barrial.

Pardiñas, Felipe. 1982. *Relaciones diplomáticas entre México y China, 1898–1948.*
Mexico City: SRE.

Parreñas, Rhacel S., and Lok C. D. Siu. 2007. "Introduction: Asian Diasporas—
New Conceptions, New Frameworks." In *Asian Diasporas: New Formations,
New Conceptions,* edited by Rhacel S. Parreñas and Lok C. D. Siu, 1–27. Stan-
ford, CA: Stanford University Press.

Pastrana, Juan Jiménez. 1963. *Los Chinos en las luchas por la liberación de Cuba,
1847–1930.* Havana: Instituto de Historia.

———. 1983. *Los Chinos en la historia de Cuba: 1847–1930.* Havana: Editorial de
Ciencias Sociales.

Peña Delgado, Grace. 2012. *Making the Chinese Mexican: Global Migration, Lo-
calism, and Exclusion in the U.S.-Mexico Borderlands.* Stanford, CA: Stanford
University Press.

People's Daily. 1996. "Chairman Qiao Shi Met with Chairman Alarcon." Editorial,
April 10.

———. 2003a. "Hu Jintao Held Talks with Castro." Editorial, February 28.

———. 2003b. "Jiang Zemin Held Talks with Castro." Editorial, February 27.

People's Republic of China Ministry of Foreign Affairs. 1987. *A General Survey of
Chinese Diplomacy.* Beijing: World Affairs.

———. 2003. *China's Stand on South-South Cooperation.* August 18. Accessed
May 3, 2014. http://enfaohn.hainan.gov.cn/swsqwywb/ForeignPolicies/200910
/t20091027_12096.html.

———. 2008. *China's Policy Paper on Latin America and the Caribbean.* Accessed
May 3, 2014. http://english.gov.cn/official/2008-11/05/content_1140347.htm.

———. 2012. "Barrio Chino de La Habana atesora nueva estatua de Confucio."
December 12. Accessed May 1, 2014. http://cu.chineseembassy.org/esp/sgxx
/sgxw/t1002717.htm.

———. 2013. "Xi Jinping Attends Eighth G20 Leaders' Summit and Delivers Important Speech." September 6. Accessed May 3, 2014. www.chinaembassy.lt
/eng/xwdt/t1074372.htm.

Pérez, Ladyrene. 2014. "Presidente chino inicia visita a la Isla: 'Cuba es un país de
peso.'" *Cuba Debate,* July 2.

Pérez Brito, Arnaldo. 1953. Vocal performance of "Chino Li-Wong," by Armando
Orefiche. Recorded by Armando Orefiche and His Havana boys on Vintage
Cuba no. 79 EP Almendra.

Pérez de la Riva, Juan. 2000. *Los culíes Chinos en Cuba*. Havana: Editorial Ciencias Sociales.

Pérez Pizarro, Renato. 2009a. "Chinese Buses Are Assembled in Havana." *Miami Herald*, December 4.

———. 2009b. "Chinese Cars Are on Their Way to Cuba." *Miami Herald*, June 11.

Pew Research Center. 2007. *Global Unease with Major World Powers*," chapter 3. Accessed April 28, 2014. www.pewglobal.org/2007/06/27/chapter-3-views-of -china-and-its-increasing-influence/.

Piccato, Pablo. 2001. *City of Suspects: Crime in Mexico City, 1900–1931*. Durham, NC: Duke University Press.

Piñón, Jorge. 2011. "Why the United States and Cuba Collaborate (and What Could Happen If They Don't)." *Hemisphere* 20: 24–25.

Pitts, Pietro. 2014. "U.S.-Cuba Deal Shows Venezuelan Oil Giveaways Running Out." *Bloomberg*, December 20. Accessed August 5, 2015. www.bloomberg.com /news/articles/2014-12-19/u-s-cuba-deal-shows-venezuelan-oil-giveaways -running-out.

Portes, Alejandro. 1998. "Social Capital: Its Origins and Applications in Modern Sociology." *Annual Review of Sociology* 24: 1–24.

Portes, Alejandro, and Saskia Sassen. 1987. "Making It Underground: Comparative Material on the Informal Sector in Western Market Economies." *American Journal of Sociology* 93 (1): 30–61.

Portes, Alejandro, and Julia Sensenbrenner. 1993. "Embeddedness and Immigration: Notes on the Social Determinants of Economic Action." *American Journal of Sociology* 98 (6): 1320–50.

Pringle, James. 2003. "Cuban Chop Suey." *Far Eastern Economic Review* 166 (27): 53.

Protocolo (published in Mexico). 2007. "Mafia China intensifica tráfico de personas en América Latina." May 5. Accessed May 2, 2014. www.protocolo.com.mx /internacional/mafia-china-intensifica-trafico-de-personas-en-america-latina/.

Putnam, Robert D. 2000. *Bowling Alone: The Collapse and Revival of American Community*. New York: Simon and Schuster.

———. 2007. "E Pluribus Unum: Diversity and Community in the Twenty-First Century." *Scandinavian Political Studies* 30 (2): 137–74.

Quesada, Gonzalo de. 1946. *Los Chinos y la revolución Cubana*. Havana: Ucar, García y Cía.

Rabinow, Paul. 1977. *Reflections on Fieldwork in Morocco*. Berkeley: University of California Press.

Rainsford, Sarah. 2012. "Cuba Oil: Offshore Exploration Brings Hopes and Fears." *BBC News*, February 1. Accessed April 25, 2014. www.bbc.co.uk/news/world -latin-america-16795321.

Ramírez, Ana. 2007. "'Traen el jaque' a los extranjeros." *La Frontera*, December 27.

Ramos Pérez, Jorge. 2009. "Cordero pide a Stiglitz leer sobre México." *El Universal*, November 19.

Ratliff, William. 2004. *China's "Lessons" for Cuba's Transition?* Coral Gables, FL: University of Miami Institute for Cuban and Cuban American Studies.

———. 2006. "Cereijo, Bejucal, China and Cuba's Adversary Foreign Intelligence." World Association of International Studies, March 4. Accessed April 25, 2014. www.waisworld.org/go.jsp?id=02a&objectType=post&o=9526&objectTypeId= 3776&topicId=10.

Ravsberg, Fernando. 2012. "Cuba Plans to Drill as Oil Rig Arrives." *Havana Times*, January 20. Accessed April 25, 2014. www.havanatimes.org/?p=60134.

Reich, Robert B. 1982. "Making Industrial Policy." *Foreign Affairs*, spring, 852–81.

Rénique, Gerardo. 2000. "Race, Mestizaje and Nationalism: Sonora's Anti-Chinese Movement and State Formation in Post-Revolutionary Mexico." *Political Power and Social Theory* 14: 91–140.

———. 2003. "Race, Region, and Nation: Sonora's Anti-Chinese Racism and Mexico's Post-Revolutionary Nationalism, 1920s–1930s." In *Race and Nation in Modern Latin America*, edited by Nancy P. Appelbaum, Anne S. Macpherson, and Karin Alejandra Rosemblatt, 211–36. Chapel Hill: North Carolina University Press.

República de Cuba. 2011. *Lineamientos de la política económica y social del partido y la revolución*. Havana: República de Cuba.

Reséndiz, Francisco. 2014. "Resalta EPN compromiso de México con transparencia." *El Universal*, September 24.

"Retiring Americans: Go South, Old Man." 2005. *Economist*, November 24. Accessed May 2, 2014. www.economist.com/node/5214922.

Reuters Havana. 2004. "News release." Editorial, November, 22.

Ritter, Archibald. 2011. "El VI congreso del partido y los lineamientos: ¿Un punto de viraje para Cuba?" *Espacio Laical* 3: 18–22.

Roberts, Walter A. 1953. *Havana: The Portrait of a City*. New York: Coward-McCann.

Rodríguez, Ivet. 2011. "Comercio ilegal acapara mercado de ropa." CNNExpansión, January 25. Accessed April 27, 2014. www.cnnexpansion.com/manufactura /2011/01/25/comercio-ilegal-acapara-mercado-de-ropa.

Rojas Peña, Alberto. 2009. "Un viaje al pasado." *El Diario de Sonora*, February 21.

Romero, José María. 1911. *Comisión de Inmigración, encargada de estudiar la influencia social y económica de la inmigración asiática en México*. Mexico City: A. Carranza e Hijos.

Romero, Robert Chao. 2010. *The Chinese in Mexico, 1882–1940*. Tucson: University of Arizona Press.

Romeu, Rafael. 2012. "Cuba: Reform Continues." In *Latin American Economic Perspectives—All Together Now: The Challenge of Regional Integration*, edited by

Eduardo Levy-Yeyati, with Lucio Castro and Luciano Cohan, 60–68. Washington: Brookings Institution.

Rovner, Eduardo Sáenz. 2004. "Contrabando, juego, y narcotráfico en Cuba entre los años 20 y comienzos de la revolución." Paper delivered at the National Autonomous University of Mexico, Mexico City, March 17. Accessed April 30, 2014. http://taniaquintero.blogspot.com.au/2007/08/contrabando-juego-y-narcotrfico-en-cuba.html.

Saco, José Antonio. [1864] 2000. "Los Chinos en Cuba." *Catauro* 2 (2): 193–97.

Saldierna, Georgina. 2014. "Mexicanos desconfían principalmente de diputados, partidos, policías y jueces." *La Jornada*, June 15.

Salinas, Daniel. 2008. "Buscan crear Barrio Chino en la 'Revu.'" *La Frontera*, March 1.

Santiso, Javier, and Rolando Avendaño. 2011. "Economic Fundamentals of the Relationship." In *China Engages Latin America: Tracing the Trajectory*, edited by Adrian H. Hearn and José Luis León-Manríquez, 67–90. Boulder, CO: Lynne Rienner.

Sato, Kanji. 2006. "Formation of La Raza and the Anti-Chinese Movement in Mexico." *Transforming Anthropology* 14 (2): 181–86.

Scarpaci, Joseph L., Roberto Segre, and Mario Coyula. 2002. *Havana: Two Faces of the Antillean Metropolis*. Chapel Hill: University of North Carolina Press.

Schambra, William. 1994. "By the People: The Old Values of the New Citizenship." *Policy Review* (summer): 32–38.

Schiavone Camacho, Julia M. 2009. "Crossing Boundaries, Claiming a Homeland: The Mexican Chinese Transpacific Journey to Becoming Mexican, 1930s–1960s." *Pacific Historical Review* 78 (4): 545–77.

———. 2012. *Chinese Mexicans: Transpacific Migration and the Search for a Homeland 1910–1960*. Chapel Hill: University of North Carolina Press.

Schneider, Ben Ross. 2002. "Why Is Mexican Business So Organized?" *Latin American Research Review* 37 (1): 77–118.

Schuler, Friedrich E. 1998. *Mexico between Hitler and Roosevelt: Mexican Foreign Relations in the Age of Lázaro Cardenas, 1934–1940*. Albuquerque: University of New Mexico Press.

Schwartz, Rosalie. 1997. *Pleasure Island: Tourism and Temptation in Cuba*. Lincoln: University of Nebraska Press.

Secretaría de Hacienda y Crédito Público. 2009. "La economía Mexicana." Paper presented at the 2009 Forum of the Mexican Institute of Financial Executives, Monterrey. June 3. Accessed July 17, 2015. shcp.gob.mx/SALAPRENSA/sala_prensa_presentaciones/acc_presentacion_la_economia_mexicana_03062009.pdf

Shambaugh, David. 2009. "China's New Foray into Latin America." Brookings East Asia Commentary, November. Accessed August 3, 2015. http://atakapa4.rssing.com/browser.php?indx=3536754&last=1&item=8.

Sharpley, Richard, and Martin Knight. 2009. "Tourism and the State in Cuba: From the Past to the Future." *International Journal of Tourism Research* 11: 241–54.

Shi Weimin. 2011. "Reforma progresiva bajo orientación política en China." *Temas* 66:17–28.

Sierra, Arturo. 2004. "Montan con $9 mil 'minilab' de piratería." *Reforma*, June 7.

Simón, Angélica. 2007. "Comunidad estigmatizada." *El Universal*, April 12.

Simon, Bernard. 2011. "Canadian Banks Eye Return to Cuba." *Financial Times*, December 18.

Simoni, Valerio. 2009. "Touristic Encounters in Cuba: Informality, Ambiguity, and Emerging Relationships." PhD diss., Leeds Metropolitan University.

Sirkin, Harold, Michael Zinser, and Justin Rose. 2014. *The Shifting Economics of Global Manufacturing*. Boston: Boston Consulting Group.

Siu, Lok. 2008. "Chino Latino Restaurants: Converging Communities, Identities, and Cultures." *Afro-Hispanic Review* 27 (1): 161–71.

Skocpol, Theda. 1996. "Unraveling from Above." *American Prospect* 7 (25): 20–25.

Smart, Alan. 1993. "Gifts, Bribes, and *Guanxi*: A Reconsideration of Bourdieu's Social Capital." *Cultural Anthropology* 8 (3): 388–408.

Smart, Alan, and Jinn Yuh Hsu. 2004. "The Chinese Diaspora, Foreign Investment and Economic Development in China." *The Review of International Affairs* 3 (4): 544–66.

Smart, Josephine, and Alan Smart. 2009. "Personal Relations and Divergent Economies: A Case Study of Hong Kong Investment in China." *International Journal of Urban and Regional Research* 15 (2): 216–33.

Solis Peña, Margarita. 2006. "Al vapor la ley antipiratería en el DF, denuncian comerciantes." *La Crónica*, May 8.

Spagat, Elliot. 2005. "Terrorist Hoax Exposes Little-Known Chinese Smuggling Route." Associated Press, 5 February.

Steele, James W. 1885. *Cuban Sketches*, 2nd ed. New York: G. P. Putnam's Sons.

Strauss, Julia C., and Ariel C. Armony, eds. 2012. *From the Great Wall to the New World: China and Latin America in the 21st Century*. Cambridge: Cambridge University Press.

Strubbe, Bill, and Karen Wald. 1995. "Start with a Dream: Rebuilding Havana's Chinese Community." *World and I*, September, 188–97.

Tai, Kuan. 2012. "La experiencia de la Expo China-México 2009–2011 y Expo Asia-Pacífico-México 2011, misiones mexicanas a China 2012." In *40 años de la relación entre México y China: Acuerdos, desencuentros y futuro*, edited by Enrique Dussel Peters, 365–70. Mexico City: UNAM/CECHIMEX.

Tan, Clement. 2015. "China Rail Stocks Sink after Mexico Shelves High-Speed Rail Line." *Bloomberg*, February 2. Accessed August 5, 2015. www.bloomberg.com /news/articles/2015-02-02/china-rail-stocks-sink-after-mexico-shelves-high -speed-rail-line.

Taylor, Lawrence. 2002. "El contrabando de Chinos en la frontera de las Californias durante el Porfiriato (1876–1911)." *Migraciones Internacionales* 1 (3): 5–31.

Tokatlian, Juan Gabriel. 2008. "A View from Latin America." In *China's Expansion into the Western Hemisphere: Implications for Latin America and the United States*, edited by Riordan Roett and Guadalupe Paz, 59–89. Washington: Brookings Institution.

Tölölyan, Khachig. 1991. "The Nation-State and Its Others: In Lieu of a Preface." *Diaspora* 1 (1): 1–2.

———. 1996. "Rethinking Diaspora(s): Stateless Power in the Transnational Moment." *Diaspora* 5 (1): 3–36.

Torres Pérez, Ricardo. 2011. "La actualización del modelo económico cubano: Continuidad y ruptura." *Temas Catalejo*. Accessed August 5, 2015. www.temas .cult.cu/catalejo/economia/Ricardo_Torres.pdf.

Trápaga Delfín, Yolanda, Enrique Dussel Peters, and Sergio Martínez Rivera. 2012. *Programa de becas ciudad de México-China: Propuestas de cooperación 2010–2011*. Mexico City: UNAM/CECHIMEX.

Tsai, Kellee S. 2002. *Back-Alley Banking: Private Entrepreneurs in China*. Ithaca, NY: Cornell University Press.

United Nations Commodity Trade Statistics Database. 2015. "UN comtrade." Accessed July 10, 2015. http://comtrade.un.org/db/default.aspx.

United Nations Development Program. 1990. *Human Development Report 1990*. New York: Oxford University Press.

Uno más Uno (published in Mexico). 2007. "Centro histórico: Bomba de tiempo." Editorial, July 17.

"US, Cuba Move toward Embassies, Disagree on Human Rights." 2015. Associated Press, January 22.

U.S. Department of State. 2010. "Key Trading Partners See No Big Economic Reforms." Wikileaks U.S. Embassy Cables, 10HAVANA84, November 28. Accessed August 3, 2015. https://wikileaks.org/cable/2010/02/10HAVANA84.html.

USGS (U.S. Geological Survey). 2005. "Assessment of Undiscovered Oil and Gas Resources of the North Cuba Basin, Cuba, 2004." Reston, VA: U.S. Geological Survey.

U.S. Immigration and Naturalization Service. 2002. *1999 Statistical Yearbook of the Immigration and Naturalization Service*. Washington: Government Printing Office.

Uslaner, Eric M. 1999. "Democracy and Social Capital." In *Democracy and Trust*, edited by Mark E. Warren, 121–50. Cambridge: Cambridge University Press.

Valdés Lakowsky, Vera. 1981. *Vinculaciones sino-mexicanas: Albores y testimonios (1974–1899)*. México: UNAM.

Van Ziegert, Sylvia. 2006. *Global Spaces of Chinese Culture: Diasporic Chinese Communities in the United States and Germany*. New York: Routledge.

Varela, Beatriz. 1980. *Lo Chino en el habla Cubana*. Miami, FL: Universal.

Velázquez Morales, Catalina. 1989. "Los Chinos agricultores y comerciantes en Mexicali 1929–1934." *Meyibo* 3 (9–10): 97–108.

———. 2001. *Los inmigrantes Chinos en Baja California 1920–1937*. Mexicali, Mexico: Universidad Autónoma de Baja California.

Vertovec, Steven. 2009. *Transnationalism*. London: Routledge.

Villalba Garrido, Evaristo. 1993. *Cuba y el turismo*. Havana: Editorial Ciencias Sociales.

Wang Gungwu. 2000. *The Chinese Overseas: From Earthbound China to the Quest for Autonomy*. Cambridge, MA: Harvard University Press.

Wang Hongying. 2000. "Informal Institutions and Foreign Investment in China." *Pacific Review* 13 (4): 525–56.

Wang, Ping. 2013. "The Impacts of China's Peaceful Influence on U.S.-Mexican Relations: A Triangular Perspective." In *China and the New Triangular Relationships in the Americas: China and the Future of U.S.-Mexico Relations*, edited by Enrique Dussel Peters, Adrian H. Hearn, and Harley Shaiken, 25–35. Coral Gables, FL: University of Miami Center for Latin American Studies.

Wang Yiwei. 2014. "Improving Relations between the United States and the Release of the Ancient Triple Signal." *People's Daily*, December 19.

Watkins, Ralph. 2013. "Meeting the China Challenge to Manufacturing in Mexico." In *China and the New Triangular Relationships in the Americas: China and the Future of US-Mexico Relations*, edited by Enrique Dussel Peters, Adrian H. Hearn, and Harley Shaiken, 37–55. Coral Gables, FL: University of Miami Center for Latin American Studies.

Webber, Jude, and Tom Mitchell. 2014. "Mexico Cancels China-Led High-Speed Rail Contract." *Financial Times*, November 7.

Weber, Max. [1922]. 1947. *The Theory of Social and Economic Organization*. New York: Free Press.

Weil, David. 2002. "The Benefits and Costs of Transparency: A Model of Disclosure Based Regulation." John F. Kennedy School of Government, Harvard University. http://papers.ssrn.com/sol3/papers.cfm?abstract_id=316145. Accessed May 24, 2015.

Weissert, Will. 2008. "China Expands Trade with Cuba." *Miami Herald*, November 19.

Werne, Joseph R. 1980. "Esteban Cantú y la soberanía mexicana en Baja California." *Historia Mexicana* 30 (117): 1–32.

Wheat, Andrew. 1995. "The Fall of the Peso and the Mexican 'Miracle.'" *Multinational Monitor* 17 (4). Accessed April 27, 2014. http://multinationalmonitor.org/hyper/issues/1995/04/mm0495_06.html.

Wilson, Rob, and Wimal Dissanayake. 1996. "Introduction: Tracking the Global/Local." In *Global/Local: Cultural Production and the Transnational Imaginary*, edited by Rob Wilson and Wimal Dissanayake, 1–18. Durham, NC: Duke University Press.

Wonders, Nancy, and Raymond Michalowski. 2001. "Bodies, Borders, and Sex Tourism in a Globalized World: A Tale of Two Cities—Amsterdam and Havana." *Social Problems* 48 (4): 545–71.

Wong, Alejandro Chiu, and Eradio Salgado Baez. 1993. "El Barrio Chino de La Habana: Una legendaria opción turística." Paper delivered at the Third Ibero-American Symposium on Tourism, Havana, May 25–28.

Woolcock, Michael. 1998. "Social Capital and Economic Development: Toward a Theoretical Synthesis and Policy Framework." *Theory and Society* 27 (2): 151–208.

World Bank. 2015a. Data: China. Accessed July 10, 2015. http://data.worldbank.org /country/china.

———. 2015b. "Gross Domestic Product 2014, PPP." *World Development Indicators database*. Accessed July 10, 2015. http://databank.worldbank.org/data/down load/GDP_PPP.pdf.

World Economic Forum. 2012. *The Global Competitiveness Report 2011–2012*. Geneva: World Economic Forum.

Wu Kai. 2006. "Breves desde México." Chinatoday.com, May 1. Accessed August 5, 2015. www.chinatoday.com.cn/hoy/2006n/s2006n5/p28.html.

Xinhua (published in China). 1994. "La Comunidad China en Cuba." Editorial, April 6.

———. 2007. "China's Top Political Adviser Voices Hope for Overseas Chinese." Editorial, September 15.

———. 2008. "Chinese President Visits Cuban Leader Fidel Castro." *Xinhua*, November 19. Accessed August 5, 2015. http://news.xinhuanet.com/english /2008-11/19/content_10378183.htm.

Yahuda, Michael. 1985. *Towards the End of Isolationism: China's Foreign Policy after Mao*. New York: Palgrave Macmillan.

Yamagishi, Toshio, and Midori Yamagishi. 1994. "Trust and Commitment in the United States and Japan." *Motivation and Emotion* 18 (2): 129–66.

Yan Jirong. 2011. "El 'modelo Chino': ¿Qué dicen las investigaciones?" *Temas* 66: 12–16.

Yan, Yunxiang. 2009. *The Individualization of Chinese Society*. New York: Berg.

Yang, Mayfair Mei Hui. 1994. *Gifts, Favors and Banquets: The Art of Social Relationships in China*. Ithaca, NY: Cornell University Press.

———. 2002. "The Resilience of Guanxi and Its New Deployments: A Critique of Some New Guanxi Scholarship." *China Quarterly* 170: 459–76.

"¿Y la soberanía?" 2007. *Reforma*, January 15.

Young, Elliot. 2014. *Alien Nation: Chinese Migration in the Americas from the Coolie Era through World War II*. Chapel Hill: University of North Carolina Press.

Yu, LiAnne Sandra. 2006. "The Reemergence of Vietnam's Ethnic Chinese Community through Local, National, and Transnational Structures." PhD diss., University of California, San Diego.

Yun, Lisa. 2008. *The Coolie Speaks: Chinese Indentured Laborers and African Slaves in Cuba*. Philadelphia, PA: Temple University Press.

Yun, Lisa, and Ricardo René Laremont. 2001. "Chinese Coolies and African Slaves in Cuba 1847–74." *Journal for Asian American Studies* 4 (2): 99–122.

Zamora, Rodolfo García. 2005. "Collective Remittances and the 3x1 Program as a Transnational Social Learning Process." Paper presented at the "Mexican Migrant Social and Civic Participation in the United States" seminar, Woodrow Wilson International Center for Scholars, Washington, November 4–5.

Zhan Lisheng. 2002. "Event Lauds Role of Overseas Chinese." *China Daily*, December 4.

Zhu Wenchi, Mao Xianglin, and Li Keming. 2002. *Communist Movements in Latin America*. Beijing: Contemporary World.